SALES ESTEEM

The Inner Source of Sales Power

". . . There is an enormous store of energy, untapped and waiting in all of us, that if discovered, and understood, will propel you to sales success you might otherwise think impossible. Today's sales mystics would like you to believe that wishing for that energy will release it. Only a fool believes in something for nothing. Wishing leads you to the entrance of success, where you can press your nose against the window, peer in and glimpse the possibilities . . . and dream. The question you need to ask is, where is the key to the door? You are about to discover the location of the key. And like all of our most worthy adventures, this journey requires something of the traveler. It requires you to use your most precious skill—your intellect. Like astronauts on a flight to the moon, science and understanding are at the foundation of our journey. Sales Esteem is the unification of sales science and the wonders of human emotion. Sales science—sales principles—give you the substance upon which you will build your stairway to the stars. Sales Esteem is the step-by-step understanding of the principles that will unlock the door, release the energy, reward the traveler, and propel you to a wealth of physical and emotional rewards you could only dream about before."

—Michael Cevanté

. . . in his opening remarks to the **Sales Esteem Conference** attendees.

SALES ESTEEM

Marc Ferguson

PAX PUBLISHING • SAN FRANCISCO • CA

Sales Esteem

Pax Publishing / October 1995

Copyright © 1995 Marc Ferguson

Editorial consultation and book design by James Arden

Cover design by Daniel Schumaker / Contrast Design

ISBN # 0-9614914-8-5

For information address: Pax Publishing, P.O. Box 22564, San Francisco, CA 94122

PRINTED IN THE UNITED STATES OF AMERICA

Contents

Acknowledgments

Distinguishing the contributions of friends and co-workers from the ideas that the author eventually puts on the page is not an easy task. For everyone who has passed on something recognizable in this book, I am grateful. In particular, I'd like to thank the hundreds of salespeople with whom I've had the pleasure of meeting over the past ten years. Among you are those who believed in the Sales Esteem philosophy and put its principles to work—thank you for the courage to travel a different path. I am fortunate to have a handful of close friends who provided professional input and, more importantly, emotional support and encouragement. A special thanks to Diane Houston, Michael Dibbert and Craig Cooper for their reflections on the concepts that went into the book. There is very little that came from other authors, and I say that so as to highlight the gifts I have taken from Ayn Rand and her philosophical writings. As it relates to marketing and sales, Theodore Levitt and his book, *The Marketing Imagination*, gave me the basis for much of the value-added sales techniques. And Howard Stevens' elegantly simple theory in *The Quadrant Solution* gave me insight on the variations of touching the customer versus touching the product. Anyone who knows these two authors will see the outgrowth of their work in this book. I have reserved comment on my brother's contributions until the introduction. And most important are the contributions made by my family: Dianne, my wife, and my two daughters, Brittany and Ashleigh. Dianne gave up an untold amount of my attention during the two years it took to write the book. And all three are the ultimate inspiration for my success, my happiness and my self-esteem, all of which they reflect back to me. My love to them.

Introduction

Oliver Wendell Holmes wrote of three types of thinkers. One–, two– and three–story intellects. All fact collectors, who have no aim beyond their facts, are one-story people. Two-story people compare, reason, generalize and use the labor of fact collectors as well as their own. Three-story people idealize, imagine, predict; their best illumination comes from above, through the skylight. This book is the realization of that thought applied to the profession of selling. Third-story salespeople know that facts have their place, and that knowledge and reason are the keys to success. They also have the added dimension of passion, which powers them to extraordinary success. This is the level closest to the stars.

The passion that motivated me to write was my own discovery of the third story and the extraordinary success I found along the way. The Sales Esteem philosophy is, at the risk of using a misunderstood word, ethical selling. But contrary to the pedestrian idea of ethical selling, it has proved to be terribly effective. By combining facts, reason and passion to overcome misconceptions about the legitimacy of a sales career, Sales Esteem forged a scientific approach to selling that dwarfed all others in terms of sales productivity. Unless I am mistaken, that is what we all seek. Greater sales . . . with a conscience.

Without this discovery, I would likely have ended up on the scrap-heap of honest people that get used up and discarded by the profession of selling. A recent experience gave me an extraordinary glimpse of this likelihood. While at a business dinner at the port city of Corpus Christi, Texas, I was introduced to an old business acquaintance of my dinner guest. The gentleman played the piano in the hotel's bar. He had the look of an eccentric millionaire. The toes of his tennis shoes were cut out to relieve an ailment, and his dress was that of a retired professor ready to walk the beach. An ex-stockbroker, he had left the business when it no longer afforded him the dignity and self-respect he needed. He couldn't resolve his ethical dilemmas and came to a fork in the road—without the benefit of directions. Rather than take the wrong path, he got off the road altogether. Now he plays the piano at a seaside resort. He told me that he never learned to read music, but he plays the piano masterfully. "I feel the music and it sounds right the way I put it together," is what he told me. *He had soul.* The same soul he couldn't find as a salesman.

When I think of the number of good people who get off the road, because they can't find their soul as a salesperson, I am truly saddened. Partly because I see how easily the same could have happened to me, but mostly because the world needs people with souls, and our profession has lost far too many.

Sales Esteem retells my own discoveries of ethical selling through the use of a story-line which allows it to be tested by critics—both clever and foolish, in the form of antagonists. I have come to truly love this method of learning as the reader will frequently arrive at the conclusions on his own, and as such, finds a source of knowledge far greater than rote learning. It's important to know that the essentials in every main point in the book had their origin in a real event, either one that I experienced directly, or those experienced by others and recreated by me for the book. *None* of the principles are without a foundation of something real. In all the years I spent selling, no one ever spoke to me of a sales philosophy. I struggled in search of my own philosophy and gradually pieced together the early thoughts of what was to become Sales Esteem. That philosophy has resulted in extraordinary sales success for me personally, and more importantly, left me with self-respect, pride, and self-esteem, not only for myself, but for the profession of selling. However, it would have remained incomplete, and intellectually inarticulate, without the involvement of a very important influence on my life: my older brother Jason. He introduced me to the philosophy of Objectivism which is at the core of Sales Esteem. But more importantly, he spent three years discussing the subtleties and encouraging my understanding of its application to the adolescent sales philosophy I had developed on my own, in a manner that was far more patient and aware than I could have imagined at the beginning. The early sales philosophy I had developed was honed and refined through his patient guidance, and his contribution to Sales Esteem is incalculable. I owe him a great personal debt.

I believe most salespeople arrive at their own sales philosophy in much the same manner that I did, but then fail to realize its full potential because they are unable to integrate their experiences into a complete philosophy. Sales Esteem provides the foundations for that integration. Theory and reality are married in Sales Esteem; it can be realized by everyone who picks up the book. The book is not without controversy, especially as it deals with the topics of company loyalty, compromise, compassion and individuality. While I might hope that the ideas here would appeal to all, the truth is, some will find its aim too high, and be uncomfortable with the theory. For those who hunger for the secrets of achievement beyond your dreams— you will be rewarded. For the rest, I can only direct you to look for the wisdom in the quote at the beginning of Chapter 20, and ask you to reconsider.

The characters developed for the book spring from personal experiences as well, both my own and other salespeople I have either trained, managed or have known as personal acquaintances. The central character, Ryan, embodies my personal insecurities about selling when I began my career some ten years ago. There are two moments when tears welled up in my eyes in writing the book. First, when Ryan agonizes in disgrace at how his son would see him if he knew the details of his sales career, and then when Ryan rediscovers his self-respect and exalts in the pride his son would have for him. It was the start-to-finish recreation of the journey I went through on my personal path to selling in a manner my own children could be proud of. This book holds many such journeys as they relate to all the various hardships— mental and emotional—of selling. I hope anyone who has ever struggled with the morals of selling can find an answer to their questions here.

1

Nowhere to Turn

We live in the present,
we dream of the future and
we learn eternal truths from the past.
—*Chiang Kai-shek*

Ryan Matthews sat on the edge of the bed and caressed his son's forehead. Although no one was there to notice, he wiped away the tears in his eyes with quick, self-conscious movements. This was the way he spent his evenings lately, sometimes for more than an hour. He wondered at the serenity and peace so obvious on his son's face. He both envied and held sacred the happiness of this little boy.

Ryan wanted Casey to live without pain, without concerns. He wanted it more than anything. He knew he was no different than other parents in the wishes they held for their children. What was different was the facade his son called Daddy every day. Ryan and Casey spent all their free time together, right up until the time Casey fell asleep under Ryan's loving eyes. Then came the silence and the painful thoughts of the truth Ryan had hoped Casey would never learn.

In the last three months, the scene had been played out practically every night and culminated in Ryan struggling to his feet in mental exhaustion. His wife Amber would stand in the doorway from time to time, weeping as she watched. She couldn't imagine the torture she saw in Ryan's face, knowing that he never noticed she was there, watching him. He wouldn't talk about it to her.

It hadn't always been this way. They had been married for twelve years. Their love had survived because their friendship flourished. Ryan, Amber and Casey seemed the vision of the way life was supposed to be. Young and vital, they were active and involved Casey in all they could. They longed for the weekends when they could escape to their lake house to splash in shallow water together, water-ski, and admire sunsets on the deck of local hot spots. During the winter, Ryan would join a handful of fathers and play street hockey with Casey and the other neighborhood kids, while Amber would cheer from the sidewalk in playful support. Lately, there had been fewer moments for cheerful laughter.

Their friends rarely witnessed an argument between them, and it was equally rare for Ryan and Amber to arrive at an impasse when they disagreed. From time to time a busy-body friend, certain that their happiness was a pretense of turmoil under the surface, would snoop for a problem, only to end up disappointed to find they didn't exist. *At least until now.*

Ryan was a bond salesman at Dremen-Russell and had become the company's top producer. He was constantly showered with praise from the firm, but managed to downplay his star status with his co-workers. Ryan liked the firm and thought highly of the company's managers, professionalism and reputation. They paid well and Ryan was frequently singled out for his productivity. He studied continuously, and helped train the rookie salesmen.

Ryan had an odd assortment of customers, which confused many people at the firm who thought specialization was the only way to succeed. He worked with municipalities, portfolio managers, corporate treasurers and a diverse group of individual investors. One might find Ryan speaking at an Optimist Club meeting, or at a gathering of savvy elderly women who would invite Ryan to their investment club, drink tea and giggle when he would grin at them. His contemporaries ridiculed his odd assortment of customers, but admired his patience and versatility. He could spend time with the elderly crowd and then jump immediately into a furious government bond auction. He had energy, enthusiasm and pride that seemed to be endless. Until now.

The slide had begun three months before when the firm's bond trader had accidentally mispriced bonds during a bid to a large insurance company. The calculations used to price the bonds were a complex series of assumptions of prepayments and interest rates, which ultimately resulted in uncertainty. There were, however, key components that could be predicted with reasonable accuracy and had a major impact on the price. If these components were off, the price was essentially no more than a lucky guess. The day following the sale, Ryan realized the mistake and went to his sales manager for advice in unwinding the trade. A flurry of angry disagreements from the trader, Ryan and his sales manager followed without resolution—except one fateful comment made by his sales manager: "Ryan," he said. "Get a grip. When did you or anyone else in the firm promise the assumptions were reasonable? And who the hell knows for sure, anyway? If the customer buys, he buys more than just the product, he buys the responsibility, and it no longer belongs to you."

Ryan sat in front of his sales manager, silenced by the statement, speechless from the implications it held, an implication that would change his life forever.

Shortly afterward, Ryan increased his studies of the financial markets and their derivative products. He had complained frequently to Amber about how little was known by his customers about the bonds they purchased, and how much they relied on his expertise to guide them. The more he discovered, the more disillusioned he became. Even experienced asset managers with years of technical expertise were frequently misinformed. With every occurrence, his sales manager's words had come flooding back: "the customer buys the responsibility." Ryan couldn't accept it. It wore on him. He seemed obsessed with a need for explanations of everything. And Ryan began to analyze every action he took, not in regret, but for its purpose.

Ryan's sales dropped dramatically. He gave many of his individual customers away to other salesmen. The "little old lady club," as it was affectionately known, was the first to go. Ryan limited his customers to the high-end of the spectrum of sophistication. His demeanor with those customers changed as well. Ryan had always been warm and friendly, but now he was developing a reputation for being as cold as steel.

Events seemed to be weighing on Ryan as well. Ryan missed a critical government funding when he was out with the flu and was harsh on himself for being away. He worried excessively about the impact of recent national elections on the economy and interest rates, often fearing a debacle in the markets. All the while, Wall Street was booming with the rush of the newest financial inventions, called derivatives, which were being gobbled up by investors. Ryan had seen several such "innovative" times—the "go-go funds" era, the "junk bond" era—and was now convinced the Street was headed for a similar debacle.

Ryan began to question his own actions closely, and the necessity to trade with a great deal of uncertainty about the future was troubling him. The idea of "hitting his numbers," always compelling as a competitive challenge, now held the specter of going off into battle to collect heads. He came into the office late and left as early as possible. When he was at the office, he would keep to himself, get his quota of sales and study at every opportunity. The other salesmen noticed the differences taking place and thought they were seeing "burnout."

The more Ryan studied, the more conservative he became. He was obsessed with the idea of losing his clients' money. He limited his riskier "plays" to his savvy portfolio managers, treating them as though they were willing accomplices in a turn at the wheel of a casino.

Initially, as he struggled to keep his sales from declining, he noticed that it required far more effort than in the past. He was fatigued. He ran to stay physically fit and alert, which helped for a while, but soon gave it up to conserve his energy. Eventually, his energy level fell and his sales began to decline. It was harder to find customers and even harder to get an order.

Throughout the fall, he noticed other travesties occurring around him. A friend was caught in a rigged government bond auction and barred from the securities industry for life. An elderly gentleman was found in the parking lot dousing himself in gasoline and mumbling about thieves at the firm. He observed for the first time, two common themes that seemed an inseparable part of his profession: do the trade regardless of the best interest of the customer, and don't worry about it because it is a required part of success that everyone accepts. The other salesmen seemed to be walking zombies, drained of responsibility, numbed by the need to succeed.

The firm hadn't noticed the collision of Ryan's values and actions. Ryan wasn't violating any laws. His numbers were down, but everyone expected him to come out of the slump. Since he spent little social time with co-workers, few noticed the personal problems. Most thought he was just bored with selling and needed a break. No one but Ryan and Amber knew of the long nights, and the tears Ryan cried for Casey.

And so Ryan sat on the bed next to his son, wondering what he had become, where his soul had gone, and what harm he was causing. His vision of being a decent father included a profession of which his son could be proud, but that seemed impossible now. Shame replaced the self-respect and pride he once felt. The guilt was so immense that it ruined his productivity at work, and filtered into every other aspect of his life.

Ryan knew he needed change, but didn't know where to turn. He was a salesman and had always been a salesman. It wasn't the securities industry he was fleeing, it was his career—his profession as a salesman. He didn't have technical skills. It wasn't as though he could start over, unless he was willing to trash his lifestyle, sell the house, and start a new career. The weight of the responsibility was enormous. He couldn't make the decision in a vacuum, and the alternatives were not very attractive.

Ryan wondered if his was the normal plight of a salesman, often thinking, "maybe we all end up this way." He knew he had to make a change, but didn't know where to turn for help.

He sat there staring down at the little boy he loved so dearly and from whom he needed love. One last touch, one last tear and Ryan was ready to leave Casey for the evening. He paused at the doorway for a glance back at his son and whispered softly, "Good night, son."

2

Michael Cevanté

Ill fortune never crushed that man whom good
fortune deceived not.
—*Benjamin Franklin*

The morning sun warmed Michael's face as he sat at the breakfast nook, nibbling on a bagel and sorting through applications submitted by candidates for the next Sales Esteem conference. He spent hours studying the applicants' questionnaires and résumés. Of the hundreds he received, just seventeen would be invited to attend.

Michael Cevanté was the grandson of an Italian immigrant who viewed America just as many of his generation had—the land of freedom of thought—not just opportunity. He was widely recognized as the pioneer of Sales Ethics, although he was a modest man. His career, however, would lend credibility to the broader opinion. The Sales Esteem conference was his creation and his passion. It had afforded him the lifestyle of his choosing, which was far from the raucous excitement of either coast, but no less energetic. He lived with his wife and two children near the site of the conference in the rolling, wooded foothills near Austin, Texas. A paradox of the global perspective of Texas, it was a scenic pleasure, dotted with recreational lakes and bathed in sunlight.

His daughter, Hallie, plopped into the chair next to his and started unloading a bowl full of cereal, toast, a glass of orange juice, and her homework onto the table in front of her. Hallie was seventeen and struggling to keep her honor student status. It wasn't easy, especially with the amount of attention she got from the boys. Michael paused to watch the balancing act worthy of a Chinese acrobat which Hallie pulled off without missing a beat.

"How do you do that?" asked Michael.

"What?" Hallie asked, as though it were as normal as tying shoes.

"That high-wire thing with breakfast and five school books," he said.

Hallie just grinned. Their relationship seemed as effortless as a Sunday morning. They talked about boys, school, and the difficulty of growing up. Mostly they talked about the wonders of life. Michael sipped his coffee and noticed Hallie tapping her pencil in rhythm on the homework spread out in front of her. "Hey, Grandma sent you a card for your birthday. It's on the counter," he said.

"No doubt she's sent more financial aid forms," said Hallie with an understanding laugh. Hallie was heading for college in six weeks, and was determined to pay for it by herself. Her grandmother had different designs. Michael had long ago put away the money to send her to school, but something was standing in the way: her ego. She had been accepted to Yale and would have to combine a scholarship and a part-time job to afford the tuition on her own. Michael encouraged her to use the money he set aside for her education to pay for living expenses, leaving the tuition for her, but she refused even that.

She jumped up from the chair to open the card, sliding her fingers between the envelope and its flap to tear it open. "Surprise! More of Grandma's special aid requests," said Hallie, raising the note so it could be read and out dropped three lottery tickets on the table in front of her father. Hallie's grandmother thought she should accept her father's generous offer and made the point by sending her lottery tickets. Hallie wasn't amused. She knew her grandmother expected to buy a winning ticket someday.

Michael returned to the applications but continued talking. "I think she's cheering you on now, but thinks you still need the motivation. You know, one of those reverse-psychology, 'generation' things," he said.

"She still sends great cards," said Hallie, as she finished the birthday card and poured milk on her cereal. Birthdays were a big deal at the Cevanté household.

"Going to scratch 'em?" asked Michael.

"Would *you*?" she said, already knowing the answer.

"No . . . but I know *why* I wouldn't want them. You don't." It was rare that Michael would make such challenging statements. Usually they pertained to one of life's lessons. Hallie didn't mind them because they were usually intriguing and never delivered in a condescending tone.

"I know why. I've just never told you, 'cause it is a secret that Grandpa and I once had."

Michael's father had passed away five years earlier. The entire family was very close to the old man, especially Michael and Hallie. They missed him terribly and with a glance acknowledged their mutual affection for him.

Michael looked up from the applications. "I didn't know that. So you and Grandpa had a little secret about self-help and that is why you insist on paying your own way to school?" asked Michael. Hallie shrugged, obviously not prepared to tell the story.

"Ever going to tell me?" he finished, trying his best to fake disinterest by returning his attention to his work.

"Nope," she said, and stuck a spoonful of cereal into her mouth. Her eyes were wide with the enjoyment of keeping her secret.

"Well, we might as well get it over with," he said, putting down an application and scratching the gum on the lottery tickets that covered the number combinations. The first two tickets had no matches, not even returning the expected $1 winner. The last ticket had three matches out of five, with one spot remaining to be scratched. Four matches won $25,000. Michael paused, realizing he could at least have a little fun by building some anticipation. "Hey. Heads up. One more 'Lucky 7' and you've got your first year's tuition," he said.

The final scratch revealed another 7 and a winning ticket. Hallie watched him scratch the winning ticket. The instant realization sent Hallie into a celebration. She jumped from her chair and repeated, "I won! I won! How much?"

A smile came to Michael's face as he watched his daughter's excitement. The momentary rush of good fortune was an excitement neither one of them could suppress. Once Hallie had finished her victory lap around the table and stopped to catch her breath from the excitement, the reality of free cash sank in. She stood, holding the ticket and looked at her father. Michael's steel blue eyes stared back.

"Want to tell me Grandpa's secret now?" asked Michael.

Hallie looked at her father, then at the ticket, and back at her father again.

"I think that would be a good idea," said Hallie, shaking her head in disbelief. She started slowly, her eyes now changing to a faraway look that gave Michael the feeling he could look straight into her soul. "The day before Grandpa died, we spent the entire morning together. He knew he wouldn't live much longer, and I think he wanted to be sure he had given me a few last bits of wisdom. We talked an awful lot about you. I don't know if you realize that you were his moral strength for many, many years," she said, ending the last sentence in a question.

"No. I didn't. He was a touchstone for my *own* moral foundations," Michael's voice choked ever so slightly.

"Grandpa said not to believe in the complex-world theory. Did the two of you ever talk about that?" she asked.

"Yes . . . it's what captured my interest in ethics . . . literally a turning point in my professional life," said Michael. Michael and his father had spent years discussing the philosophy that was to lay the foundation for Michael's work. He was impatient to learn more of Hallie's conversation. "What else?" he asked.

Tears began to flow from her eyes, but she smiled proudly. "He said that there were only a handful of principles that would guide me through my entire life, no matter how complex things seemed. We talked about them for hours. It's really the same stuff that you and mom talk about, only it really hit me hard since he said he knew he was going to die."

Hallie looked out the window to the backyard where her younger sister was swinging on a playscape in the pleasant summer morning air. It's one of the principles you know," she said, watching Hanna. "He said you would understand, but that you might not have an opportunity to teach me about it."

Michael reached over and cupped his hand over Hallie's. He expected it to be shaking, but it was firm. Hallie was more determined that ever.

"Grandpa said that life was about *living it* . . . that it wasn't a destination, but a journey. He said that the things he truly valued in his lifetime were those things he earned on his own, no matter how difficult or how simple." She paused. "It's one of the most treasured memories I have. It's the reason I want to pay my own way through school. I believe in what he said. It seems so noble an idea, living life—no matter what the outcome—but living it on the basis of experiencing it along the way," she said.

"You're facing your first moral conflict, sweetheart. Money has no intrinsic value—it represents value. In this case, its value is in freeing you from the hundreds of hours of work needed to pay your own way through school. Its value is that it has returned the time you would have spent earning the money," he said.

"So you think Grandpa would understand that I should take it?"

"No. That's the conflict. You know why?"

"Yeah . . .", she said dejectedly. "This is exactly what he was talking about. He would say I am cheating myself of the experience. That just getting there isn't living—but a shortcut." She paused. She was sitting now and staring down at the ticket.

"But it doesn't mean that I will just be sitting around watching television in place of work . . . right?" she asked.

"No. I'm sure you will fill your days."

"So wouldn't I be living more by spending the time doing something more worthwhile than working? I mean, I would study or play the piano or lots of things more rewarding than work."

Michael deliberately avoided making a judgment for her. "You could make that argument," he said.

"But you wouldn't buy it?"

"It's not my decision. I will pay for your education. The lottery can pay for your education. Or you can work to pay for your own education. I would suggest that you reconcile your values, though."

"I want so much to believe in Grandpa's vision. But I'm having a real hard time ignoring all that money. It's easy to refuse to take more from you and Mom. But there is nothing attached to this. It's faceless. It doesn't belong to anybody. And if I don't take it, it will just go to waste."

"That's all true," said Michael.

"It's a dilemma."

"No, sweetheart. There are no true dilemmas. You either live your beliefs or you abandon them. A dilemma is a contradiction and this is not a contradiction. You can't choose both," he said.

"I don't know what to do."

"You will. Take your time."

"That means you don't want me to take the money."

"I won't say. It's got to be your decision. Whether you take it or not, what you learn from the decision will be far more valuable than the money itself."

3

Jock Shaw

There's none so blind as
those who won't see.
—Jonathan Swift

James Shaw sat at his desk sifting through the month's sales figures. He ran his finger along the printed data in a manner that would lead an observer to believe he could divine something unwritten by his touch. At times he would speed across the numbers, his fingertip pressing lightly. Other times, his finger would bend from the pressure exerted and slow down as though he were trying to rub the name and the numbers from the printout.

Shaw knew the numbers inside out. He would flatter every new salesperson by knowing his or her first name, then blow the illusion by droning on about their individual sales figures, averages, trends, and ratios, betraying the fact that his true interest lay in the numbers. A sports gambler, he would spend hours working the statistics for athletic competitions, which earned him the nickname "Jock." If it were possible, Jock Shaw would do away with the human side of sales and just focus on the numbers. Most of all, Shaw disliked personal problems.

As far as Shaw was concerned, Ryan Matthews had a lot of personal problems, and he wanted very little to do with them. Shaw had joined Dremen-Russell two years after Matthews. During those two years, Ryan had set the world on fire. Soon after Shaw had joined the company, he had a noticeable influence on Ryan. It had been an unusual relationship from the start, one that few who knew them both could explain. For Ryan's part, he had come from a military family where authority was respected, especially when it was his direct supervisor. Besides,

Shaw was smart, and, perhaps even ruthless, which Ryan did not necessarily assume to be a negative. He would soak up any advice Shaw had to offer, good or bad. Several people had cautioned Ryan about Shaw, but the message was never fully received. Had any of them known of Ryan's problems, they would have made an immediate connection to Shaw's influence. Ryan, on the other hand, never thought of Shaw as part of the problem.

The knock on his door shook Shaw from his concentration. Ryan walked in without hesitation, as was his custom. Shaw looked up from the printout, pushed himself back from the desk, and nodded at the empty chair for Ryan to occupy.

"What's up, big hitter?" asked Shaw.

"Jock, I wish you wouldn't call me that. You know my numbers are way down, even worse than last month."

"Ah, come on. It's just a slump. I've had 'em myself, and I always came out of them," Shaw lied. He had never been a successful salesperson, although he had worked very hard to convince his employers otherwise.

"That's why I'm here. My slump just isn't going away, and I think I need some real analysis of what's going on. I just don't know how many more times I can strike out." Ryan wondered to himself why he was using stupid baseball analogies, but realized Shaw had started them.

"What do you have in mind?" Shaw saw one of the dreaded personal discussions coming, and hoped he could dodge it.

"There's a professional sales conference I would like to attend. It's called Sales Esteem, and it runs for about a week. It's not cheap."

"You think you need help with your sales skills? No way. You're one of the best I've ever seen. It's not the answer," Shaw shot back, partly worried about the price, and fully offended that Ryan would look outside for sales training.

"This conference is different. It develops the philosophical side of selling. The 'why' instead of the 'how.' Anyway, I started calling around to ask people what they knew about the thing and I couldn't believe the response I got. I would swear that everyone I called had been tipped off that a potential student was calling, and was paid handsomely for a good referral."

"Big deal. So a couple of people liked it. How much does it cost?" asked Shaw, seeing that his best defense would be the cost.

"More than a couple people liked it, Jock. In fact, I was so intrigued with the response that I decided to keep calling until I found someone with something bad to say."

"And?"

"I called three dozen people that I had selected randomly from their full roster. I finally called a guy named George Maxwell and realized he worked in our LA office—you know, the one who is either second or third biggest producer for us on the West Coast."

"Yeah. So what did Maxwell have to say about 'em?" asked Shaw.

"Everyone I called gave the conference high marks. Everyone but Maxwell. He said that he didn't think I should go."

Shaw sat up straight. Now he was intrigued. He knew Ryan well enough to realize he was setting the trap, and when he did it this way, it was usually rather well executed. "So . . . come on, let me have it. Why doesn't our West Coast hot dog want you to go? Is he afraid you'll catch up?"

"No, that's not it at all. He said he didn't think my career would survive it. He thought it would cause what he called a 'philosophical meltdown'."

"Screw him. Who does he think he is anyway, giving you an answer like that?"

"He was sincere, Jock. He said I should prepare myself for questions I might not want to answer. His exact words were, 'You'll either ignore everything you hear, or quit the minute you get back because you can't reconcile how your life is, with how it should be.' Christ, it's like this guy knows all the turmoil I'm going through right now," Ryan said, wishing immediately he hadn't added the turmoil part.

"What turmoil? Are you in trouble? Why haven't you said anything to me? Come on, Ryan, what's going on?"

"Listen, Jock, you don't like all that crybaby stuff, so I haven't said anything to you. Anyway, I truly think I'm the only one who can resolve it now. And I think I need this conference to do it. I came in here prepared to tell you that I either go to the class, or I start looking for something else." Ryan's hand was shaking slightly, but he pulled himself together enough to make it sound convincing.

"How much?" It was Shaw's last chance to kill the idea.

Ryan slid the invoice across the desk and waited for the expected response.

"No way!" said Shaw. "We don't spend this much to train the whole staff for a week. It's not in the budget."

"Jock, listen to me. There are two certainties in my life right now. One, I have no more answers . . . and no more excuses. I'm ready to quit and check groceries if that's the only alternative. And two, this conference is my last hope to avoid leaving the business. If it's not in the budget, advance me the money. It's my last chance."

Jock Shaw didn't give a damn about Ryan Matthews' psyche. But he did care about the revenues that Ryan generated. Still, he was opposed. He thought he would press Ryan on his suggestion for an advance.

"I don't believe in this stuff. These things are always a waste of time," he said. It was quite an ugly contradiction coming from a sales manager who had never been a successful salesman. "If you think it's that important, all I can do is to give you the time off, and advance you the money against bonus."

"Will you go upstairs to see if I can be reimbursed?" he asked, referring to Shaw's supervisor in senior management.

"Yes, of course. But don't expect it to happen, okay? I can't promise to tell them I support the idea," said Shaw.

"Why, gee, thanks Jock. I really appreciate you going out on a limb for me," he said in exasperation. "When can they cut the check?"

"I'll take the invoice and have them send it out right away. But look for it to show up on your monthly commission statement."

"Yeah, yeah, yeah . . . just make a dignified effort to get me reimbursed, will you?" Ryan said, knowing that he was on his own and had lost his argument. At least he had gotten Shaw to agree to the time off.

"I'll do my best," said Shaw.

After Ryan had left, Shaw spun his Rolodex to find Jason Smith's extension. Smith was Director of Corporate Training and Development, and would be the best candidate for scapegoat in turning down Ryan's request. He punched in Smith's four digit extension and waited for it to ring.

"Smith," came the answer at the other end.

"Jason, it's Jock. Quick question for you." Shaw and Smith were not fond of each other so Shaw could afford to get right to the point. "Do you know anything about a sales conference called Sales Esteem?"

"Yes . . . I do, in fact. Why?" asked Smith in an unusually suspicious tone.

"I have a guy in my group who is willing to pay his own way and wants us to consider reimbursing him the cost. It's incredibly expensive."

"Who is it?" asked Smith.

"I'm not sure who holds the conference. I figured you might know them."

"No, no. . ." Smith said impatiently. "I know all about the conference. Who in your group wants to go?"

Shaw was caught a little by surprise. "Uhm . . it's Ryan Matthews. He was just here."

"Can I call you right back on this?" Smith asked and then hung up without waiting for an answer.

Shaw had just enough time to light a cigarette, move around his desk, and sit on the other side to gaze out the window when the phone rang with Smith's reply.

"We'll pay the whole thing in advance. Send the invoice up to my office for approval," said Smith.

"*You've got to be kidding.* Do you know how much this costs?"

"Yes, I do. Bill Mallory approved it himself. Oh, and Jock. This is a special deal, because we want to help Matthews get things straightened out. We can't afford to send everyone on these things. Please ask Matthews to keep it quiet," said Smith, and then hung up.

Shaw was mad. He picked up the phone and re-dialed Smith's number.

"Smith," came the voice at the other end.

"Jason, it's Jock. This Sales Esteem thing. Shouldn't I being going to it as well?"

Smith hesitated, but not long enough to expose his initial uneasiness at the idea. "Your budget?" he asked.

"No way. If you'll pay for Matthews, why not me? Maybe I'll be able to bring something back for the rest of the group. As a matter of fact, maybe I should go instead of Ryan and see if it is worthwhile," said Shaw.

It wasn't Smith's intention, or responsibility, to address the problems the organization had with Shaw. He knew he couldn't turn down the request without exposing the company's unhappiness.

"I'll approve it on one condition," said Smith. "Ryan goes for the help it will give him. You go as an observer. I want you and Ryan to remain separated throughout the entire thing. I'm going to tell him he is to experience this on his own without your influence or interpretation. Agreed?"

Shaw didn't like the sound of the request. "Wait a second. I don't get it. Won't it help if he and I can analyze it together?" he asked.

"No," said Smith.

"That's not good enough. Why not?" insisted Shaw.

"Listen, Jock. I'd rather not have to say this, but if you have to know . . . Ryan will get a much different perspective of selling than what you normally present," said Smith.

"What the hell does that mean? I don't want these guys messing up all the work I've spent developing Ryan," he whined.

"Jock . . . We'll send him to help reverse what you've done," Smith's voice finally betrayed Shaw's fears. The rest was quite clear. The company was not fond of Shaw's sales approach, and they no longer felt compelled to hide it. "You go only if you agree to leave Ryan alone. Agreed?" asked Smith.

"I can't promise that," said Shaw.

"The decision to go is yours. If you go, leave Ryan alone. If you can't—stay home." Shaw was not about to retreat. He knew he had friends who would support him . . . or at least one friend, and a powerful one at that. Mike Carter was Marketing Vice President and had promoted Shaw to his current job. Carter liked the predictability of the sales numbers Shaw produced and had been quick to support him in the past.

"Listen. When Carter tells me to lay off Ryan, I will. Otherwise, he still works for me," said Shaw, throwing the challenge right back at Smith.

Smith was silent. Mike Carter was a very powerful person in the company, and still a supporter of Shaw's. He hadn't had the chance to confront Carter with his growing resentment of Shaw's self-serving managerial manipulations.

"Jock, it's simple. I approved Ryan's application because it came down from the very top. I say he will learn more without your involvement. If you mess him up you may have to explain it to someone above Carter. I'll go on record as having told you as much. The choice is yours," said Jason, hanging up the phone without waiting for the response he was sure would come.

Shaw started to speak but the click of the receiver cut him off. He held the phone out in front of him, staring at it like it as though it were alive. "Damn it. Who are these guys to always be pushing their way into my department, anyway," he said aloud. No one was going to decide how he ran his team, he fumed. Carter is strong enough to keep them away. If I need to, I'll call and ask Carter to push back.

He slammed the phone down hard on the receiver and spun in his chair to catch the view from the window behind him. Maybe the conference would be a good opportunity to discredit Smith and anyone else lined up with him. Shaw was certain he could short circuit Ryan's adventure. The thought never occurred to him that he might damage the last chance Ryan had to recover. Shaw didn't think in those terms. Shaw thought in terms of staying one step ahead of the pack, cleverly outmaneuvering them, and never paying much attention to the damage he caused along the way.

The corner of Shaw's mouth curled up in a cynical smile as he spoke out loud. "Yeah . . . this little conference may turn out to be even more expensive than they think."

4

The Sales Esteem Conference

Beaten paths are for beaten men.
—*Eric Johnston*

With one motion, Ryan slid into the waiting cab, pulled the door closed and called his destination to the driver. "The Summit," he said. As usual, Ryan was running late.

He stared down at the brochure which had the requisite map on the back panel with a star depicting the location of the conference. The cab slipped out of the traffic of the city and began a gradual climb into the suburban hills to the west. Large oak and cedar trees towered above the cab as the rolling hills became more dramatic. The road curved as it approached a white granite outcropping that rose out of the ground as though it were part of the earth it was built on. The building sat on a bluff high above a large reservoir that filled the surrounding canyons. Its windows pointed toward the west to take in the view, as well as the locally legendary sunsets. It looked more like a vacation mecca than a conference center.

As Ryan hopped from the cab, he found his spirits already on the rise. At least the surroundings would be pleasant. Inside he located the conference room and walked in slowly. The room looked functional but comfortable, and bright from the natural light that poured in through the windows that formed the entire west wall. It overlooked the spectacular view as well. Most of the other conference participants were there and had taken a place in one of the plush seats arranged to face toward the front of the room. Ryan nodded a wordless greeting to a few as he passed. He picked a chair next to Katherine Kelly, a confident-looking redhead, who offered the kind of smile that Ryan recognized as both friendly and business-minded. He hoped his colleague would be as interested as he was in making the most of the conference. On the table in front of Ryan was the typical assortment of pads, a pencil, a water glass and the conference brochure neatly arranged next to a plastic package that contained expensive lycra cycling shorts and a matching runner's jersey.

The large table at the front was stacked with backpacks and other mountaineering equipment. More equipment lay around the table—enough packs for everyone in the class, which meant they wouldn't be sitting around in chairs struggling through monotonous lectures all week. That was, after all, one of the promises made by the conference brochure. The others in the room had started a conversation about the equipment and it was clear that no one knew its purpose.

"No one said a thing about mountain climbing to me," said Katherine, who looked like she spent plenty of time working out at the local health club. her friends called her Kat and she didn't mind a little dirty work, as long as it was in a controlled environment. The thought of scaling a mountain was not her idea of fun.

Stanley Fischer was an investment banker who had obviously eaten more than his share of bagels and cream cheese. It earned him the nickname "Tug." "You didn't read the literature. It said this would be an experiential conference," his voice was rough with a cynical tone. "Gotta read between the lines, honey."

Kat Kelly despised the term "honey" and never missed an opportunity to let it be known. "Listen, Pal, if I were you I'd check to make sure they packed enough trail mix. For all you know, this is one of those health excursions where they starve you half the time."

"Oh no. Murphy Brown in pinstripes. Didn't mean to set you off, dear."

Kat didn't answer. She had hoped this conference would be a chance to meet the most talented salespeople from around the country, and had expected them to have decency that mirrored their talent. The exchange with Fischer seemed more fitting for a singles bar.

Shannon Shelley was a literary agent from Philadelphia and single mother of three wonderful little girls. She specialized in representing the authors of children's books where the clientele was typically as kind hearted and meek as she was. She was at the conference to find her "nerves of steel" in order to be more aggressive in locating publishers for her clients. Everything about Shannon was soft and gentle, which made her clients comfortable, but seemed to have the opposite affect with publishers, whom she believe paid her little respect. The idea of mountain climbing made her nervous. "Has anyone here ever done any mountain climbing? I'm not sure I can do it," she said.

Bobby Green had done some mountain climbing, but it had never held his interest. Bobby was a computer components salesman who had an appetite for performance. He liked speed and efficiency. Anything that could be put into a formula, repeated precisely in the same manner—and then timed for speed—captured his interest. He overheard Shannon's comments and came to the rescue.

"I don't think we'll be doing any mountain climbing—it's not the right gear for that—but it looks like we'll be staying overnight," he said.

Two other class members stood near the window staring out at the water below. Kyle Mitchell was a junk bond trader who had survived the Milken Meltdown because he had never strayed into the euphoria that swept most of his companions. It was his major achievement so far: surviving the junk debacle that collapsed companies and the investment bankers that escorted them along. Kyle had made a name for himself by keeping his feet on the ground in an industry where most had their heads in the clouds. He puzzled both his friends and family by his critique of the very business in which he excelled, although the fine line he drew was no more of a conflict than others made between quality and cheap junk. The difference they failed to see was Kyle's criticism of those who seemed incapable—or unwilling—to distinguish between the two. Kyle had recognized, and avoided, the sensationalism that blurred the senses, and it had served him well.

Glen Bailey was a friend of Kyle's from college, and the two had been stunned to meet each other at the conference. Kyle knew him as "Tip", a reference to his days as the dorm bookie for local school sporting events. Bailey was a sports agent who had just lost a handful of stars to a competing agency after a misunderstanding with a sponsor. Bailey had blamed himself and had taken a three-month sabbatical, which would culminate with the Sales Esteem conference. The sabbatical hadn't helped. He still felt to blame even though he had been consoled by management to the contrary. His company wanted him back but he didn't know if he could find the drive. If the last three months were any indication, he was in trouble.

The remaining class members sat silently waiting for the morning to get underway. Rick Kincaid was bored with the small talk about the backpacks. They would know soon enough. Kincaid was a labor relations arbitrator who never quite felt comfortable with the idea of selling, although he could see how people would characterize his job as selling solutions to problems. He relied heavily on changing the perceptions of the parties involved, on both sides, and forging a compromise so they could move forward. He liked to wait for the problem to arise and then solve it. The backpacks were no different, just another small mystery that would present itself in full color when given time.

Sally Holiday and Madison Porter sat silently next to Kincaid. They had arrived the night before and met at the hotel's registration desk. Sally was a corporate recruiter with a heart of gold. If she had ever made an enemy, it would be a surprise to anyone who knew her. Everything about her was warm and comfortable, which typically lead her to become more personally involved than most with her clients. She befriended anyone who opened their arms to her.

Madison Porter was the picture of health. Blonde and athletic, she was a track athlete from USC who could have doubled as a cheerleader. She was a sales rep for the world's largest maker of athletic shoes and had become a top performer by landing large international accounts through acquaintances she had made during a brief track career overseas. Madison also held an advanced degree in fluid dynamics, the result of four extra years in school and much prodding from her father. "A living, breathing, walking paradox" is the way her father referred to her. She broke all the stereotypes—she was a beautiful rocket-scientist who was selling shoes instead of sending people into outer space. Her father had always supported her and always would, even if there were no stars in her future.

Jock Shaw hadn't arrived yet. Ryan wasn't looking forward to the inevitable encounter with Shaw now that he had been asked to keep his distance from Ryan. He decided not to confront Shaw immediately with the order to keep his distance. Instead, Ryan decided to keep it in reserve, like a veto, in case Shaw became too much of an irritant.

The discussion about the backpacks was ending just as Michael Cevanté walked into the room. Michael knew how to build excitement, and it was especially easy with a room full of smart and enthusiastic professionals. The group quieted in anticipation of his opening comments. Most of the class members were familiar with the reputation of the Sales Esteem conference. All of them had pored through the literature they had received in preparation for the week they would spend at the Summit. All of them knew how expensive it was to attend. They expected to get their money's worth.

Michael approached the podium in front of the room giving no more than a brief sweeping glance and confident smile at the class. His demeanor was like someone preparing to lead them on a courageous journey. Once at the podium, he arranged the class biographies into a stack in front of him. Pictures were a requisite part of the application process for the very purpose of recognizing them without a long drawn-out introduction period. With each face, he had associated a name, the sales specialty and a potential sales problem. Michael prepared diligently, studying for hours the individual personalities as they had been laid open through the pages of the application. They were the cast in what would become a week-long drama. It was Michael's job to write the script and direct it.

There were a mere seventeen people in the room; all had different expectations for the conference, and vastly different experiences. The introduction was critically important in setting the theme and tone of the conference.

"Good morning . . .," he said in a voice that was warm, strong and full of purpose. " . . and welcome to the Sales Esteem Conference. My name is Michael Cevanté."

Michael paused for a brief moment.

"What lies ahead for you in the next six days can best be described as a 'journey'; a journey of self-discovery, of enlightenment, of terrible difficulty from time to time, and one that I cannot promise you will complete successfully. This journey is the continuation of a pilgrimage made many times by others like you. Sales Esteem is a philosophy—but hardly the kind we all suffered through in school." A few nervous laughs greeted the reference.

"Sales Esteem is the antithesis of today's 'feel-good' sales philosophy, and the long-awaited response to a culture that thinks of selling as undignified and distasteful. Sales Esteem is unique in its core premise. *Please etch this in your mind. 'Sales Esteem is the philosophy of ethical selling that results in increased productivity'.*" He paused.

"There is an enormous store of energy, untapped and waiting in all of us, that if discovered, and understood, will propel you to sales success you might otherwise think impossible. Today's sales mystics would like you to believe that 'wishing' for that energy will release it. Only a fool believes in something for nothing. Wishing leads you to the entrance of success, where you can press your nose against the window, peer in and glimpse the possibilities . . . and dream. The question you want to ask is, 'Where is the key to the door?' You are about to discover the location of the key. And, like all of our most worthy adventures, this journey requires something of the traveler. It requires you to use your most precious skill, your intellect. Like astronauts on a flight to the moon, science and understanding are at the foundation of our journey. Sales Esteem is the unification of sales science and the wonders of human emotion. Sales science (or sales principles) give you the substance upon which you will build your stairway to the stars. Sales Esteem is the step-by-step understanding of the principles that will unlock the door, release the energy, reward the traveler, and propel you to a wealth of physical and emotional rewards you could only dream about before.

"When those words were first uttered seven years ago, they were met with incredulous cynicism, or more often, hysterical laughing." Michael paused to offer a battle-worn smile that seemed to recall the inevitable criticism heaped upon pioneers.

"Those who have been through the journey laugh for a different reason, however. They laugh joyfully at their discovery of what others believe to be a paradox—increased sales are proportionate to the practice of the Sales Esteem principles.

"Sales Esteem finds its root in science, which is to say, proof and validity when applied to the real world. Ultimate sales performance has a foundation . . . a reason . . . a cause. A positive self-image or a rush of enthusiasm is shallow and short-lived unless it rests firmly on substance. Selling is a process, a process of well-designed principles and their corresponding actions. Like the difference between wishing to 'float to the moon' and the principles that allowed NASA to put man there, Sales Esteem is a set of principles that *work*. Principles that realize success through a passion for excellence, and then celebrate that success through earned emotions. The crucial part is the assembly of principles. Good principles result in success, bad principles fail. The essence of Sales Esteem is the sum of its principles, the enormous gains in productivity brought about by an extraordinary process, and the resulting rewards of Self-Respect, Pride and Self-Esteem."

The class was engaged now, and Michael hurried to bring his opening statements back into the framework of learning and away from preaching. "The Sales Esteem conference relies on experience. We will spend six days learning through experiences. *We will be up to our ears in experiences.* The foundation of Sales Esteem will be something you can reach out and touch. It won't ask you to have faith, or to believe in something that you can't readily grasp. And if you grasp it, its implications will be obvious. You'll understand the enormous opportunity to increase your sales. Both the content and its resulting benefits can only be learned by your thoughtful participation." Michael's tone was blunt but sincere.

He continued. "The most important thing to understand as we begin our journey is that Sales Esteem deals in substance. An ethic which condemns success is self-defeating; yet many of us associate success with excess—and guilt. An ethic that insists we respect authority is doomed when the authority fails us and leaves us stranded to fight on our own. An ethic of company loyalty is immoral if it requires coercion and deception. Sales Esteem will question the substance of these ethics and offer a more realistic approach. In a word, Sales Esteem is *practical*, but not necessarily in the sense that the word is normally used. Sales Esteem is practical in the sense that when it's practiced, it works. It has no contradictions. It is practical because it doesn't require you to take two steps forward and one step back. It's practical because you waste no time. It's practical because it recognizes that every action has a component of emotional energy attached, and that impractical actions waste energy. It is practical because keeping a customer takes less effort than getting a new one. It's practical because fixing messes costs more than avoiding spills. Sales Esteem has value for only one reason—it's a smarter way to sell. Without a gain in sales, the effort to be here wouldn't be worth your time."

Michael paused. It was a lot to dump on them in the first fifteen minutes. He knew the most immediate impression of ethics in sales was that it was impractical—that ethics was viewed as inaction instead of action. He knew the common perception of ethics was "second place." He knew they all wanted to believe differently.

"Please look around the room and admire the quality of the people gathered here. You are among the most talented people in corporate America. Your companies have spent thousands of dollars training each of you, and this is a continuation of that training. However, that is where the similarities end. It has been my experience that we have failed in giving you the essence of selling. We have failed in helping you to develop a comprehensive philosophy of selling. The result is that you have been shortchanged; you've been given just part of the picture.

"Without a philosophy of selling, you're left with nothing but the mechanics. Without practical ethics, you have just half the picture.

"You have the courage of the astronaut without the wonder of the adventurer. You have the skills of a technician without the passion of the artist. You have the body of a champion, without the soul of a winner."

Everyone in the room was infused with the energy of Michael's comments and their implications. Michael's tone was anything but condescending. Nothing they had ever heard had been spoken with such easily felt confidence.

"Doctors save lives," he continued. "Teachers give the gift of knowledge. Judges dispense justice. But what does the salesperson do?" he continued. "Sales Esteem is a journey to discovering the answer to that question, and the rewards are enormous.

"The sales philosophy of the past delivers techniques of persuasion, but fails wholesale in delivering a philosophy of selling. In its place is a disguise called *inspiration*, which is the modern-day equivalent of a sorcerer's incantations. It can be compared to a skyscraper without the first five floors; the penthouse that pokes through the clouds and is bathed in the sunlight seems like paradise, but there is no foundation. It delivers tricks, and scraps of ideas that you are asked to take 'on faith.' Unfortunately, there is no foundation upon which they can rest. It is no wonder they crumble to the ground when tested.

"The trend today is to overcome the 'obstacle' called the customer by subverting the negative emotions considered to be an unavoidable part of selling. The Sales Esteem philosophy will steer clear of mind games."

Michael paused to let the air rush out of his attack on false sales motivation. He had a particular dislike for the recent fad of motivational sales training that invoked frenzied emotions, and trance-like states of mind that were aimed at blanking out emotions. He knew hundreds of thousands of salespeople had been affected by the technique, hoping to find new sources of sales success, and he didn't want to go on the attack without exposing its emotion-based fallacy first. After all these years, Michael still had to work to rein in his passionate dislike for the fraudulent.

He regained a calm voice.

"Through your own experiences, you have come to recognize hype for what it is: empty and shallow. But once you have rejected it as a sales foundation, you are left to fend for yourself in arriving at your own sales philosophy. I am certain you have one; those who don't rarely make it this far. And I am equally certain that it relies on honesty. We rarely have class members who are less than honest. Sales Esteem will encompass honesty, but move far beyond it. Most of you have elevated yourself to a place of dignified sales. You arrived there on your own. What your organizations realize, and the reason you are here, is that your own discoveries are often only partially developed. With the benefit of the learning of others, you can finish building that philosophy."

Michael didn't like to lecture. Try as he might to avoid it over the years, the introduction always required it. It was like the cover of a book that described the journey ahead, only this journey was waiting to be written. Michael firmly believed in learning through personal discovery. And he believed that truth was delivered by experience. The success of the conference relied on two principles: more doing, less preaching. He enjoyed watching intelligent people discover the answers on their own with no more than a few gently guiding questions. He used this approach as the framework for the conference.

"To demonstrate the depth of the type of search we will be conducting, I'd like to ask a straight-forward question. We've concluded that all of you are likely to be honest. But is there anyone in the room who refuses to lie, no matter the circumstances?"

Hands shot up throughout the room. "Why?" Michael asked, pointing to Shannon Shelley, who was in the front row.

"Everyone knows you don't lie," she said, somewhat indignantly.

"But people do lie?" asked Michael.

"Yes, of course," she said, realizing suddenly that this conference probably demanded more than just simple answers.

"But you don't," Michael continued.

"Honestly . . . ?" she asked, which generated chuckles from the class members who recognized the absurdity of the response. "The only time I knowingly lie is when I think I would cause more damage by telling the truth. Sometimes I bend the truth a little if I think it will help the situation."

"How do you decide when to bend the truth? And how do you determine whether the damage you avoid by telling the occasional lie isn't actually exacerbating something much more damaging?" His voice had the tone of objective questioning, even though it was obvious he knew the questions were practically unanswerable.

Shannon was caught, and smart enough to know when to cut her losses. "I suppose that's the reason we're here," she said.

"Yes, partly," he said. "You see, we *know* it's not in our best interest to lie. It's *floating* out there in our conscience. The problem is that it's floating instead of being grounded in a principal. If we focus on discovering the principal, we will have a guide to determine whether there is *ever* a reason to lie," he said, hesitating.

"These are the type of questions Sales Esteem seeks to answer. Lying is not bad simply because an authority figures say it's bad. Lying is impractical for a far more obvious reason—it doesn't work. It falls apart when it bumps into reality. Reshaping reality is difficult.

"If I were to define honesty as the *absolute adherence to reality*, would it be easier to guess at the consequences of lying?" he asked.

A smile came to Shannon's face. "Sure. I can see that a lie does nothing to change the facts, and only helps me to temporarily avoid something that won't go away."

"Very good," said Michael. "Does honesty take on a different meaning when you realize the risk of a lie is *not* in being caught?" He paused before elaborating. "The risk is that you are trying to push reality around, trying to change things that can't be changed by words or feelings, or illusions. Ultimately, you bump into them and have to change course."

Michael's face softened. "Actions are half-empty unless we understand the underlying reason. That reason becomes a principle. We are here to discover the principals that guide your sales actions, not because an authority said it is the way it should be done, but because reality rewards it.

"Everyone has principles. Some of these principles are sound, and others are misguided. From your principles come actions, or your ethics. Good principles generate good ethics, poor principles lead us in the wrong direction. The results, either way, are emotions, or energy. It's a cause and effect chain reaction; principles . . . guide your actions . . . and result in energy—both to move us and reward us," he concluded.

Michael picked up an electronic remote control for a slide projector positioned in the back of the room. He pressed it several times to turn the power on and engage a slide. The screen lit up with a diagram.

Sales Esteem
Values, Principles and Motivation

"This slide is a skeleton outline of the science behind Sales Esteem. It's a model of human motivation, developed to explain where the increase in sales productivity of the Sales Esteem philosophy actually comes from. We all start at the bottom with a litany of values—the things we pursue in order to maintain life or enhance it. For instance, food, shelter . . . even love. Once we have identified our primary values, we rely on an assembly of *principles* as a 'master-plan' to guide our effort to get the basic values. Finally, like any other movement, the effort to achieve our primary values requires energy, or motivation."

Tip Bailey liked to make comparisons between the motivation of the professional athletes and salespeople. He raised his hand as Michael ended a sentence.

"Yes, Tip?"

"It seems to me that we need some motivation before we form our principles," he said.

"It's a good observation. It requires that you start at the point in life when an infant recognizes hunger and discovers the principle necessary to satisfy that value," Michael said with sincerity, while suppressing the urge to laugh.

The others had no reason to hold back their laughter and Tip immediately understood the implication of Michael's comment. He covered quickly. "I guess more than one value is established at that point," he said to more laughter.

Michael continued. "From there it's a continuous spiral. Once we understand that attaining values requires a plan and energy, we follow a basic pattern that leads us to identify the things we believe will be of value to us. We form a plan to get those things, and exert the energy needed to reach them." He paused.

"Please keep in mind that this is a preliminary discussion. We'll delve into motivation more thoroughly later. For now, what I want you to consider is the substance behind the Sales Esteem philosophy. It lies in the principles." He pressed the remote control to bring up the next slide.

"Principles are sorely misunderstood, but we're going to fix that. For now, it will be enough to know that all action requires a process. That process is the assemblage of knowledge about the way things work. The knowledge comes in the form of principles. And keep in mind, the knowledge can be right or wrong. In this slide, the principles all hang together and keep our upward movement intact. The power of Sales Esteem comes from the process of good principles, actions that execute those principles and the motivation that is generated in the continuous cycle of each sales opportunity." He pressed the remote for the next slide.

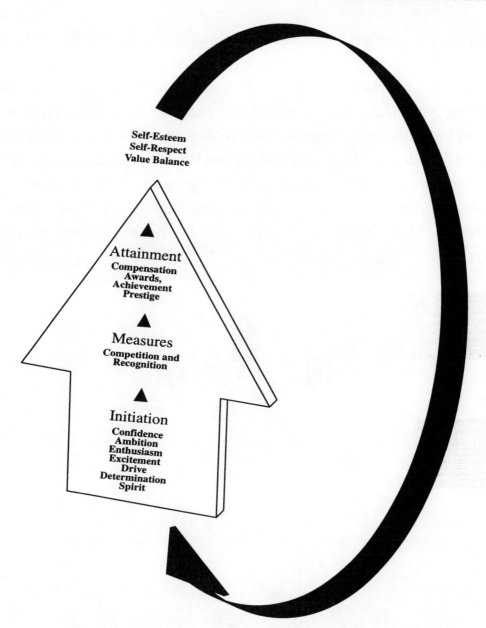

Self-Esteem
Self-Respect
Value Balance

▲
Attainment
Compensation
Awards,
Achievement
Prestige

▲
Measures
Competition and
Recognition

▲
Initiation
Confidence
Ambition
Enthusiasm
Excitement
Drive
Determination
Spirit

Motivation Cycle

"This slide illustrates the cycle of motivation. The arrow represents the stages of motivation from initiation to the all-encompassing view of your actions. We'll spend more time on that aspect in the days to come. If you complete the arrow with sound principles in place, you return along the circular path to start again. If your principles are right, your actions guarantee success, and the emotional energy of motivation builds upon itself—you've completed the cycle. When you start at the beginning for the next cycle, you have an expanded energy source. But if something goes wrong along the way, if your principles are ineffective, ragged and torn, and it's more difficult to make the sale, then all the things that motivate you begin to fade. If you get to the top and are unable to look back on all that you have done and can't feel the self-focused emotions of self-respect, pride and self esteem, the return to the beginning of the arrow is difficult at best. You zap energy and motivation. Here's how it might look on a slide," he said, pressing the remote again.

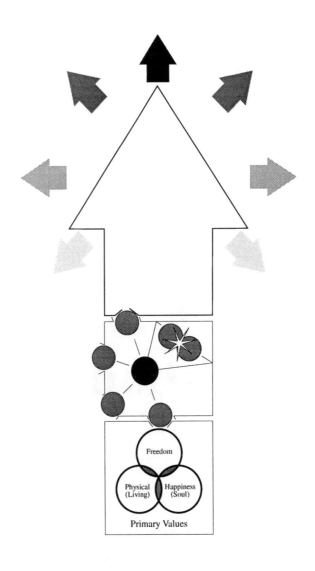

"Here the principles don't work . It may be that they fail to work together—what we would call a lack of integrity—or worse, they contradict one another and cause a conflict. The result is a bad 'master plan' and actions that fail to realize our goals. It's as though you have all the wrong tools, or the wrong road map. The result is a diffusion of energy—wasted or misdirected. It's interesting to note that it's impossible for every principle to be wrong. Any movement requires a minimum of the right principles. So you can realize partial success even with a handful of the wrong principles. The question is, how much more successful can you be with all the right principles? That's the basis of Sales Esteem. Grasping the principles that work—and grasping those that work in harmony—that's integrity. It's perfectly logical, then, that the efficiency of the right principles adds to your energy. Efficiency and more energy are the reasons your sales will increase." Michael stopped there, waiting for a response. This was the moment of the conference where the class members realized they were in for something truly extraordinary. Michael beamed at them as though he had just shown them a treasure, and was about to share it with them.

"Our week will be devoted to discovering the principles that work in selling. And identifying the counter-principles, or those that fail." He pressed the remote to bring up the next slide.

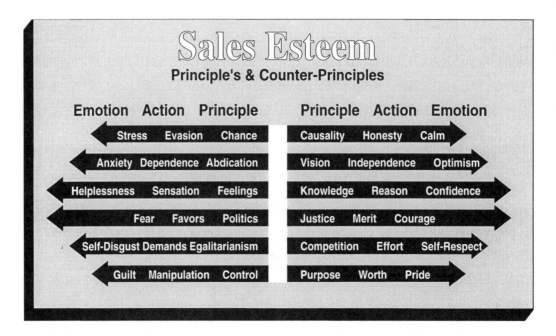

"There are six primary principles—on either side of the equation. Each leads to an action, and results in an emotion. Those emotions will either contribute to your motivation or detract from it." He paused.

"Ultimately, we'll end up here." Michael brought up the next slide.

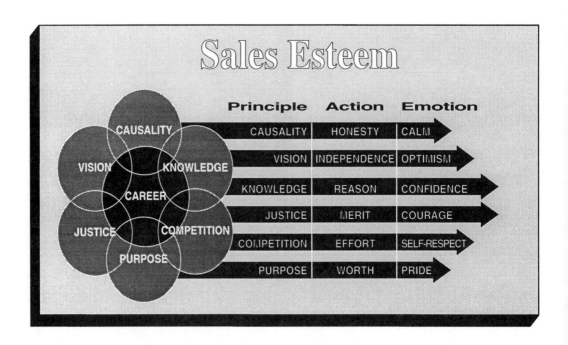

"All that you'll see right now is the emotional results that ultimately come from your principles and actions. The principles can be good or bad and move either right or left, as they did on the diagram before. Principles are formed for just one reason—as a guide to action. Emotion is the result. Good principles result in good emotions . . . bad result in . . . you get the idea," he said. "This is our outline for the week."

It was enough motivation to get everyone but Tug Fischer, jotting on the paper placed on the table in front of them. Fischer sat with his arms folded across his chest, rocking back and forth on the legs of his chair. Michael paused, glancing around the room until he reached Fischer, who was staring at him waiting on a response. A smile came to Michael's lips. Every class needed someone to contrast the ideas being presented. The greater the contrast the better. Michael spent a great deal of time on the résumés he reviewed when selecting conference members to make certain he would include someone certain to argue. This time it looked like he had found a perfect candidate.

"Very good, Mr. Fischer," Michael said, with just the right change in tone to signal acknowledgment of Fischer's defiance. "I see that you are either an excellent listener or have arrived at these steps prior to joining us. I think you will find the conference very interesting."

"Oh. I'm sure," he said, pausing. "Can hardly *wait* to get started."

Rick Kincaid could recognize a conflict from any distance. He raised his head and glanced back and forth at Michael and Fischer as though he were watching a tennis match. He had seen it many times: two individuals so different that virtually nothing could be agreed upon between them. "If there was chemistry between two people . . ." he thought, ". . .then there must also be its opposite."

The group finished their note-taking and Michael continued. "The Sales Esteem conference is designed to mix experiences and discussion, view something real and concrete and then analyze it thoroughly. When possible, we will create an experience for you directly. And when necessary, we will invite a guest lecturer to discuss their experiences. Regardless, we will take real examples and apply them to selling. Typically, we'll experience it first, then tear it apart here in the classroom. Nearly all of the experiences will come from something other than a sales environment. As the brochure explained, we leverage experiences in other endeavors that can be nicely translated to apply to a philosophy of selling. Other than the minimal but necessary amount of lecturing, most of what you learn will come from the experiences and the subsequent analysis as we discuss them as a group. If it isn't real or based on reality . . . it's worthless. I will help you to analyze and apply the principles to selling, but you must make the integration," he said.

"I should tell you now that our journey will become a little more rigorous. No doubt you noticed the hiking gear when you came in. After lunch, we will have a guest who is going to lead us on a little expedition into the desert—or was it the mountains?" Michael feigned a loss of memory to pique their interest. "Or maybe there are mountains . . . *in a desert*. Yeah. . . that was it," he ended with a coy smile.

A new face appeared at the door. Jock Shaw had a simple personal rule, "being on time to a meeting was directly related to the control the individual expected to have at the meeting." Shaw had attended many sales seminars in the past, and was generally obnoxious and disruptive. His plans were no different for the Sales Esteem conference.

"Hello, I'm Jock Shaw from Dremen-Russell. Hope I didn't miss much," he said, as he walked to an empty chair and sat down.

"Mr. Shaw," Michael said in a tone that sounded much more in control that Shaw would expect. "I'm very sorry, but the beginning of the conference is *essential*, and to repeat it would be unfair to the others. We will refund your tuition and enroll you in the next conference if you wish."

Shaw was caught off guard. "I'm sure I can catch up," he said.

Michael knew of the circumstance surrounding Shaw's attendance. Jason Smith was an old friend, who had called Michael to warn him of Shaw's possible influence on Ryan. Michael, in fact, wanted Shaw to attend since Smith had fingered him as the most likely culprit in Ryan's struggle. Michael walked around to the table where Shaw was sitting. Shaw was a large man, but Michael suddenly looked much larger as he loomed over Shaw. "Mr. Shaw. May I be blunt?" he asked.

"Fire away," said Shaw.

"The conference information emphasized the importance of arriving on time. Did you have travel troubles?" he asked.

"Nope. Everything was on time," said Shaw defiantly, looking down at his watch, and looking back up at Michael with a smirk.

It was just what Michael would have expected. He went on. "Let's see then . . . there can be just two other reasons for you to be late. Either you're incapable of managing your life, or you have a lack of respect for what the rest of us came here to accomplish. Either way, it leads me to believe you will fail here. I suggest you take my offer to refund your tuition while you have the chance," he said.

Shaw looked surprised. "I guess my flight was late after all," he said, with a slight chuckle that he expected would gather a few laughs from the rest of the class members. It didn't.

"Mr. Shaw, we've already discussed the futility of dishonesty this morning. You should understand that you're here at my pleasure, and at the pleasure of the rest of the group. I can see no benefit from your participation to this point. If you would like to stay, you'll respect the others in this class, and stop wasting our time. I would be fascinated to hear your honest explanation for being late today . . . ." Michael's tone had changed to hint at forgiving Shaw.

Shaw was clearly embarrassed, but not about to be humbled completely. He glared at Michael. "My plane was late," he said.

Michael turned to walk back to the front of the room. "We're going to break for a few minutes," he said. "But first I would like to tell you about a tradition we have here. Accepting anything at face value is a mistake. Whenever you get the chance, question the content of the conference. Poke at it, dispute it, criticize it, tear it apart. It's the only way to learn. Nothing is off limits. Breaks are an excellent opportunity to be a critic, but not a cynic. There *are* dumb questions, but there are no unfair questions."

The words were liberating. There was no hiding behind definitions and statements made in a manner that implied they were sacrosanct. A sense of excitement was beginning to spread over the group. The combination of the unknown of the journey ahead, and the freedom to explore the essence of questions never raised, gave them a feeling they hadn't experienced in many years—the feeling of discovery.

"Before we break, may I ask if it was clear from the promotional pieces that the conference would be physically challenging?" he asked, as he surveyed the responding nods.

"Good. Does that mean that each of you have found a way to exercise over the last four weeks?" he continued.

The group members quietly shook their heads in guarded agreement.

"Good," Michael continued. "As part of the experience of the conference, we're going to jog each morning. There is a purpose for this, and it applies directly to Sales Esteem. If anyone is physically unable, or finds great discomfort in running, they are exempted," he said.

"It is now 10:00 AM. After the break, we'll take our first jog. We've provided running gear for you and the hotel has a small health club downstairs where you can change. After you are dressed, please meet me at the building to the back. There is a grassy area where you can stretch. See you in twenty minutes," he said, with a smile on his face.

The group was generally young and vibrant; few complained about exercising. At 10:20 the group had gathered and stretched. Michael came down to the grassy area to join them. "How many of you run regularly?" he asked. More than three-quarters of the group raised their hands.

"Excellent. We are going to make time to run everyday. I would like you to consider the question, Why do you run? It will be part of our discussion throughout the week. Some of you are going to fall in love with this type of running. Others of you may wish you never have to put on a running shoe again, but I think all of you will understand its application to selling—as strange as that may sound right now. Our path starts behind us here and runs for approximately three miles," he said.

The class turned towards the thick wooded area behind them to see a brown dirt path that quickly disappeared into the forest. Michael continued, "It goes downhill from here to the valley floor. Then it winds along a tributary stream back to the top of the ridge. It crisscrosses the dry stream bed. It's not easy, so please be careful. It has been cleared of branches so you can run upright, literally as fast as your feet will carry you. The path itself is mostly flat and well-worn, but where it crosses the creek, the footing becomes a little more treacherous," he paused for questions.

"I would like you to time yourselves, but be cautious until you are familiar with all the obstacles on the path. Be curious about where you are and what you are doing. I'll lead to begin with. Each of you should follow at thirty-second intervals. Everyone ready?" he finished.

Michael took a quick glance around and noticed that Carol Simpson, Tug Fischer and Jock Shaw were missing. The run was not mandatory, but few chose not to participate. He started off towards the path in a slow jog and was quickly out of sight. Madison Porter followed after him and the rest of the class joined one by one, checking their running watches, and guessing at the thirty-second increments Michael had suggested.

Madison Porter had run on tracks all over the world, but had never run through a forest. The thought occurred to her as she inhaled the fresh smells of the cedar, pine and the wildflowers that covered the forest floor. Her pace was fast and she quickly closed the gap on Michael. She yelled ahead to him, "Guess I should have given you a minute head start."

Michael grunted, "Hah. Would you like to pick up the pace?"

Madison was just twenty feet behind him now. "If you can," she said.

They had reached the bottom of the downhill section where the path turned and began its climb. Michael ran the path frequently, and knew that the uphill portion, which danced across the creekbed, was a test of agility and leg strength, and not speed, which was the forte of a world-class athlete like Madison. He increased his pace.

The creek flowed heavily during the spring runoff, depositing large boulders which formed stepping stones, some two feet high, on which to cross the creek. The path darted back and forth along the creek's banks. It rolled up and down, through the jagged surroundings, accelerating the runner's pace on the downward side of each hill and then pushing him into a short upward climb on the next rise.

Madison was pushing hard now, but didn't seem to be catching Michael. She slipped frequently until she realized keeping her arms lowered gave her more balance. The short downhill stretches and the uneven rock-covered creek bed made it a difficult course. Once she had a feel for the new technique, she could tell that she was covering ground more rapidly. By now, Michael had pulled away from her and she could no longer see him or hope to catch him. She decided to give up the chase and enjoy the run. Her immediate thought was a feeling of freedom. It occurred to her that she had never thought of running in those terms—running for the joy of it. A rush of adrenaline hit her and she recognized it as the sudden jolt of energy a runner gets when the body releases endorphins. She was puzzled. Commonly referred to as 'a second wind,' the body produced endorphins only after long strenuous periods of exercise. This couldn't be the same thing. Yet, she felt a release of energy that had to be explained by something. It didn't matter just then, as she was completely engrossed in the love of running.

Thirty feet in front of her she saw the trees open into a clearing. Michael stood there, fidgeting with his watch. She covered the ground quickly, and asked as she slowed to a stop, "Where did *you* run off to?"

"It won't take you long to get used to it. That will probably be my biggest margin of victory," he said.

"I can't remember the last time I enjoyed running that much," said Madison.

"You've never run through a forest before?" Michael asked.

"No. And I felt something I haven't felt in a long time. It was really amazing. It was like a second wind, but I couldn't possibly have gotten it from the exertion. My mind just opened up. It was a kind of a mental high."

"I'm not surprised," he smiled.

Kyle Mitchell finished next. Tip Bailey was right behind him. They were breathing hard and Mitchell started to complain. "Why . . . are we running . . . through that . . . mess?" he said in a jerked rush of words that were interrupted by his breathing.

Michael laughed out loud. "Be patient—and inquisitive," he said.

The rest of the group was finishing the run one by one, and christened it with variations of either positive or negative comments. There was no middle ground. The run was either terrific—or terrible. As was typical, the group was engaged in arguing the merits, the purpose, and the difficulty of the run. Michael had achieved the desired result. The group was "thinking" about the reason for the run, and the various theories included everything from health fanaticism to out-of-body experiences, neither of which were right.

Michael raised his hand to plead for the group's attention. "I hope everyone enjoyed the run. Please keep track of your times. We will run at 8:00 in the morning from now on. I'll be anxious to hear your first reactions to the run when we get back to the meeting room. You have plenty of time to shower and eat lunch before we get started at 1:00," he said.

The group, some moving more slowly than others, returned to the locker rooms for a shower. Madison waited for everyone to leave, stretching on her own, away from the rest of the group. When the last person had disappeared into the locker-rooms, she turned and entered the forest to run the path another time.

Lunch was served on the balcony just outside the conference room. It was a large suspended decking that had been cantilevered so that it extended out over the face of the ridge. It stepped down from the building so as not to obscure the view from within, and gave one the feeling of being detached from the rest of the building. The decking hugged the curves of the rock wall, revealing nothing but natural surroundings in all four directions, except for the deck itself. The wooden staircase was all that joined it to the conference center.

Kyle, Rick Kincaid and Fischer stood next to what looked to be a free-standing bar, although no one was tending it. They held their plates of food and faced each other, oblivious to their surroundings. Kyle Mitchell was thirty-three years old, making him the youngest of the three. He had been raised to respect experience and age, and assumed a deferential role, even though he was quite comfortable when the roles were reversed.

"What do you think?" he asked, speaking first to Fischer.

"I'm glad I didn't pay for this out my pocket," Fischer said.

"Yeah . . . wasn't cheap, was it? But if we get the results he says, maybe it will be worthwhile," said Kyle.

"Uh-huh. When was the last time you got a damn thing out of one of these? Just clever head-games that never apply to selling. This Cevanté guy has got people fooled into believing this stuff and has to convince us so we'll go back and keep the story going," said Fischer.

Kincaid ignored him. "I will say this. He has set himself up to either win us over, or leave us in a fog. It's a big promise he's made," he said.

"Lambs," said Fischer his voice falling in an accusing finish.

"What?" asked Kyle.

"Lambs. Anyone who goes for this can be led to believe anything."

"Yeah . . ." said Kyle. "I can tell by the way that he insists we think for ourselves that he wants us to be mush in his hands," Kyle said, shaking the wide-eyed kid routine. "What do you do for a living, Tug?" he asked.

"Investment banking," said Fischer. "I find dreamers like Cevanté who look for the intangible value in things and are willing to pay dearly for it."

"I don't get it. If dreamers make your world go 'round, what's the hang-up with Michael?"

"I don't *buy* the deals. I arrange them. I only buy when the price doesn't include a premium for the dream. I'll let you pay full price, kid, and I'll come in and pick up whatever I can without the emotional buy-in."

Fischer was a street fighter who had grown up in the Bronx and struggled to make his way to Wall Street. He knew his acidic tone was insulting—just as he wanted it to be. Kyle had seen more than his share of "bankers" during the junk bond frenzy. He wondered if Fischer had been involved in any of the "deals" he had seen.

"Deals, huh? Initial offerings or mergers?"

"Buyouts, kid," said Fischer, realizing suddenly that he had no idea what Kyle did for a living.

"What do you do?" asked Fischer, trying to get back on equal footing.

"Nothing that sophisticated. Are you familiar with the Beckman acquisition?"

"Yeah . . . My firm did the deal. I was mostly on the sidelines though," he lied. Fischer was the architect.

"No kidding," said Kyle. "Wasn't there something wrong with that deal?"

"Somebody claimed the pension plan was undervalued and the whole thing ended up in a lawsuit. The court decided it was baseless and dismissed it while it was being settled out-of-court," Fischer lied again.

Kyle Mitchell was the "somebody" who showed his analysts the discrepancy in the pension valuation. He had been a hero at his firm, but a bane to some on the

"Street." The court had no intention of dismissing the suit. The case was settled quickly and quietly. There were enough lies in Fischer's story to raise suspicion about his involvement, and Kyle decided not to let him know that his accuser would be spending the next six days with him.

"Oh . . . really. I guess I had heard a different story," said Kyle. He was stunned at the circumstance that would put him in the same class as a potential culprit in the fraud he had uncovered. Especially a conference that dealt with topics of ethics and morals in selling. His thoughts stopped right there as though a light had come on in a dark room.

"No . . ." he thought. "There's no way Michael could have known . . . and then . . . planned. Naw . . . no way."

Ryan Matthews stood alone, looking off into the distance. He had plotted the direction he would travel if he could be where he wanted to be at the moment—pushing his son in the swing at preschool. Kat Kelly stood chatting at one of the groups when she noticed Ryan standing alone. It struck her that he was terribly unhappy. He hadn't noticed as she approached him and touched him gently on his shoulder in an unconscious sign that she had recognized his pain. It was an unusual thing for a stranger to do, and Kat was suddenly embarrassed. Ryan turned slowly and smiled at her. "Is it time to go in?"

"Soon, I think. It's beautiful isn't it?"

"What's that?"

"The view."

"Oh . . . yes . . . it is," he said. "My mind was somewhere else."

"I could tell. Is everything okay?"

"Oh, yeah . . . sure. Just thinking about my son. He's why I'm here."

"Really," said Kat, hoping for an explanation.

"It's hard to explain," he said, suddenly realizing he was talking to someone he barely knew.

Just then a bell rang, surprising them that anyone would actually watch time in such a beautiful setting, but reminding them of the reason they were there. Ryan was thankful for the interruption and turned to join the others.

Kat and Ryan returned to the conference room and found the others in small groups, talking quietly, but with a palpable anticipation. Michael joined them, causing the small groups to break up and sending each class member to find a chair. Michael's manner was now one of partner, not professor. His introduction to the conference demanded more traditional lectern speaking, and even a little preaching, which he tried to avoid when possible. Now he sat on the edge of the table at the front looking relaxed but purposeful.

"What do you say we begin with the run on the path . . . one of my favorite topics. Did anyone enjoy it?" he asked.

Madison looked for signs that someone else shared her joy of running on the path. About half the class had raised their hands in response to Michael's question.

"And, did anyone dislike it?" asked Michael, knowing there would be a flurry of negative comments.

Grumbles rose from half of the seventeen people in the room. Michael smiled and held his hand up in a manner that signaled he knew what the responses would be.

"Would someone like to elaborate on either side of the question?" Michael asked.

Bobby Green was an avid weekend long-distance racer. He spoke first. "I run an awful lot of races, and frankly, I've never known that I could dislike running so much. Thanks, Michael, for taking running to a new low for me," he said. There was laughter from the group at Bobby's blunt answer.

"Yes. I've been accused of that before," said Michael. "Why has it ruined your love of running?" he asked.

"There's no opportunity for speed. It's like a formula-one car in the jungles of Peru. Who really cares about bouncing up and down through the hills when they could run on a smooth surface and cover the distance in half the time?" replied Green, obviously passionate about his running.

"Well stated, Bobby. Can I ask if you know your personal best for the five-Km run?" asked Michael.

Bobby was quick to answer. "You bet, it's sixteen, thirty-one, three."

A smile came to Michael's face. "Bobby, I have to tell you that you are the first to give me times in tenths of a second," he said with a slight chuckle. "Is it fair to say that your times are important for you?" he asked, already certain of the answer.

"Without a doubt," Bobby said proudly.

"Do you think time stands still in the forest?"

"No."

"Would you mind if we chart your times each day for the rest of the group to see?" asked Michael.

"Sure . . . that would be okay," said Bobby, a little surprised.

"And what was your time for the run this morning, Bobby?"

"Uh. . . eighteen, fifteen, six," he said a little sheepishly.

"Not bad," said Michael, as he turned and jotted it in big numbers on a tote board behind him. "And, Madison. You ran the path twice today. What was your time on the first run?"

Madison smiled at him for finding her out. "Nineteen, thirty, something," she said, her casual tone contrasted Bobby's seriousness.

Michael scribbled it on the board. "And the second run?" he asked.

Madison protested. "You didn't ask if you could keep track of my times."

"That's right," he said. "What was your second time?"

"Eighteen, ten or so," she said with a smirk.

"A few seconds better than Bobby's time. But before I start a conflict, I need to tell you that Madison is a world-class track athlete, or least she used to be," he said, looking at Bobby.

"Is there someone who runs consistently as a part of their normal routine? Someone who is not a world-class athlete. Someone who would be willing to share their times with the group?" asked Michael.

This was of particular importance in Michael's analysis of the run. Typically, the group was full of such people. This group was no different. A third of the class raised their hands to volunteer. Michael pointed to Sally Holiday, a corporate recruiter from Philadelphia. "Sally. How about you? What was your time?" he asked.

"Twenty-six minutes, and I didn't look at the seconds. Sorry," she said.

"It's okay. We'll put you down for twenty-six even," he said, scribbling.

Michael paused and turned to address the group. "The path will be a regular topic of ours. I think you'll notice some interesting things when you run on the path. Please do yourselves a favor . . . analyze the hell out of the run. I welcome your comments throughout the week. We'll put our experiences on the path under the microscope on Friday."

"Time to move on. The first part of our journey is just that. Late this afternoon we will board a charter flight to our base camp at the foot of a small mountain range in New Mexico." Michael paused to let the inevitable whispers breathe slightly more excitement into the room.

"By tonight, we will be sitting before a bonfire having one of the best steak dinners ever served in the wild. We'll sleep in the cool weather of the desert night, and begin a five hour excursion over the mountain range tomorrow."

The trip over the mountain had become legendary among sales managers throughout the country. The thought of the expense and difficulty in moving seventeen people to, around, over, and then back from, a mountain was staggering. From the very first conference, Michael had insisted on the importance of the trip over the mountain. One of his favorite memories came from the conference's early years when he was arranging financing: the look on his banker's face when he first explained the mountain excursion, and how he would be spending part of the bank loan. The mountain was the epitome of his conviction of experiential learning. But the mountain trip was far more important for another reason. It provided a concrete foundation of objectivity. Most errors in sales philosophy were rooted in "mind-over-reality" mistakes that weren't tolerated well by nature. The mountain gave rise to the cornerstone of Sales Esteem philosophy—reality can't be changed by wishing it away. It was impossible to fake it on the mountain, especially when a one-hundred foot fall loomed nearby. Regardless of one's definition of honesty, the experience on the mountain proved that adhering to reality was ultimately unavoidable.

Michael continued, "The trip over the mountain is very expensive . . . it's a pain in the tail logistically . . . it's ever so slightly dangerous, and it is the *most crucial aspect* of the entire conference," he said.

"In the morning, you will be divided into three groups. You've probably noticed the hiking gear," he said with a smile. "You'll select a team leader, chart your course, and then cross the mountain as a group." He paused.

"We will be joined by Kevin Keller, a knowledge engineer, and an experienced mountaineer climber, who happens to get a kick out of city slickers slipping and sliding around desert canyons. Once there, you will have very little guidance from Kevin or myself, unless you happen into a dangerous situation." Michael grinned. "We'll be finished and on our way home by late afternoon."

Tug Fischer was already annoyed. Fischer rarely did anything that could be called exercise, let alone climb up and down canyons. He had ignored the pre-conference request to exercise in anticipation of the physical exertion during the conference. "You're going to pack all these people up and fly them four hundred miles to New Mexico so they can wander around in the desert? You've got to be *kidding!*" he said.

"Sounds extreme doesn't it?" replied Michael. "Tug, you're a sharp guy. Want to guess the reason for such an extravagant effort?" he asked.

"Not really," said Fischer, who didn't have a legitimate guess. Fischer was smart enough to avoid speaking just to be heard. Michael was a little surprised. He had hoped Fischer would be a consistently sharp adversary, and he was being let down at the moment.

Ryan knew the reason for the mountain trip. But then, Ryan was at a crossroads and had been surveying his life, backward and forward, for months. He waived his hand, two fingers held out casually, to get Michael's attention. "Michael, I'll take a chance and guess it has something to do with gaining perspective on our sales careers," he said.

"Extremely close, Ryan," said Michael warmly. "You have captured one aspect of the mountain crossing, but do you think it's possible to plan an entire career?" he asked.

"Exactly!" interrupted Fischer. "You guys are nuts if you think you can plan your career that far into the future—and to go to New Mexico to do it. This is great."

Michael was truly disappointed in Fischer now. It was an obvious mistake that any worthy adversary wouldn't make. Maybe Fischer needed a poke to get him in the right frame of mind. Michael's tone changed to that of a school teacher. "Come on, Tug. Everyone in the room has been through goal-setting. This is the advanced class. Catch up," he said with a mix of gentleness and annoyance that was just right.

Fischer shifted upright in his chair. "Advanced? Wandering around in a desert doesn't sound as though it will be recognized as progressing the species to me. If you really want to know my guess, I'd say you want to convince us that we need to see the long term—getting over the entire mountain. Isn't it a little too predictable?" he huffed.

"That's better," Michael thought to himself, then said aloud, "Sure, but that's obvious. There's something far more important to be discovered on the mountain."

"I know. We'll make all kinds of mistakes because you won't explain enough about planning the trip. Then we'll get to hear all about how to plan our entire career," said Fischer.

"The mountain is analogous to your career, all right, but your guess runs into trouble after that. You won't make very many mistakes because you already know how to walk, and you'll have detailed maps to guide you. Also, I have no interest in *telling* people how to plan their careers. I enjoy seeing people figure things out on their own. They frequently do it better than I would. But there is a bigger issue yet. One that I won't betray until after we have come back to discuss our trip. For now, I would ask that you all make an association between how you expect to tackle your careers and the way you tackle the mountain tomorrow. We are going to have dozens of insightful analogies, almost all of which will come from tomorrow's experience and your own reasoning," Michael said.

"Please grab a backpack on the way out. You have a half hour to change. We'll meet in front of the building at 2:30 and board a bus for the airport."

Forty minutes later, they were on their way. It was a thirty-minute ride to the airport, where they would board a commuter flight to the mountain range.

Rick Kincaid was the last to board the bus. Tug Fischer was sitting alone. Fischer had never bothered to pay much attention, but people generally avoided him. Kincaid took the seat next to him.

Once the bus was underway, Kincaid asked, "What do you think of this stuff?"

"Not impressed. You?" inquired Fischer.

"I think it's kind of interesting. I've heard of Kevin Keller before. He's quite well known. I'm anxious to see how all of this is tied into selling."

"I think it's hokey," said Fischer, staring out the bus window.

Kincaid was quite good at guessing moods, and Fischer's was easy to read. He wondered why Fischer always displayed his anger. "Tug, who paid for you to be here?" asked Kincaid bluntly.

Fischer turned to him for the first time. "Why do you wanna know?" he said.

"I don't know. I get the feeling you would rather be somewhere else."

"I'm here because the Securities and Exchange Commission is playing Gestapo and needed to find a scapegoat," Fischer lied.

"I don't understand," said Kincaid, although he was getting a pretty good picture.

"My deals are over their heads. If they can't understand them and then some fool loses a little money, they look for a scapegoat. I'm the scapegoat. They know just enough to understand that it's the fools who lose their money who are wrong, not me. This just makes them feel better," Fischer snorted.

That gave Kincaid enough information. "What do you think about the conference?" he asked.

"Like I said, it's hokey. Just a bunch of weak salespeople trying to feel good about what they do. Me? I have no illusions about who I am, or what I do to make a buck."

"There's a chance to learn something. Even if you don't agree with it, it's a new perspective that might help you somewhere. Why be so negative?"

"Listen, pal, you do this labor relations thing, right?" growled Fischer.

Kincaid nodded.

"Well, your thing is to see different perspectives. Good for you. My thing is to do cutthroat deals where most times there is a winner and a loser. I don't need anyone else's stinking perspective."

Kincaid had run into the likes of Fischer before. "Wow . . . so you've got the whole thing figured out," said Kincaid.

Fischer was sitting right next to Kincaid so that when he turned his head to face him, he was uncomfortably close, practically staring into Kincaid's ear. "Can I make something perfectly clear? I don't give a damn what you think of me. You're the one who asked why I won't play this little game. You *asked* and I *told* you!"

Kincaid was silent. He wasn't used to being attacked. Kincaid had gotten into labor negotiations because he had a knack for understanding two conflicting positions and finding a common thread. He knew it could only happen if there was some reason for common ground to be found. He also knew that there were conflicts that just couldn't be resolved—when two philosophies were so different that they were virtual opposites. He guessed correctly that the difference between Michael and Fischer was one of those conflicts. Then it occurred to him. Michael Cevanté was the foremost authority on ethical sales practices. His reputation for honesty and integrity was about as high as they came. It was his business. If Kincaid was right about opposite philosophies, what type of philosophy did Tug Fischer possess? Suddenly it occurred to him that he was going to have a chance to watch it play out. "And that," he thought to himself, "should be truly enjoyable to see."

5

Kevin Keller

Anything will give up its
secrets if you love it enough.
—*Dr. George Washington Carver*

The bus pulled into the charter section of the airport and rocked back and forth as the class members filed off. A Fairchild Metroliner III waited thirty feet away. The ground crew helped to unload the backpacks and direct the class onto the waiting plane.

Michael stood next to Kevin Keller, who was directing the crew, sharing an occasional laugh and barking instructions for the flight's preparation. He was slightly over six feet tall with the build of a welterweight boxer, and wore a leather flight jacket and aviator glasses. He looked like a "top-gun" flight instructor without coming on too strong. His confidence, humor, and sincerity were always in balance, making him an immediate hit with practically anyone he met.

Keller was an ex-fighter pilot who had spent time training Navy pilots in emergency actions. His preparation had saved many lives, although most of them were during routine training flights in peacetime. He had been recognized as a pioneer in the study of controlling panic. Keller was now the lead engineer at IntelliOne, a commercial venture that provided knowledge engineering, more commonly referred to as artificial intelligence. An expert in human cognition and logic, he had helped Michael with the early ideas of experiential learning for the Sales Esteem conference. Michael had sought Keller out after learning of his work in human emotion studies, and, with Keller's help, had developed the Sales Esteem principles of managing emotion in the sales process. Keller had been fascinated that such a traditionally emotional profession would prosper by forming a rational base. Salespeople also represented an unusual opportunity for Keller's work—they had a great deal of autonomy, which translated to authority to make ethical choices in their daily decisions. He applied much of his observations of the Sales Esteem class to his work in artificial intelligence.

Keller's electrical engineers had demonstrated the functionality of mathematical reasoning in the laboratory, but were decades from integrating the element of human emotion into their computer models. His team was dedicated to discovering the basis of emotion, not to discard it, but instead to build it into their models of artificial intelligence. Keller was most fascinated with high performance professions like selling, which traditionally sought to expel science and replace it with emotions.

Keller himself was a fascinating blend of reason and emotion. He was thirty-four and had never been married. This, however, did not leave him without companions. Keller was handsome and charming, and left many girlfriends wondering what they were unable to give him. Most surprising to Keller's new acquaintances was his love of adventure, and his seemingly childlike joy in the thrill he would find in disciplined diversions like martial arts and high-speed airplane racing.

The moment people met Kevin Keller, they realized they were in the presence of a genius. Before long, however, they would feel as though they had known Keller for years.

Michael and Keller formed a bond quickly after their first meeting which would last a lifetime. They had a supreme amount of respect for one another that was rooted in identical values and an identical thirst for life. Keller had agreed to help Michael with the original Sales Esteem conference and never stopped coming. Keller would spend the week at the Cevanté residence during the conference, and fight off Michael and Dianne's not-so-well-disguised attempts to find him someone to marry.

Keller would be leading the "trip over the mountain." He and Michael finished the conversation and with a slap on the back, left Michael to continue directing the ground crew.

Within fifteen minutes the plane was airborne. The New Mexico mountain range was a two hour flight to the west. The ride was comfortable but noisy. The group chatted about the trip over the mountain in voices strained by the roar of the engines, and the stress of the unknown. Finally, they all settled in to read or take a quick nap before arriving at the site.

Ten minutes out from their destination, the pilot throttled back to begin his descent. The plane leveled off at 2,500 feet above the floor of the high desert with the mountain range visible off the right side. Below them were rolling, high-desert plains interrupted by single mountain ranges. Millions of years earlier, this had been a basin submerged by an ancient sea, and the land was still rugged enough to give the impression of life's struggle. The mountains were carved with the canyons caused by run-off from the spring rains. Sparse desert vegetation covered the plains but retreated from the canyons. It was the perfect movie set for a Hollywood western, but had few other valuable uses. *Their* mountain stood alone, perhaps five miles from one end to the other. It looked strangely contrived, as though it had been built for this very purpose. Keller took a stack of single pages of paper and handed them backwards throughout the plane. The paper had a detailed topographical map and instructions. Keller grabbed the plane's cabin microphone and began an explanation. "In just a few minutes, we'll land real close to our little mountain," he said. The group members strained to look down as they circled.

The plane finished the circle at altitude above the range, and then started to descend towards its eastern slope. A few minutes later, the wheels touched down on a dirt runway and the plane bounced to a stop near what looked to be a deserted gas station at the base of the range. Behind the gas station was a flurry of activity. Large grills made from halved oil-barrels were filled with charcoal and glowed red in the twilight. A staff of six was busy preparing the meal, and readying the camp sight. Now it looked like a Hollywood set, without the lighting and camera equipment, but with all the comforts expected of people not used to sleeping under the stars on the hard desert floor.

The group members staggered down the short ladder, stiff from the small cabin space, and lined up to collect their packs and be shuffled off in the direction of their campsite. The sun was beginning to set, and there seemed to be a quickened pace now as the ground crew hurried their dinner preparation. Michael gathered them around a large unlit campfire.

"Please pair up with someone and set up your tents. If you need help, just wave," he said. Small cliques were beginning to form so that choosing a partner wasn't difficult. They did so quickly and began unfolding the tents from their packs, and assembled them as clumsily as a father with new toys on Christmas morning.

It was an invigorating environment. The sky was a clear blue, a few stars could be seen over the eastern mountains, and the desert floor was dry and cool. Other than the mountain range, which was now just a blackened outline against the horizon, the whole world seemed to open up to the night sky.

Soon the group was seated at large boulders that had been collected over the years and placed in a circle around the campfire. They began devouring a sizzling steak dinner. The atmosphere was festive and relaxed—almost surreal. Just a few hours earlier they had been in an air-conditioned conference center in the middle of civilization. Now they were a world away but still carrying on as though the changed environment was nothing more than a scene change in a movie. When dinner was nearing its end, Michael stood to speak and the noisy and boisterous group went silent. Michael paused just long enough for them to notice and remember their surroundings. The crickets chirped and the bonfire crackled against the background of desert sounds. The light from the fire flickered across Michael's face, making his eyes glow brighter and seem larger with the changing shadows. It was a captivating environment, perfectly set for the evening's closing comments. Michael enjoyed the contact with the real world and liked to use its impact in setting the tone for the trip. "Every year I get mail from our past participants who remember this moment as the beginning of a new chapter in their lives. They write of the strangeness of seventeen city slickers dropped into the middle of nowhere and suddenly vulnerable. They speak of an awakening of their minds to the possibilities symbolized by the endless vista of the night sky. And they ask me to send them a copy of the toast I will leave you with tonight."

He raised a bottle of beer to the sky. "To each of you:

'You are unique in the world, to look forward and back.
You can learn from your mistakes, you can learn from the past.
You can choose to replace any weakness with strength,
Strength that each of you possess, deep inside and awake
And realize the secret that alone you can know
Whether your soul is alive, and how far you can go.
Happiness comes not from just reaching the end,
But from making the journey, which on reason depends.
The march you make toward your dreams and away from your fears,
Starts here with a clear mind and a horizon that calls without limits—
Bounded only by your imagination
and your willingness to keep it grounded in honesty.
Wise and fortunate are those who see life this way.'"

Michael tipped his raised bottle to a group as they sat in silence. Slowly they followed him in the toast, their eyes locked on the figure before them as their minds rolled with thoughts of the words he had spoken. All but Fischer were captivated. He took a drink, looked up at the stars that dotted the sky, and without another word, turned and left for his tent. The group hesitated for just a moment and slowly rose to retire for the night. They were left with their thoughts, and no one broke the silence.

6
The Mountain

Nothing splendid has ever been
achieved except by those who dared believe that
something inside them
was superior to circumstance.

—*Bruce Barton*

Kat Kelly rolled over and pulled the thermal bag up over her head to keep the morning chill away. "Why . . .", she thought, "does morning come earlier in places like this?" Madison poked her head out of her bag. Kat started to giggle and struggled to stop, holding her hand to her mouth.

"What?" asked Madison, knowing Kat was laughing at her.

"I'm sorry, it's just that . . . well, you look mortal this morning," said Kat, breaking into more laughter.

Madison tossed and turned at night, which left her flowing blond hair looking like an electric mop in the morning. She laughed too. "Thanks a lot. I'm glad someone gets a kick out of how I look in the morning," she said.

The group slowly came to life as they caught the aroma of fried eggs, bacon and coffee. Makeshift showers, their first true inconvenience, were waiting for them. The pace was slow, as though they had been sleeping much longer than they had. The sky was steel blue with the sunrise blazing over a rim of the mountain range. The desert life was stirring, seemingly unaware of the people among it. Breakfast was gobbled down and the ground crew helped to break camp as they prepared for the trip over the mountain. Keller moved through the group with a tin coffee cup in hand and pointing to his watch to signal they were ready to gather.

When the group was assembled, Keller began. "I've passed out a map and instructions for forming your teams. There will be three teams. I've asked Bobby Green to mountaineer Team I. Michael and I will mountaineer Teams II and III. Mountaineers *are not* team leaders. The groups are responsible for selecting team leaders. The team leader is responsible for organizing the trip over the mountain. The *mountaineers* will not lead unless there is a danger to someone's safety. Seriously, we have never had anyone injured on one of these trips, but that doesn't mean you won't be the first. You will face some risks," said Keller.

Keller directed them towards their groups, helped some with their gear, and spent time walking them through the specifics of the map he had provided. It was still early in the day, and the crossing would likely require five hours of hiking, depending on the terrain of the route each group selected. The instructions on the map indicated the teams must leave by 10:00 AM. They would have eight hours to accomplish a five-hour trek.

Team I selected a former U.S. Marine Captain as its leader, giving them a great degree of confidence they would cross without any problems. The team included Kyle, Bobby and Jock Shaw. Team II included Madison, Sally Holiday, Tug Fischer and Kat Kelly. Kat suggested Madison be team leader, since she looked fit and had an athletic background. Madison declined, and to everyone's surprise, Tug Fischer volunteered. Perhaps caught off-guard by his offer, the group named him leader for Team II. Team III named Ryan team leader and included Kincaid and Tip Bailey.

Inevitably, there was always a group that seemed destined to fail, usually due to the selection of the team leader. Keller typically took the risk groups. Fischer's was the suspect group on this trip. The only potential medical concern they had was for Shannon Shelley of Team II, who was three months pregnant. Shannon was in great shape, but Michael wanted to be especially cautious. Normally, Keller would be assigned to Fischer's group, however, after a quick discussion between Michael and Kevin, they decided Kevin should keep a close watch on Shannon. That left Michael as mountaineer for Fischer's team. With that settled, Kevin asked them to formulate their strategy for the crossing.

It was 8:30 AM, and they should take no more than an hour to arrive at their plan. The teams formed into circles, earnestly looking over the map and making suggestions. As was typical, the designated leader in each group watched for a moment before assuming control, trying to organize the discussion. Soon the groups settled down into a thoughtful exchange of suggestions and strategy, with the team leaders exercising various degrees of control. Ryan listened thoughtfully, waiting for good suggestions to be offered, directed the team's attention to those he felt had merit, and then, glancing from one member to the next, waited until he got a silent nod of agreement.

Cleave Benson was the Marine Corps Captain that headed Team I, and he assumed complete control, shunting most of the ideas off as foolish in a brusque, but inoffensive way. It wasn't long before he was doing all of the talking and simply directing the group as to the strategy they should take. The other team members complied without much resistance, since Cleave had clearly been in similar situations before and seemed willing to command.

Fischer's team was a different matter altogether. Fischer displayed a peculiar mix of disinterest and domination. He asked the group to make suggestions, listened without much interest or response, and then ridiculed most of the group's suggestions. It was a group with very little actual experience and only trial-and-error suggestions, which were difficult to arrive at, but extremely easy to criticize. Fischer made no suggestions but was quick to criticize.

Michael and Kevin listened as the teams plotted their strategies for the assault on the mountain, neither making suggestions or raising concerns. When they were finished, they all gathered together once again to review the various strategies. Teams I and II took conservative routes. Fischer's team chose a more aggressive route. Kevin quieted the groups to ask, "Okay, how did you arrive at your chosen routes? Cleave, you first."

Cleave seemed to come to attention and for a moment it looked as though he would salute Kevin. "I . . . uh . . . I mean, we. . . selected a route that considered points of danger to be avoided, like rivers, steep grades and canyons," he offered. "Then, we selected three potential routes which would avoid as many danger areas as possible and settled on the shortest."

"Ryan? How about your team?" asked Kevin.

"Practically the same, except we reversed the process and selected the three shortest routes and then discarded those we thought might be too difficult."

"And what about you, Tug?"

"Short routes are smart. We didn't spend much time worrying about the danger zones because we are confident we can overcome them. We'll be the first team to finish," said Fischer.

Keller didn't like Fischer's route. It skirted a ridge on the most dangerous part of the mountain and added far too much risk for the small gains in time. He was close enough to speak quietly to Michael without the others hearing. "What do you think? Should we let them take that route?"

Michael glanced down at his map. "It's not the one I would take, but it looks like there are enough alternatives if we have to reroute along the way. Let's try something to see if we can shake Fischer's confidence."

"Listen up everyone. Team leaders are to be in the point position. Routes can be changed at any time. Is everyone comfortable with the routes they have chosen?"

Fischer spoke up. "Yeah, yeah, yeah. We're all ready. Would anyone like to make a wager on the first to finish?"

Rick Kincaid was still seething from the comments on the bus, and saw an opportunity to humble Fischer a little. "Sure, Tug. How much?"

"My hundred against yours?" Fischer replied.

Kincaid extended his hand, which Fischer refused. "I know where you live," he grunted.

Kevin looked at Michael, who could only shake his head in a resigned look of anticipated trouble. "Let's go," said Michael.

The three groups made their way from the base camp towards the first canyon. They split there and started on their individual routes. Fischer's team crossed a ravine in order to climb up the side of the canyon to its high wall. The three teams hiked through the washouts, dry river beds and along the sides of canyon walls. The first couple of hours were uneventful. The teams were performing quite well in keeping track of their location, maintaining directions, and even making some excellent assessments in timing their arrival at certain points they thought were critical along their route. Michael was pleased. His goal was to get them to recognize that no matter what they wanted to do, they couldn't change reality, and they possessed the ability to consider actions far into the future. He would develop that point in the classroom the following day using some of the experiences they had encountered along the way—washouts that couldn't be crossed, bluffs that caused them to make adjustments to their planned course, a once-dry river bed that had flooded and forced Team I to retrace its course back up the mountain and try an alternative path.

Three hours into the hike, Cleave's team stopped to have "lunch," even though no one in either group would call it that. Fischer's team pressed on. Just after 1:30, Ryan's team caught sight of Fischer's across a large valley, perhaps 300 yards apart. The terrain on Fischers' side of the valley looked rather treacherous, with steep canyon walls, and dramatic washouts. They spotted each other and waved with large sweeping arm motions. Kincaid was a member of Ryan's team and was not pleased to be so far behind Fischer. He could imagine Fischer's pleasure at having such a large lead.

As he stared across the valley a sudden gust of wind swept through the group and whipped itself into a small funnel of dust that disappeared over a ridge. Kincaid turned to the west and confirmed what he had expected. His eyes scanned the sky as it darkened with thunderheads. These storms, or squalls, formed rapidly, brought gusting winds, and heavy downpours called "gully-washers" by the locals. They were usually gone as fast as they came, and the approaching storm looked to have all these characteristics. The first few raindrops were beginning to fall.

Kincaid turned to join the others and saw that Keller was surveying the sky. Keller motioned for the group to gather around him. "Ryan, you're the team leader. What do we do during a thunderstorm?" he asked.

Ryan glanced around the group. "Does anyone know anything about desert storms?"

No one answered. Ryan looked at Keller for a suggestion.

It was clear that Keller would provide only a minimal amount of direction. "This one looks like it could be nastier than most. What do you think we should do, Ryan?" pressed Keller.

"My inclination is to pull out the ponchos and find some high ground for the next twenty minutes. Any disagreements?" Ryan asked surveying each group member quickly as they started to fidget with their backpacks.

"Keller, do you agree?" asked Ryan.

"Yep," said Keller.

Three hundred yards away, on the side of a canyon wall, the scene played out in a slightly different way. Fischer's team was not in agreement. By this time the winds had picked up to thirty miles per hour with forty mile an hour gusts, and the rain was heavier.

"Tug, I think we should wait it out," said Kat.

Fischer glanced back, preparing an insult, but getting a face full of pelting rain that stopped him short. "Uh . . . " he stuttered. "Uh, yeah. Maybe it's not a bad idea."

Michael motioned to the rest of the group towards an overhang that protruded away from the canyon wall and extended over the path they were on. The group quickly huddled there, glancing back and forth at each other and commenting about the ferocity of the pounding rain.

The squall was getting worse, with the wind lashing the rain against the ground, which had turned to a reddish-brown mud. It didn't look as though it would let up soon. All three teams were worried about the storm's onslaught, but it was the members of Fischer's team that were most concerned. They were perched on the same canyon wall Michael and Keller had worried about. The ledge where they stood wrapped around the high side of the wall, which dropped off dramatically to the floor some ninety feet below. The gullies formed by past storms, which had seemed harmless when dry, were now flowing with gushing water. Large chunks of red mud swept away down the gullies like a melting candle. The entire mountain seemed to be washing away with the storm. It was now clear that they had been caught in an unusually strong thunderstorm, and were in the worst possible place to sit it out. The sky seemed to be getting darker with each passing moment, and the lightning strikes were closer than before. The rain came down in slanted sheets, popping and bouncing on the ground when it struck. Water was flowing down the side of the canyon wall in small, but powerful streams.

With a sudden, ear-shattering crack, a bolt of lightning struck the side of the canyon wall fifty yards above them, and twenty yards in front of the overhang. Just as the brilliant flash of light ended, a torrent of brown mud rumbled down the side of the wall in an avalanche of chocolate-colored water and red rock.   The sound was nearly deafening as the avalanche roared by. It spanned twenty yards across and boiled up and away from the wall, engulfing everything in its path. The avalanche flowed for nearly a minute before stopping, shaking the ground and rumbling by them as they perched under the overhang. They were frozen in fear watching the slide that could have swept them all away.

The storm was passing. The winds had slowed and the rain was now just a soft drizzle that would be gone in another thirty seconds. The group rose from their crouched positions and moved to the edge so they could observe the damage. The ledge that was there just moments before had washed away completely. They stood just twenty-five feet from the cut of the path which was now ripped away and opened up to the a forty-foot, nearly-vertical drop to the canyon floor. Their route had vanished.

They turned—almost in unison—to check the condition of the path behind them. An audible sigh of relief came up from several in the group. The ledge looked to be in reasonably good shape, although it had been narrowed in several places. It wound back down the canyon wall for several hundred feet before disappearing around a rock slide. Several in the group started back down the path right away.

Michael looked at Fischer. "Would you agree that we should retrace our steps until we find another route?" he asked.

Fischer was clearly shaken. "Yeah. I wo. . would say that's a good. . . iii-dea," stuttered Fischer.

Sally Holiday was near panic and started back down the ledge. Her first few steps sunk her ankle-deep in thick red mud that spread away from her hiking boots far more than normal. With a sudden 'whoosh,' the dirt supporting the ledge beneath her feet gave way into another slide. Sally was unable to react quickly enough, fell to her backside, and slipped with the slide down the side of the wall. A scream followed her down a narrow crevice, but ended abruptly when she came to a slow-motion stop, resting against a large boulder that caused a bottleneck and stopped the mud like a cork in a bottle. Sally was thirty feet down—stranded on what remained of the debris that had slid down the canyon wall. Her position looked stable for the time being, but she clung to part of the rock outcropping in terror. Michael shuffled to the edge and called out for Sally not to panic. There was no direct route to Sally and he surveyed the situation closely. Madison came sliding down next to him, slipping and bumping him slightly.

Madison looked calm, but her eyes were wide with the excitement of the moment. "Can we reach her?" she said, even though it was clear they couldn't at the moment.

"Not from here," said Michael, looking over to see that Madison was far less calm than he would have expected.

"The ledge could give way at any moment!" said Madison.

"Yeah. But we still can't reach her from here. What do you say we *don't* panic, Madison?" Michael said in a intentionally calming voice.

"Right . . . right. Okay. What do we do?" asked Madison, settling down a little.

Cleave's team had not seen the avalanche, and had continued their trek once the storm had passed. Keller's team had watched much of the avalanche and he had taken off towards them to help.

Keller was jogging as quickly as possible through the mud towards them, leaving the others behind. He reached them just shortly after Michael and Madison had scurried back up to the ledge where the rest of the team waited.

Keller and Michael hurried through the packs and dug out the ropes and climber's picks. Without saying a word, they knew they would have to descend by rope and pluck Sally from the side of the canyon wall. Keller grabbed a harness and moved around Michael to strap him in as Michael was routing a rope through metal clips and the dead-head that would anchor both climbers' ropes. After snapping Michael into his harness, Keller attached his own harness and began helping Michael with the second anchor. Madison was struggling to fit into a third harness. Keller looked over and caught Madison's glance. She stopped for a moment to gauge his reaction and to argue should he object to her joining them. He reached down, picked up a rope clip and tossed it over for her to use. Madison smiled at the instant compliment of equality—especially coming from a hero-figure like Keller. She couldn't get the harness to fit properly and was struggling in frustration. Keller walked over to her, grabbed her with both hands at the waist and turned her around with mock forcefulness. "Here," he said. "Let me give you a hand."

Madison let him turn her around, and when he was done cinching her into the harness, she turned partially back around to face him. Their eyes met and remained fixed for a moment, sharing an instant of interest in the midst of the adrenaline and excitement. Kevin's hands were still on Madison's hips and they both suddenly realized they had remained there much longer than they should have. Madison felt herself blush and they both turned to join Michael in preparing for the descent.

Michael said to Keller. "What do you think?"

Keller was surveying the side of the wall and Sally's precarious position. "You lower yourself directly over her from above. You'll carry her out. I'm going to position myself below her about ten feet in case her movements cause another slide—I can try to catch her. I'll talk to her as you edge toward her and keep her calm. I don't want her to move until she can take your hand. I think the whole thing can move again at anytime. Madison, you position yourself to the side of Michael and follow him up as he ascends with Sally. Agreed?"

Madison nodded. Michael said, "Kevin, make sure you explain to Sally that we'll count down before she moves to take my hand and then make one slow movement. She's got to be panicked."

"Right," said Keller.

They moved around to their positions and sunk their anchors into the soft mud. Michael used the sledge to pound both his and Madison's anchor-deep into the rock below the mud. When they had clipped their ropes onto the anchor, they began to rappel down the slide area. Keller was already moving down and talking calmly to Sally as he descended. Sally was terrified. She clung to the rock outcropping that had halted her slide. Her eyes were closed and tears were running down her cheeks. She was shaking uncontrollably, and wasn't answering Keller's questions.

Keller made it to a position below Sally as Michael edged to within a few feet. Madison was just to the side of Michael, making certain she didn't do anything to cause another slide. They were ready. Sally *wasn't*.

"Okay, Sally. We're going to get you out of here, but we need your help," said Keller.

"I can't let go! Please! Help!" she cried.

Keller said, "Sally, listen to me. At the count of three, I want you to reach out and grab Michael's arm at the elbow. From there you'll be able to stand on the rock using Michael to help keep your balance. He's going to lower himself far enough for you to put your arms through the back of his harness. Clasp your hand over your wrist. The two of you will walk back up then. Okay?"

Sally didn't answer.

"Sally? Did you hear me?"

"I can't do it! I can't move!"

"Sally. You *have* to do it. Come on now. Reach up and take Michael's arm."

"I can't!"

With a cautious but determined release of her rope, Madison lowered herself closer to Sally. Sally clung tightly to the rock. "What if I get on the rock and put Sally in my harness?" she suggested.

"No!" said Keller. "We don't know if the rock will hold that much weight."

Madison was stretching her leg toward the rock outcropping. There was just enough room for one person to stand. It would be a difficult maneuver for Madison to release her harness as she stood on the rock, and then stand beside Sally as she tried to help fix it around Sally's waist.

"Sally?" said Madison softly. "Will you please reach up and take Michael's hand?"

"I can't!"

"I'm going to try it," said Madison.

"No! Madison, it's foolish," said Keller, edging closer as he sensed a disaster coming.

"Well then *you* do it! You're close enough now," said Madison in frustration.

"Madison. Stay calm. The rock won't hold the weight, *damn it!*"

Madison lowered herself within range and her foot made contact with the rock. Michael and Keller moved toward them simultaneously as Madison stepped onto the rock. The rock slipped slightly but stopped. Sally screamed. Madison unhooked her harness as she reached down and helped Sally to her feet. The rock slipped, and then stopped, throwing them off balance for a moment. They stopped themselves from falling by steadying themselves against one another. Sally stepped through the legs of the harness as she clung to Madison's shoulders. Madison hooked the harness just as the rock slipped again. Michael and Keller moved instantly. The rock fell out from beneath Madison's feet and she plunged, stopping suddenly in a painful jerk as Michael reached out and grabbed one of Madison's outstretched hands at the wrist. He held on tightly as the force of the movement slammed Madison hard against the side of the wall. Keller pushed himself off from the wall in a sideways swinging motion towards them and wrapped his arm around Madison's waist for the second time that day. This time however, it was not so gentle. Madison clung to Keller and Michael as the three of them came to a stop suspended above the canyon floor. The rest of the group had pulled Sally up and began lowering the harness again. They swung it within Michael's reach and they helped Madison put her arms through the leg-straps. The group towed Madison up as Michael and Kevin climbed on either side of her; one hand on the rope, and the other hand held with two fingers through the belt loop of her jeans. The wall was sloped enough that all three could plant their feet and climb using the help of the rope. It was a difficult and slow climb but one that would end without tragedy.

"Damn it, Madison," said Keller on the way up. "That was stupid!"

Madison was shaken, but recovering quickly now. "I didn't think the rock would slip," she said, her heavy breathing masking the trauma.

"You didn't *think* at all!" said Keller.

"At least I *tried*," she said, her voice trailing off as she realized her argument wouldn't win a lot of admirers.

The other members of the team had carefully found a path that would lead them from the canyon ledge and soon the group was on their way. They were nearing the end of their trip over the mountain. Sally was recovering well, able to walk, and even offer up some gallows humor. They had another hour of hiking before they would join the others for the return trip.

7

On Wing to the Stars

Life has no smooth road for any of us; and in the
bracing atmosphere of a high aim the very
roughness stimulates the climber to steadier steps,
till the legend, 'over steep ways to the stars',
fulfills itself.

—*W. C. Doane*

Madison dipped her shoulder and turned her body around a tree like a ski-racer bending around a gate. The morning air was crisp and a slight trickle of water was running through the stream as she rushed over the rocks that made a dry crossing possible. Her steps were uneven over the creek, but her pace didn't change; she glided across with surprising speed. She felt as though she were in pursuit of something, but what it was, she didn't know. She could hear her own heavy breathing. And her imagination was filled with the memories of running when she was a child. Madison finished the path in less than seventeen minutes.

The others were much farther behind. Bobby Green had decided to run behind Sally so that he had a target to catch and pass. He did, and as he went by he patted her gently on the shoulder and greeted her with a sincere "Good morning," and a smile.

It was Sally's smile that couldn't be mistaken. She had labored to keep her weight down. At forty-two she was still in decent shape, but only because of her dogged determination to continue jogging. The normal trip around her suburban neighborhood in Chestnut Hill was always painful. She viewed jogging as a retribution for her eating sins and the only way she could keep from feeling guilty was with a stoic dedication to her morning run.. Deep down, the only thing that got her out of bed for her jog was the desire to keep her figure. On the surface, she put on a cheerful face, and somewhere in between, she hated to run.

But something was different on the path. She felt good from deep inside to the surface this morning as she admired both the natural beauty of the path and its difficulty.

The group gathered at the path's exit from the hills as they cooled down. Many were still burning with criticism for the path—especially Bobby Green. Others were resigned to it as part of the conference, still more were beginning to enjoy it. Some, like Madison, were consumed with the enjoyment they found in running the path.

Soon they were showered, finished with breakfast, and milling around their tables in the conference room. It was an unusually brilliant morning due to the low humidity, and the bright blue sky seemed to burst into the room through the wall of windows. Michael and Kevin were chatting and drinking coffee as the group settled in.

Michael returned to the front of the room, anxious to start. "Good morning. We obviously have some fascinating things to talk about today."

"Sally," he said as he stood at her desk looking down at her. "It is *truly, truly nice* to have you here this morning." Sally smiled as the rest of the group allowed some nervous laughter. The near tragedy had the effect of bonding the group together and tactful humor only strengthened that bond.

"Thank you. It's good to be here," she said.

"How are you feeling?" he asked.

"I'm *really* okay," she said. Slightly irritated at the number of times she had been required to answer the question.

"Before we get into the heart of our discussion about the mountain, I'd like to run through the times for this morning's run. Sally? Did you run this morning?" he asked.

"Yes," she responded.

"How was it?"

"I stopped to pick up some flowers," she said, knowing the absurdity of it. The rest couldn't help but notice her budding love for running on the path, and they laughed with her. No one yet understood how Sally's example would affect them.

"And your time?"

"Uhm. . . Twenty-two minutes and thirty-three seconds."

"Did you enjoy it?" asked Michael.

"Oh yes!" was all she said.

"Well you lopped three-and-a-half minutes off your time." He smiled at Sally and then glanced over at Bobby. Bobby was disinterested. He had passed Sally on the path that morning, and figured he would *always* pass Sally. The improvement in her times slipped right past him.

Michael returned to the board and put Sally's time in.

"Bobby? How was *your* run this morning?"

"*Just* as enjoyable as the first time, Michael," said Bobby sarcastically.

"You love it *that* much. Any improvement on your time?"

"Sure. Put it on the board at eighteen, nine, eleven."

"Let's see! That's a whole *six seconds* faster that last time." Michael rolled his eyes.

"I chip away at my times consistently—a few seconds a day." Bobby was rubbing it in now.

"Uh-huh," said Michael, adding Bobby's time to the tote board.

	Bobby	Sally	Madison
Run 1:	18:15:06	26: ?	18:10 ?
Run 2:	18:09:11	22:33:?	

As he jotted Bobby's time in, he guessed correctly that Madison would be making a mental comparison of her times with Bobby's. He swung around to catch her smiling and said. "Okay. Let's have it."

Madison whipped up the most innocent looking expression she could. "What?"

Michael said nothing, instead waving his hand toward himself in a coaxing manner.

"A little better than last time . . . 16:55:12," she said. She could see Bobby's reaction, and she enjoyed every microsecond of it.   Michael caught both expressions and smiled at Madison's competitiveness. He had to remind himself that Bobby's reaction came from his competitive nature as well. There was no doubt that Madison was going to leave Bobby behind.

"Madison. If you keep going, you're going to set a new course record."

"Who holds it now?" she said.

"I do," said Michael. "And if I had thought you were going to break it, I would have thrown your application into the 'declined' pile."

That brought smiles from the group—except for Bobby.

"Comments about the run?" Michael asked to the entire class.

"I hate it," said Tip Bailey .

"Yes. . . "

"It's too damned hard. I have this image of Walter Payton running through sand dunes," said Bailey .

"Who's Walter Payton?" It was Sally.

"Only the best football player to ever play the game," Bailey said.

"Tell us about the dunes," asked Michael.

"His pre-season training was legendary. Used to lace up his army boots and run up and down sand dunes. Unbelievable!"

"Why?" asked Michael.

"Can you imagine the agony of the workout?"

"Tip, do you think Payton had a purpose for working out like that?"

"I heard him say in an interview once, without blinking, that he wanted to be remembered as the best running back in the game." Bailey wasn't getting it.

Michael waited. No one spoke. Michael was staring at Bailey, who was becoming quite uncomfortable. No one spoke. The class was beginning to stir. *No one spoke.*

Finally, Michael relieved the silence. "Tip? Did you ever play football?"

"Yeah."

"Did you ever take a *very hard* shot to the head?"

No answer. Some quiet snickers.

Michael crouched down right in front of Bailey. "Tip? Do you think there is any connection between Payton's hard work, and a purpose to become the greatest running back of all time?"

"Yeah. Sure" he said.

"So *why* is it unbelievable? You said his purpose was to be the best. Anything short of the most demanding effort would be '*unbelievable*'. Do you see?"

Bailey shook his head in agreement.

Michael rose back to a standing position. "Running on the path is harder than running on the street. *Is* it too damned hard, like Tip said? Yes . . . and no. You tell me." Looking out over the group, Michael could pick out the yes's from the no's.

Bobby shifted in his chair and said, "I don't mind that it's hard. I run long, grueling races every weekend. The path is much harder over the same distance than anything I've done—but that's not my beef."

He went on. "It's the terrain. It's not conducive to achieving the fastest time over the distance. I *live* for refinement, for the level when improvement comes in tenths of a second, and squeezing the last ounce out of my gear, my training, and me," he said passionately.

"Bobby, you said you live for refinement. We're talking about running here . . . or are we?" asked Michael. "I admire your drive to improve, to refine. Is it running you refine or your life? Or both?"

Michael hit a chord with Bobby. His throat got dry and his eyes watered ever so slightly. "Both," he said with certainty.

"It would appear that some interesting things are happening on the path. Or should I say running the path has caused some interesting things to begin happening in your heads. So far, so good."

8
Values

Since the beginning of time we have sought three things: Survival in an ever-improving style; freedom to choose our own path in life; and happiness in all our relationships, including how we see ourselves.

—*Michael Cevanté*

"We have many interesting things to talk about today. And our first guest will be the gentleman who lead us over the mountain yesterday—my partner, Kevin Keller." Michael rolled his hand towards Kevin with his palm open in the traditional welcoming salute. Kevin nodded, acknowledging the applause from the group.

"Let me reintroduce him formally. He is this country's leading 'knowledge engineer,' which means he spends his time discovering how people acquire their knowledge so he can build a similar process into a machine—'a thinking machine.' When we talk about the substance behind Sales Esteem, much of the credit for its 'scientific base' can go to Kevin. He's going to be with us for the rest of the week.

"The near-tragedy on the mountain is the most dramatic example we have ever had to amplify a key part of Sales Esteem. I wouldn't have planned it, but it has given us an unmistakable example to use," he said. Michael switched on the projector and the Sales Esteem graphic came up.

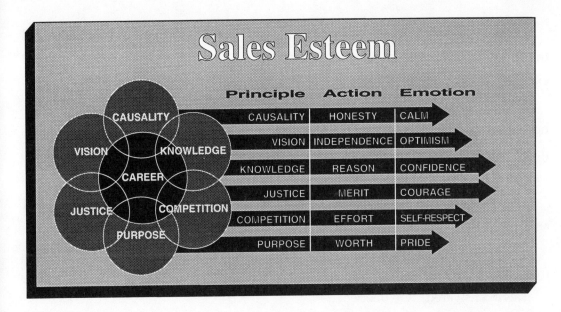

"Our goal today is to tackle values—your values. We'll begin with the value at the center of the diagram—*career*. And another that always comes up—*honesty*. But we're going to define it a little differently than you might have in the past. We'll also look at the antonym of honesty—*evasion*, and consider the results of both. We'll explore another point made from the experience on the mountain: *vision*—what it means and its ultimate value to you. And finally, perhaps one of the more controversial aspects of Sales Esteem, the choice between *independence* and *dependence*.

"But before we begin, we have to establish the validity of using experiences from one context, and applying them to another. In other words, can we really apply the mountain's lessons to our philosophy of selling?

"We have spoken highly about the value of experiential learning," he said. "But we haven't asked the reason why. Who cares about experiences on a mountain when we work in an office building? Who will ever use the knowledge gained in watching Sally cling to the rock yesterday? Why are experiences from one aspect of life valuable for another?"

Keller joined Michael at the front of the room, leaning against the table with arms folded in front of him and his legs crossed. He spoke first. "Maybe it has to do with those troublesome natural laws, Michael?"

"Naah. Gravity is just as strong on the sixtieth floor of an office building as on the mountain. Maybe human knowledge is nothing more than memories—and experiences are good memories that can be relied on in the future," said Michael.

"Yeah . . . hey! . . . maybe the next time Sally wants a raise, she can just wrap herself around her boss' leg and not let go until she gets one," Keller said, with a quick glance to be certain Sally's sense of humor would allow it. She was smiling, as was the rest of the class at Michael and Kevin's playful routine.

"I'm not sure this memory thing sounds so good," said Michael. "Let's pose it as a question. What do we gain from experience, and why is it useful?" he asked.

The class was warming up now. Kat Kelly spoke first. "You draw an analogy from your experience which will also apply to other circumstances."

Kevin answered, "Go deeper."

Rick Kincaid was next. "The experience can be analyzed for its different parts—its *causes* and *effects*, and whether the principles used were effective or not."

"Now we're getting somewhere," said Kevin. "Give me a definition of a principle."

"A principle is kind of like a . . . it's like . . . a fact—you know, something that can't be avoided," Kincaid ventured.

"Sure they can," said Fischer. "Where do you think the phrase 'acting only on principle' comes from? People only act on principles when they have no other choice, otherwise they'll massage reality all day long."

Michael and Keller shared a glance. "Whoa," said Kevin. "Let's get back to a definition of principles and then we'll examine whether people ever use them."

Madison answered. "A principle is mental shorthand that takes all of your existing knowledge and forms it into a broader *generalization* that can be applied to virtually any circumstance."

Kevin smiled warmly at Madison for an instant longer than he might with others in the room. "Good. That's right. We can shorten it slightly. Principles are the integrated summation of our knowledge. They're our intellectual blueprint. We sort objects and their *actions* into categories to form a generalization which can help us solve problems in the future. Here's an example—people use cars to move around. Streets were constructed to accommodate people moving around in cars.

If I recognize that I am standing at the edge of a street, what reasonable conclusion could I draw?" he questioned.

Kat answered in a sing-song rhythm of a child's voice. "That you're going to get run over if you don't look both ways."

Kevin laughed softly. "Yes, I know it's rudimentary. But it's quite marvelous when you consider the amount of 'programming' required for something so simple. Because there are so many objects in the world, and so many varied actions they can take, and so many different circumstances, we form generalizations, broader categories, and from these we derive our principles. Memory is critically important, but it fails us if we try to use it solely as a guide. *There are no formulas that can be applied to every circumstance.* Principles, however, are used for that very purpose. They give us broad operating guidelines that allow us to accumulate knowledge, integrate it, and then solve a variety of similar problems—that's a principle."

"So why is experiential learning valuable?" asked Kat. "If we're never going to find ourselves in the same circumstance again, and what you say is true, our memories aren't going to do much to help us act when we are confronted with a different set of problems?"

"You're absolutely correct, Kat. So you tell me. You've had experiences before—most of which you never applied exactly the same way again—but from which you drew valuable knowledge?" he asked.

"Sure. They're not that precise. My experiences have always been useful in telling me 'why'—instead of 'what,'" she said.

"Excellent. Experiences help to *connect* our knowledge. It helps us to identify the cause and effect. It allows us to generalize, integrate and form principles that we can then use later. Have you ever known a teacher who instructs a five-year-old about crossing the street, and then merrily points the direction to the nearest intersection?" he asked.

"Of course not. They need to see it to understand."

"What happens, cognitively, is that the child makes the necessary connections with cause and effect, completing the formulation of the principle." Kevin's eyes got wide and he swept his arms in dramatic motions. "Think of the calculations going on inside a child's mind." He spoke in distinct sentences, separating one from the next.

"Cars are large and made of steel. They're bigger than my brother and it hurts when he runs into me. They're noisy and move fast. They run faster than I can. They move around on these streets, back and forth, just like the teacher said. If I get in the way when they're moving fast, I may get hurt—worse than when my brother runs me over. I don't want that to happen so I will wait to cross until they stop moving, or go away altogether.

"*A principle is born.* 'When I am near a street, there is the possibility of cars driving about. If I am hit by a car, it will hurt. Watch out for cars, especially near streets,'" he said. "The principle is the result of dozens of bits of knowledge. If we had to go through each piece of knowledge every time we came to the street, it would take us forever to move around. Instead we use principles. The integrated summation of our knowledge generalized so that it can be applied to any circumstance." He paused.

"Experiences are more likely to help us make the connections. They help us solidify principles. It doesn't mean that we can't form principles through abstraction, we must do that as well, but somewhere in the chain of knowledge, an experience is more valuable, because the cause-effect relationship is far more evident." Kevin paused.

The group was silent. Few of them had given the thought of principles much consideration. Some had gotten a few bits and pieces of epistemology in school, but that had been covered up by the conventional wisdom that memory-like experience was all that mattered. Now that they were given the subject some consideration, it all seemed so terribly obvious—and the word "principles" began to take on an entirely new meaning.

Kevin continued. "Principles are the foundation of our current knowledge, and we apply them to almost everything we encounter in the world. They form the master plan before we take action. Principles are dynamic. They can change—hopefully only to be refined and improved. Do you suppose we can have poor principles—or perhaps a better way to say it is, can we have ineffective principles?" he asked.

There were nods from most in the room. Kevin wasn't satisfied.

"Can we act without principles at all?" he asked.

Kat laughed grimly. "Lots of people do."

"Can people act arbitrarily?" asked Madison thoughtfully. "I kind of doubt it."

"It's an important question. There are times when principles are thought of as a luxury. Do all actions presuppose some principle?"

Ryan was shaking his head. "It would seem we need something to guide us," he said.

"Regardless of whether we realize it or not, we form principles. They're a necessity of a volitional being. We can have really bad principles, but we can't survive with them for very long. For instance, the child in our example before who formulated a principle that held he could outrun the car would probably have some difficulties.

"We can have confused principles which we fail to integrate—if the child in our example, noticed that the cars seemed to pass in threes, and decided that counting the cars would help in deciding when to cross the street. As soon as the fourth car zooms by, he has to reformulate his principle.

"Or we can have effective principles; those that work and are constantly refined and improved by gathering more knowledge, or by making further integrations with existing knowledge. It's important to note that effective principles don't change dramatically—that's why they're effective. They are consistently effective and can be applied to a wide range of related problems.

"And finally, arbitrary actions are rare. Even what seems to be a whim, typically is the result of some principle—no matter how poorly constructed it might be."

Kat shifted taller in her chair. "So we all act on principle, some of us just have *better* principles?"

"Yes, Kat. That's it precisely. Poor principles can be innocently arrived at—or they can be knowingly embraced—those are the bad guys. Good principles are simply those that work. Those are the ones we want to discover. Bad principles fail, not because some authority has decided they are 'bad,' but because they don't work. Those are the principles we want to avoid. That's what this conference is all about. Discovering which principles of selling work, and which principles fail—

and more importantly—why?" And that leads us to our discussion of the mountain, if I'm not mistaken. Michael?"

Michael rose from his chair and spoke as he walked back to the front of the room.

"If we were to try to extract the most essential aspects of yesterday's trip, what would they be?"

Jock Shaw was the first to speak. "Teamwork."

Michael was standing at a table in the middle of the room now. "Jock, would you mind helping me out by writing our answers on the flip charts at the front of the room?"

Shaw shrugged, stepped to the front and scribbled it on one of two flip charts that were placed eight feet apart at the front of the room.

Kat said, "Survival."

"Jock, put 'Survival' on the *other* flip chart, please. Keep going," he said.

"Goals and direction," Kyle Mitchell said. Shaw looked at Michael with an annoyed frown wondering which chart to add it to.

"Under 'Survival' on the second flip chart," he said.

"The fragile nature of men," said Fischer, as his mouth curled into a cynical smile.

Michael replied, "Insightful . . . I think. Can you explain it a little more thoroughly?"

"Our lives were in the hands of Mother Nature. No matter what, if the side of the mountain was going to fall, it was going to fall, and there was nothing we could do to prevent it."

"Okay, but let's refer to it as something a little less threatening, shall we? Man is fragile if he fails to be alert to the world. On the other hand, man has found he can contain risk as long as he respects and plans for the risk. In other words, man changes from fragile to *agile* so long as he adheres to the nature of the physical world—or reality. Can we use the word 'Reality'?" asked Michael.

"It's your show."

"Under 'Survival,' Jock," directed Michael.

"Unselfishness," said Rick Kincaid. Michael pointed to the chart to the first chart, and Shaw put it under teamwork. Michael walked to the other flip chart and scribbled 'Selfishness' below 'reality.' "Does anyone object to that?" he asked.

The room erupted in chatter. Each of the various tables broke into instant discussion. Michael let it flourish for a few minutes. Out of the melee came barbed comments. "Maybe on a desert island . . . ," "Society couldn't afford . . . ," "My mother would go berserk . . .," "Who'd want to live in a world where . . ."

Michael stood at the front of the room and forged an embarrassed look on his face which was clearly theatrical. "I've done it *again*." He had to repeat himself to quiet the chatter. "Yes. I've *done* it again." He shook his head side to side to add emphasis. "I need to remember that our culture has redefined that darn word. Can I scratch it out and start again?" he asked, not waiting for an answer before drawing a line through 'selfishness' and scribbling 'rational self-interest' in its place.

The room quieted, not because they were satisfied with the change, but because they were confused and uncomfortable with the term self-interest.

"Without going into detail now, let me say that I believe you'll like the explanation of rational self-interest and how it applies to your selling," said Michael. The class was anxious, and not at all satisfied with the answer. Michael went on knowing the void would generate thought.

"What else should I put on the flip charts?" he asked.

"Planning," said Tip Bailey. Michael pointed to the same flip chart as 'teamwork' and 'unselfishness.' Shaw obliged.

Ryan Matthews joined in. "Perspective," he said.

Michael smiled knowingly. "Explain what you mean, Ryan."

"The mountain gave us the chance to look at the whole thing. We need to do that with our sales career as well." Michael was still standing by the chart and he turned and put 'Perspective/Vision' under 'Rational Self-Interest.' He turned and faced the class. "Ryan, why do you want to look at the whole thing?" Michael asked.

"Because we can learn from our mistakes, and it's not very difficult to predict what result our actions will have in the future," he replied defensively.

"That's very well stated," said Michael. "Let's frame all of these in a broader topic. Step back far enough to consider why we take *any* journey, expend *any* energy, put forth *any* effort. Why do we take the 'trips' over 'mountains'? Why do we pursue our sales career?"

Madison answered. "We do it to achieve something of value. Isn't that our topic?"

"Sure seems simple, doesn't it?" Michael scribbled 'Values' at the top of the chart that listed survival, goals and direction, reality, rational self-interest, and perspective.

Values

Survival	Teamwork
Goals and Direction	Unselfishness
Reality	Planning
~~Selfishness~~	
Rational Self Interest	
Perspective/Vision	

"And it's there that I would like to start. *Values.* Of course, we are all so thoroughly familiar with the concept of values that we probably don't even need to discuss it . . . right?" Michael paused. "Someone throw out a couple of values that we can all agree on?"

The groups broke into conversation once again, offering up various suggestions to Michael's question. What emerged was a chorus of the standards: family, honor, honesty, faith, love, friendship.

"Okay, let's see. Among those, which is the *primary value*?" he asked.

At nearly the same moment came an eruption of different answers, followed by a short silence, then self-conscious laughter. Michael smiled knowingly. "You don't mean to tell me that you have different values?" he asked.

"Sure we do. But some are more important than others, and some take on different meanings to different people," said Kat.

Michael shook his head in tentative agreement and said, "Perhaps it will help if we define value. Would anyone like to take a stab at it?"

Ryan Matthews had asked this question many times over the last six months. "Values are those things you find important. The things that you pursue in life. And the things you fight to keep once you have them," he said.

"Good. Can we shorten it a little?" asked Michael.

Ryan nodded. "Values are those things we act to attain or keep," Kat said.

"Kat, is there one value that *must* supersede all others?" Michael asked.

"I don't know what you mean," she said, embarrassed that she was unable to offer an answer.

The group was quiet. Michael waited. He knew that the process of learning was work—hard work—and he knew the great value in letting his students struggle to learn on their own. He paced in front of the group, showing he would wait for the answer.

Finally Madison asked, "One primary value from yesterday?"

"Yes, Madison, one primary value," he said.

"Well I suppose this sounds a little ridiculous, but I guess life was the primary value," she said sheepishly.

"Why do you think that sounds ridiculous?" he asked.

"I don't know. I guess it sounds so obvious," she replied.

"Yes. That's right. It's probably obvious," said Michael. "It would be irrational to risk your life on the mountain. Life is the precedent value to all others. Let's keep our analogies tightly drawn. If life is the primary value, how does that apply to the sales process?"

"If we have no career, none of the other values of selling can be pursued."

"Yes Kat, exactly. The primary value of our sales career is *the continuation of our sales career*—just as the primary value on the mountain is the continuation of life." Michael paused. By now the class could tell which of his pauses were done in search of a question. This was one which begged a response.

Tug Fischer had received the equivalent of a life sentence by the SEC. The Sales Esteem conference was an ironic rehabilitation for his disbarment. If there was anyone in the group who should appreciate the potential death of a career, it was Tug Fischer.

"I think you've taken this life and career thing too far," said Tug Fischer. "Life is life. I sell to live. Not the other way around. If one career falters, I'm not done, I just move on to the next. How many people in the room have had the same job all their careers? None, I bet. You use a career to make your life livable, that's all. It's nothing more than that. You take advantage where you can—when you can," he said.

"To begin, Tug, a career is just that, the combination of all the jobs you have held in any single industry. Moving from one to another does not change the fact that a career can end. And, more importantly, both have an enormous emotional stake. This is what I like to refer to as the psychological life and death of a career." Michael turned away from Fischer and continued his discussion with the rest of the group.

"The psychological element of your career is found between the two extremes of self-esteem and self-disgust. Self-disgust is the equivalent of dying. Those things that contribute to your self-esteem have value. Those that create stress, anxiety or guilt slowly make you miserable . . . or worse, are self-destructive. I would like you to take a few minutes to discuss the emotional side of selling among your groups," he said.

The group flew into a flurry of conversations. Emotions were a hot topic judging from the intensity of the conversations. There was a tension in the room that came from lurking around the unknown in one's mind, poking at fears and distant, detached motivations. They spoke of ecstatic moments of success, and the injustice of the brother-in-law sale, where the reward for hard work is learning that another salesman would be collecting the fees—and probably eating Sunday dinner at the buyer's home as well. There were the moments of reaching new heights, filling the bank account—and the terror of beginning all over the following month with a blank sales log. They spoke about customers who ranged from grateful to disdainful, practically treating the salesperson as though they were a criminal. Everyone had a story regarding the emotional trauma brought on by sales managers with lashing tongues and outrageous production demands. What of companies that intentionally misstated the value the product provided and sent their sales staff off to pitch it anyway? Some mentioned the extraordinary degree of self-management inseparable from the lonely accountability of hitting the numbers, great pay offset by a scarcity of security.

Michael let the conversations continue for some time. Finally, he spoke. "Would I be too bold to say that the emotional content of selling is a hot topic?" he asked.

Nervous laughter came from the group. Many of them had come to the conference to find an emotional grounding. Others had been oblivious to the impact of emotions, and had closed them out, refusing to deal with them, and giving up the potential upside that positive emotions could extend. Ryan Matthews came to the conference to save his selling life. He was drowning in guilt. For him, *it was the only topic*.

"May I revisit the point that the primary value you must have is the continuation and enhancement of your career. It *is* the standard of your sales activities. Every action taken moves you either towards, or away from, your professional happiness. Actions are the result of principles. If the principles work, the actions are successful in acquiring the things we value, and specifically, in furthering your career.

"Let's try a quick game as an example. Everyone from this side of the room please gather in the far corner," he said as he carved an imaginary line down the middle of the room with his hand. "The rest of you are on the team on this side. Now, please pair up with someone of the opposite sex."

The groups stumbled around clumsily for a few moments. Madison looked for Keller who was watching her when she turned to him. Madison blushed slightly as her smile sent an obvious message. She waved him over to her table.

Michael continued once they had finished. "Let's set the context and the stakes. Both will change as we go. The setting is that of a blind date. Each of you are single. The game is strip poker. The stakes are that you will eventually undress."

Kat Kelly burst into juvenile laughter. "Can we change partners?" It was good natured and the rest of the class enjoyed it. "Sorry, Tug," she apologized.

"Don't tell me that some of you wouldn't want to play?" Michael asked with a grin.

They broke into rollicking chatter.

"Okay. The things you value are already at work in this context, as are your principles. Some of you see your values in your partners . . . other don't. If there is value, your principles of behavior will take over, and your actions will follow; some would play, while others would leave the party."

Keller glanced over to Madison who was seated at his side. Madison smiled. "I'll stay," he said.

"Some of you would play no matter what because of the *social element* of the party. That value is of more importance than the embarrassment of being undressed in public. Perhaps being undressed doesn't necessitate any other actions, so it's harmless," said Michael.

"Who said being undressed would be embarrassing?" It was Kat. More laughter.

"Ooookay, better be moving on," said Michael. "Let's change the context. Your partner is now a teenage son or daughter. We are still at the strip poker game, only now, you are a silent observer. The proverbial 'fly-on-the-wall.'"

The intensity of the chatter that followed was of a different tone. Reservation mixed with nervous anger.

"Does anything change?" asked Michael.

Shannon Shelley said. "Everything changes. We'd probably send in the Marines."

Kat was enjoying herself, playfully taking the role of mother watching her son. "Yeah. My boy wouldn't do this kind of thing. Can we send the little sluts home now?"

Now they broke into laughter at the levity Kat had brought to the seriousness of the idea.

"I think everyone gets the point. Let's change the context and stakes yet again," said Michael. "Your partner is a celebrity, and an attractive one at that. As long as we have shed our clothes, we'll leave them off. You're single and so is your partner, so we're not breaking any vows. Everything seems perfect. Physical attraction, fame, fortune . . . the whole nine yards. But then you discover that your partner is a control freak—and not just an everyday control freak. Your partner literally wants to determine everything you do . . . or say . . . or think."

"What could be worse?" said Madison. She looked over at Kevin. He had a perfectly neutral look on his face as though the question was too sophomoric to consider. Clearly, he was confident enough that he didn't feel compelled to patronize her with a nod, nor did her comment stir disagreement. It was a great test, although she quickly scolded herself for using it for that purpose. A great relationship wasn't made up of tests.

Kat concurred. "Yeah, I agree. Personal freedom and independence aren't less important than the physical, or the emotional aspects of a relationship."

"Emotions are an evaluation of whether or not we have attained the things we value. The little exercise we went through demonstrated how easily emotions could change depending upon the values associated with each circumstance. The starting point for each was practically identical—we were undressed. But the emotional result was dramatically different depending on one thing—and one thing only—the realization of acquiring or losing something of value," he said. "So values are important. At the very base is the value of preserving life—or our sales career. It's precedental. It's required to realize any other value associated with that career. It should be obvious by now that all principles, and all actions, should be consistent with enhancing or protecting your career." He paused. It was an easy point to grasp and the group was in agreement.

"Once we have satisfied that precedental value, what comes next? What are the primary human values?"

Kat Kelly had her MBA, and hated to admit it. She was the first to ridicule symbolism in place of substance. But she had a good deal of formal education, much of it centered around the topic they were discussing. She said sincerely, "Classic management theory puts food, shelter, and safety at the base of human values."

"You're referring to Maslow?" asked Michael.

"Yeah, Maslow's hierarchy," she said.

"How many of you find food to be an important value . . . ?" asked Michael rhetorically. "And of course, shelter . . . and a second home on the island, . . . and a cabin cruiser, . . . and a bigger car," he said to a room full of light chuckles. "Can we call them *living values*?"

Nods of agreement.

Michael spun around to flip on the slide projector. He punched the control pad a few times to bring up the desired slide.

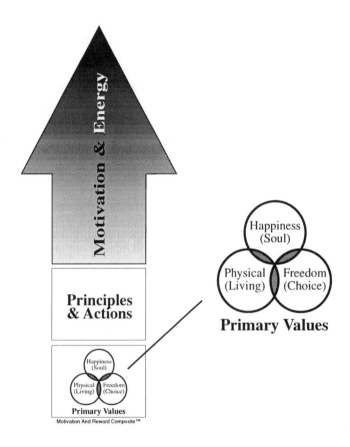

"All except . . . safety. That belongs to a different category. Let's take another look at our motivation diagram. The primary values consist of three groupings: Living Values, Happiness Values and Freedom Values. Kat, I think you're going to find this interesting. Maslow was mostly correct, but he missed some crucial pieces. For instance, his theory would be completely incapable of explaining the idea of 'give me liberty or give me death,' or hunger strikers. Maslow believed values fell into a hierarchy, which necessitated pursuit of the more base values. In his theory, those base values were food, shelter and safety. His assertion was that we give up all other values when those three are threatened. Then he moved up his hierarchy to add social values, which would be pursued only after the base values were realized. I think self-actualization completely confused him so he set it way up on top as though he were hoping no one would ever have enough time to get to it." He smiled gently to cushion the criticism.

"Our model of motivation treats each of three values as fundamental. Living values are like Maslow's base values—food, shelter and the betterment of anything physical we value. But that's where the likeness ends. Maslow treats safety as a base value—and it is probably the 'biggie'—but it is part of a larger set of values, one that I call Freedom Values. Specifically, safety for the Sales Esteem model is simply 'freedom from physical threats.' Other Freedom Values that can be extremely important—like the phrase—'give me liberty or give me death.'" He repeated it. "It's quite powerful, isn't it?

"And finally, Sales Esteem is not only *willing* to deal with the abstract values of happiness, it recognizes them as 'equally important.' These values include relationships with others, including friends and loved ones—like Maslow's theory. But Maslow believed that these would always be sacrificed for the base values. Once again, he's mostly right, except he can't explain the father who would exchange his life for his daughter's. Clearly, there are many instances when we value others so highly, that they supersede our other values." He paused to punch up another slide.

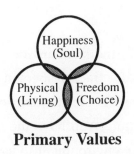

Primary Values

"Each individual places emphasis on one of the three, but so far, I've yet to find anyone who can exclude one of the three completely."

"People try all the time," said Kat.

Michael nodded his head in agreement. "And the result?"

"Doesn't work."

"Not true," said Fischer. "I don't need friends—and my family is more trouble than they're worth. I do just fine, thanks," said Fischer.

Kat's reaction was all that was needed. Her mouth dropped at his statement. Her eyes narrowed thoughtfully. Then she moved her head from side to side as though she understood the emptiness in his life. Fischer sat with his arms crossed, not realizing how pathetic the statement was.

"Okay, Tug. You're the first," Michael said, intentionally patronizing him so as to avoid a discussion in which reality would be discarded. It was said in a manner that would leave no doubt among the others that Tug was a shining example of failure by trying to eliminate one of the three values.

"Let's go back to the lists of values from the mountain and see where they fit," said Michael.

Values

Survival	Teamwork
Goals and Direction	Unselfishness
Reality	Planning
~~Selfishness~~	
Rational Self Interest	
Perspective/Vision	

"Yesterday on the mountain, the standard of value was your safety, and for Sally, her life. The same is true for the salesperson in regard to his career. If you hold the principle that your career is the standard of value, every action serves to enhance or detract from that value. You have the ultimate guide in protecting it, and therefore the most foolproof environment to assure honest, ethical actions. If you undervalue your career, like ignoring the importance of safety on the mountain, it will almost certainly be damaged. On the other hand, if you treat your career as the primary value—you'll never put it at risk." Michael paused.

"Let me ask," Michael continued. "Who has claim, and who should benefit from your career?"

Kincaid spoke first. "The company, of course."

"On what principle, Rick?"

"You work for them."

"Hmm. I'd have guessed your experience in labor negotiations would lead you to believe the worker has claim to the benefit of their work. Isn't there an exchange?"

"Sure. The company receives the benefit, the worker receives compensation. It's a collaborative arrangement."

"Let's define our semantics, shall we? An employee-employer relationship is a negotiated matter. It's work for pay . . . yes?" he asked.

"Right," said Kincaid.

"Both exchange something of value. The worker his skill, the company, its capital in the form of compensation."

"Yes."

"If it's equitable, they're both happy? If not, what happens?"

"There's a dispute."

"So you agree, then. The company must exchange something of value for the work. If it requires an exchange, then the company can't possibly have a 'claim.' True or untrue?"

"I don't follow," said Kincaid.

"Could the company force the employee to come to work?"

"No."

"Then the company has no claim over his career."

"Now that you put it that way, I would agree."

"Could the company choose not to pay?"

"Of course not."

"Then the employee has both the claim to his career, and the right to benefit from his effort?"

"I wouldn't disagree with anything you've said."

"An appropriate perspective of the claim to your career and who should benefit from it is *truly* important. We spent a lot of time talking about your career as the standard of value. It's lip service to yourself unless you understand that you have *all* of the rights attached to your effort, including the right to benefit from it."

Michael paused. This reasoning was contradictory to conventional corporate thinking. It was easy to skip over, without realizing the trap it could become.

"I will make a quick wager, and if I lose, I buy lunch," he said, which brought smiles to a few in the room. "I'll bet there is no one in the room who can explain the importance of this last topic as it relates to the perspective you hold of your career."

There were no takers.

"No one interested? Okay, but before we go to lunch, I want you all to help me out with one of my *company* objectives. We're going to make some fund-raising phone calls so we can counter the unfair treatment of Saddam Hussein."

The class practically burst into laughter at the absurdity of the statement. Michael was stoic. "I'm serious. I am asking for your help. You agreed to be part of my conference. We negotiated it. I am giving you something of value in exchange for the money you paid. And you came here under the agreement that you would participate. It's just a half-hour, and we're calling Iraqi expatriates so it's real easy to do."

Near the back of the room sat Ashfar Khan, an Iraqi who had fought against the aggression in Kuwait. The example was intentionally designed. Michael was counting on him to speak up, and he did.

"Mr. Cevanté. I know this is an exercise, so I will remain calm, but you have offended me, sir. I would ask to decline," said Mubarrel.

"Why, Ashfar?"

"I would forsake my principles, and my honor."

"Rick," Michael said, turning to Kincaid with a theatrical tone. "Can you help me out of this? All I want is a little loyalty. No one seems to respect authority and loyalty anymore." Michael moaned.

"Not me, Michael," he replied.

"Kat?"

"I'm just as offended. I'm not making any calls," she said.

"Where does loyalty fit in here?" Michael said, returning to his normal tone.

"It doesn't," said Kat.

"Oh, but it does," said Ashfar. "Loyalty *is* at stake. The loyalty is to *my* values, *my* principles, *my* honor."

"Mr. Mubarrel, I was *wrong*. You win the bet, and lunch is on me," said Michael. "And thank you. I hope my example did not offend you too deeply. It's *your* career. It's *your* value. And if you are submissive to any call for loyalty, or allow authority to intervene, which conflicts with protecting your career, you have every right to say 'no.' In fact, the perspective of your career as the standard of value would lead you to decline *any* request that would damage it. As Mr. Mubarrel stated, there is just one application for what we call loyalty—and that is to your own values, or company values that are synonymous to your own," he said.

"We'll stop here. Lunch is on the balcony. See you in an hour."

The group unwrapped itself from their chairs and wandered out on the balcony. A squall could be seen on the horizon, and it looked as though their lunch could be interrupted by the storm. Keller grabbed Madison by the arm on the way out.

"Still need a partner?" he asked with a smile.

Madison nodded her agreement. The others paired off into small groups. There were two odd men out—Shaw and Fischer. They ended up together at a small table near the rail.

Fischer spoke first. "Cevanté really got to ya, huh?"

"The son of a bitch," said Shaw.

"How did you get roped into coming to this thing, Shaw?" asked Fischer.

"I asked to come."

"You're kidding. Well, then you deserve it."

"What's that supposed to mean?"

"You don't get it, do you?"

"Get what?"

Fischer was forcing salad into his mouth, waiting for the server to move away. "You and I are out of place here. Worse, we're probably here as an example to the rest of these weenies—bad examples."

"Speak for yourself," said Shaw.

"Yeah? I'll bet we see eye to eye on most everything about sales—the way it's supposed to be, the way it's always been."

"I sure don't like the things I'm hearing. If it weren't for Ryan, I'd pack and get the hell out of here."

"Ryan works for *you*?" asked Fischer.

"Yeah. He caused a scene at my firm about coming, so I had to follow him all the way out here."

Fischer leaned forward. "Wouldn't it be interesting to see a little disruption here? You know, something that would throw Cevanté and his crew off track a little."

"Sure. But what would it be? He seems to be in control."

"Something *out* of his control. If only Ms. Holiday had fallen yesterday, we'd all be heading home. Listen, maybe there'll be another opportunity for disaster."

Fischer leaned back as the busboy approached them holding a pitcher of iced tea. He and Shaw sat silently and watched while their glasses were refilled. When they were left alone again, Fischer said, "This little morning run they do. I think it may be slightly more dangerous than they think, don't you?"

Shaw nodded at Fischer without saying another word. They stared at each other for a moment, each of them forging a vicious smile before finishing the conversation.

At the other end of the balcony sat Keller, Madison and Kat Kelly. Kat was officiating their flirting. They weren't paying her much attention, but she was having a ball.

"You know, Madison," said Kat. "I'll bet all the girls fall for this guy."

There was no answer. Madison looked more deeply into Kevin's eyes.

"Kevin, you should see her in the morning. *I have*—and it's not pretty."

Nothing.

"I read somewhere that two eggheads should never try to be a couple," said Kat.

"Shut up, Kat," said Madison, without turning away from Kevin's face.

"Okay, but don't say I didn't warn you. By the way, if you two are going to hit it off, you'll probably need to work on your mountain climbing skills," she added.

With that they both turned and looked at Kat. Kevin had been upset with Madison, and it was still unresolved. "She climbs okay, it's her sense of safety that concerns me," he said.

Madison looked away for the first time during the last twenty minutes as her thoughts returned to the mountain incident. She stared out over the lake. "I'm curious," she said. "You were trained as a fighter pilot. I thought they were supposed to be courageous."

"Do you think it's courageous to die?"

"For something you care about, yes. Don't you?" she asked.

"Yes," he said flatly.

"So why were you upset at me?"

"You care enough about Sally Holiday to give up your life?"

"Well . . . yes! Any human life is important."

"Uh-huh? Hitler's, Lenin's, Hussein's?"

"Obviously she's *not* any of them," she gritted her teeth in anger.

"You're right. So how do *you* decide when to sacrifice your life for someone else?"

Kat suddenly realized what she had begun. "Wait, guys," she said. "I was just kidding about the mountain climbing stuff."

Madison brushed the comment aside and continued. "You don't make value judgments, you just act if the circumstances are right?"

"Madison, you're wrong. People make value judgments all the time, on the spot. Some are rational, some are emotional. You were emotional and you almost got yourself killed," he said.

"So you wouldn't have tried to save her?"

"I did try. But that has nothing to do with courage or emotion. I wouldn't have traded my life to save hers, if that's what you're asking."

"I thought you were a hero or something. I guess I got the wrong idea," she looked down and then back to the lake.

Kat plopped her head down into her hands. "Look what I've done," she moaned. "A perfectly good start and I go and mess it up. Can't we talk about something else?"

"NO!" They both replied at exactly the same time.

"When would *you* trade *your* life?" demanded Madison, returning her glare to him.

Kevin sat back, paused for a moment, and then leaned forward again. "If it had more value to me than my own life. Do you have any *idea* how few things there are that are more valuable than your own *life*?"

"Answer my question."

"I don't know. Maybe my wife, if I were married. Or kids."

"Would you have traded it for my life if I had started to fall?" she asked the fateful question.

"No," he said, shaking his head slightly.

Kat let out a groan. All he had to do was say "yes" and the whole thing would be over.

"I guess I see where I fit in your scheme of things." Madison got up, dropped her napkin on her plate, and looked as though she would say more. She opened her mouth to speak, but nothing came out. Tears welled up in her eyes instead, and she turned and hurried away.

Kat and Kevin sat there in awkward silence. "Sorry," said Kat.

"It's not your problem, Kat."

Kat nodded and the two of them got up from the table and headed back to the conference room. Others were joining them, anxious to continue. Michael was talking on a phone in the back of the room; it was his daughter Hallie. She was struggling with the lottery tickets.

Michael was answering questions shot at him in machine-gun fashion. "No, I would understand if you decided to use them . . . Grandma would be happy. . . Yes, there would still be a lot of expenses for you to pay on your own. . . No, Grandpa wouldn't be hurt. Yes, sweetheart, let's talk more about it this evening. Good-bye."

Michael hung up the receiver and returned to the class, waiting for them to take their seats. He stood at the front, staring at the white boards. "Are there any questions about the importance of career as the central value?" he asked, bringing the class back to the topic. "If we agree career should occupy this position, then we have placed an important burden on career that will impact all of our other principles. Can anyone tell me what that burden is?" asked Michael.

Ryan answered. "It's like the core of an apple. If it's rotten, the rest of the fruit dies quickly. Likewise, the purpose of the fruit is to support and nurture the core. In other words, the core of our career has to be protected, and everything else we do has to enhance our career."

"Not bad, Ryan. I kind of like it. The key is that our principles support the primary value of our career and then those values that rest upon career. They must never contradict it. They must always enhance it."

"Okay. Back to the board. The first of those principles is *causality* or certainty. Michael went back to the projector and flicked the switch.

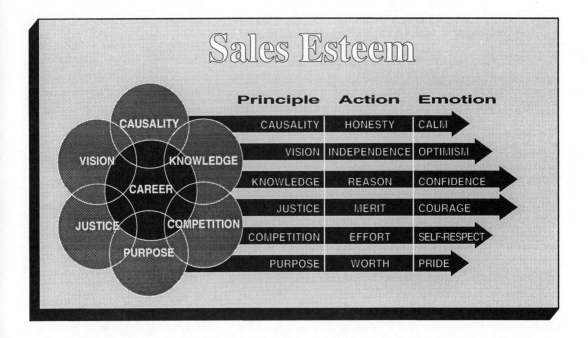

"Someone refresh my memory on the definition of a principle," he said, gaining energy.

"It's the sum of your knowledge, integrated into a master plan of action, all designed to achieve some goal or value and the resulting emotion," said Ryan.

"Great, Ryan. Thank you. Would someone take a stab at the meaning of certainty?"

"You can never *be* certain," said Shaw.

Michael had been looking the other way, and turned suddenly to face Shaw. "You're joking, right?" asked Michael, which should have been a clear sign to back away from the statement.

"Haven't you studied the great philosophers? When it comes down to it, nothing is certain."

"Actually, the only worthwhile philosophers take the exact opposite position," he said, and then paused to formulate an example for Shaw.

"Jock, . . . yesterday on the mountain—was there anything that you would say was an absolute certainty?" he asked.

"No, not really," he shrugged.

"Sally? Would you disagree?" asked Michael.

"Yeah. I was certain I was going to fall," said Sally.

"Jock?" asked Michael.

"Nothing is certain until you look back. Obviously, she didn't fall, so how was she certain?" he asked argumentatively.

"Jock! That is an absolutely arcane answer. If you were back on the mountain, standing on the ledge, and took a step forward, could you be certain you would fall?" Michael was standing at Jock's desk and looked directly, with a penetrating stare, into Shaw's eyes.

"I'd be certain, only after I fell."

"Jock, that's not an answer," Michael said, trying to remain patient.

"Listen, it's my opinion, okay. I don't operate under the *arrogance* that things are certain. I see amazing things, everyday, that have no explanation," said Shaw.

"Jock, I have just one requirement of this class, and I apologize because it's not advertised anywhere. The goal of the conference is concrete conclusion arrived through rational discussion. You can hold *any* position you want as long as you are prepared to *defend* it logically, refine it, or change it. Can we discuss certainty under those guidelines?"

To everyone's surprise, Shaw didn't answer. He said nothing—as though Michael had never uttered the question. Michael stood there for a moment, waiting. It was an impasse.

"Mr. Shaw?" asked Michael.

"I'll choose when to abandon my opinions, thank you!"

Michael's expression had not changed throughout the exchange. He waited a moment longer, still looking deep into Shaw's eyes, as though he were allowing one more chance for Shaw to admit his was a weak position. When the moment was up, he turned and walked to the back of the room and opened a cabinet.

He looked back over his shoulder at Shaw. "Mr. Shaw, some people insist that their opinion is worthwhile simply because it *is their* opinion. They couldn't be more wrong. The only worthwhile opinion is one that carries the explicit agreement to accept the consequences of the opinion—all others are trash," said Michael, still calm.

Michael reached into the cabinet and retrieved an Air Force standard issue, Colt 7mm sidearm. "Kevin?" he said, addressing Keller. "This is yours, right?" Keller nodded.

"It's loaded?"

Another nod.

"What would it do—*in your humble opinion*—to a man at close range?" asked Michael.

"It wouldn't be pretty," said Keller.

"You're certain?" asked Michael.

"I couldn't be more certain."

Michael walked back over to Shaw's desk, popped the clip into the handle, and locked a shell into the chamber with a swift, violent motion. He motioned the others at the table to move away—which they did hastily. He set the gun on the desk in front of Shaw.

"Mr. Shaw. Do you share Kevin's opinion that this is something very dangerous?"

Shaw was white as ash—still not speaking, but this time it was from the shock. He nodded his head up and down.

"You've seen me load the gun, yes?" asked Michael.

Another nod.

"If you were to unlatch the safety, point it squarely at your head and pull the trigger, what do you suppose would happen?"

"Hhhhh . . I wwwould put a hole in my hhhead," he stammered.

"Are you certain?" asked Michael, without a change in the tone of his voice.

"Yessss."

"Then you agree that you *can be* certain? And you can be certain before an event occurs?"

"Yesss," Shaw was shaking.

"Would you agree that an *opinion* to the contrary is not only worthless, but very dangerous?"

"Yesss."

"And finally, can you and I agree that opinions are fine so long as you are willing to accept the consequences of that opinion?" asked Michael.

Shaw had gathered himself enough to shake his head in agreement and clear his throat.

Michael picked up the gun, reholstered it and handed it over to Kevin, who was smiling. One more jerk with some in-your-face reality to think about, Michael thought as he returned to the front of the room and continued, "Mr. Shaw has helped to demonstrate something of particular value to us. For our immediate discussion let's use opinion and principle interchangeably. As we have discussed, there are two kinds of principles: those that work, and those that fail. You can choose to hold failing principles, and then attempt to ignore the consequences. It only works for just so long. Ultimately, they catch up with you. I believe Mr. Shaw is beginning to change his opinion about certainty. So let's move on now and try to define it, realizing that the notion that *nothing is certain* is trash."

"Kevin, help us out, will you? Are there physical laws that give good cause for accepting the principle of certainty?" he asked Keller, bringing him into the conversation.

Keller had ejected the shell from the gun's chamber, removed the cartridge and clip and returned it to the cabinet. Walking to the front of the room Kevin said, "Certainty is a derivative of the law of cause and effect." Keller scribbled the words "cause" and "effect" on the white board. "Everything has an origin. Every effect, a cause. Every action, a result. They are inextricably linked. The opposite of cause and effect is random—and nothing is random," he said.

"What about the weather?" asked Kincaid.

"A lack of knowledge doesn't mean that certainty is impossible. In other words, you can identify what you don't know. Everything that occurs in nature can be pinpointed to a cause. What makes some people believe weather is random is the number of variables involved and the complexity of predicting the interaction of all the variables. If you had enough information, even the weather could be predicted," said Keller.

Michael joined in. "The connection to be made here is that you have a reason to hold the principle of certainty. Absolute certainty is difficult to realize, but contextual certainty is not. The principle of certainty relies on our understanding that everything has a cause. And every action a result. Stepping over the ledge will result in the same outcome every time it is repeated in that context. What I hope you will grasp here is we can rely on the law of cause and effect. And like the gun at Shaw's head, we have to be aware that our actions have consequences. Life is not chance or luck, and neither is selling.

"Let's explode some myths about cause and effect, and the principle of certainty. How many of you believe that anything is possible?" he asked

Hands shot up all around the room. Michael nodded his head to show it was what he had anticipated.

"Tip?" He said. "Is it possible to be in two places at one time?"

"No, of course not."

"Kat, can you sprout rainbow-colored wings and fly out of the window and over the valley?"

"In my dreams," said Kat.

"Jock, could you blow a hole in your head and get up and walk out of here without any trouble?"

"No," Shaw said, still shaking.

"Ryan, you miss your son?"

"A lot."

"Can you kiss him goodnight tonight—from Austin?"

"No."

"Madison, the record in the 200-meter run for women is what, about 22.30?"

"21.19."

"Is it possible that *you* could run it in 12 seconds?"

"No."

"Could I see the hands of those of you who believe anything is possible?"

The group reacted like a deflating beach ball.

"Does anyone think the idea of walking on the moon was once considered to be impossible?" Michael asked. The class lit up with renewed hope. "Does anyone know the difference?"

Kyle Mitchell dealt with the high-tech world of medicine daily. He often fretted about the way some competitors stretched the conceptual facts of the effect of their drugs. "Michael? This is hard to understand because we all 'want' to believe that anything is possible. Our whole history is full of achievements that people said couldn't be done, yet there are dozens of real examples of things that we would all agree are impossible. I have to battle everyday against guys who play on the human condition of 'wanting to believe.' It's hard to understand the distinctions," he said.

"Let's start with the moon walk. It seemed impossible 100 years ago. Was it?"

Blank stares. Madison answered at last. "The idea of walking on the moon *was* impossible 100 years ago . . . contextually. There was simply no means to do it. Knowledge caught up, though. Walking on the moon was never an impossibility. It couldn't be done at the time because other conditions had not been met. Once things like rocket engines powerful enough to escape the gravity of the earth were built, the realization of walking on the moon became more likely."

"So a hundred years ago, we could be certain that it was possible, but in the context of lacking the necessary constituents of space travel, it was impossible contextually?" countered Michael.

"That's right. The context makes all the difference. It's very difficult to apply anything out of context, on the other hand, context lets you define, precisely, the way things really are," said Madison.

"Let's apply it to your competitor's willingness to prey on the admirable human condition of 'wanting to believe,' Kyle. How do you know their drugs won't deliver?"

"Everyone knows," answered Kyle.

"Huh-uh. *Somebody* doesn't know."

"Okay. My competitor knows, and I know, but the doctor doesn't."

"Why not? Are you guys really that much smarter than the doctor?"

"No, we're not *that* much smarter," Kyle said with a grin, realizing how absurd it sounded. "But since our companies are on the brink of innovative discoveries, the doctor is willing to consider the chance we've made a breakthrough—some new bit of knowledge that he perhaps didn't know before. We have the research and tests. We have knowledge that he doesn't."

"So *you know* based on scientific facts. You know, in the given context, just like the idea of space flight 100 years ago, that your product has its limitations?"

"Right."

"The guys you know, Kyle—who stretch the willingness to believe—how well does it work for them?"

"It works often enough to cost me sales."

"Uh-huh. Can you think of someone who's used it for years, successfully, and is still working?"

Kyle hesitated, eyes rolled to the ceiling, literally searching his memory. "Most of them seem to move on," he said. "Although one guy I know seems to stick around."

"In other words, it works for a while, and then it stops working, except for this one guy?"

"Yeah . . . that's probably right."

"Why do you think one guy can get away with it?" Michael asked with sincere interest.

"Well, the buyers don't respect him very much. They know he doesn't shoot straight all the time. All they buy from him are the things they know about," said Kyle.

"Ahhh. Do you know the guy?" asked Michael.

"Not really. He's a real party hound. Lives his life like it's going out of style— you know what I mean?"

"No."

"It's like he's expecting things to change anytime."

"Hmmm, like being found out and fired?"

"Probably. I haven't thought about it very much."

"If you were to think about it, how would you feel?"

"I think I'd party while I could before someone figured me out."

"So Kat can't fly but she could throw herself over the balcony and have the illusion of flight for, oh, say about 180 feet," said Michael.

The class laughed aloud. Each and every one of them had lost sales to the unscrupulous competitor—despising the perpetrator, and damning the business for its ills. Each of them had felt cheated at one time or another, frustrated at the injustice of lies, and never fully realizing that justice catches up in time.

"Kyle, how long have you been selling in this market?"

"Quite a while, given the normal span."

"Do you think it has anything at all to do with your resistance to lying?"

"Sure."

"Why?"

"Well . . . my customers believe me. I never lose one."

Michael stepped closer to the overhead projector and pointed to the word "certainty." "Please everyone, listen closely to this. Honesty has no intrinsic value. And being honest because someone else said you should is hollow, at best. Honesty is valuable when its underlying principle is certainty. Honesty is valuable because it attaches itself to the physical world, and the physical world doesn't care about the 'wishes' or 'good intentions' of human beings. Honesty is the *uncompromising recognition of reality*—nothing more and nothing less. Honesty is valuable because it works. True honesty can only come from certainty, and likewise, certainty provides the basis for honesty. Certainty is the principle—honesty is the ethic," he said.

The explanation of honesty poured out over the class like a flood. Some, like Ryan, smiled in satisfaction. A few, like Fischer, moaned subconsciously at the restrictions imposed, and the limits the definition would place on them personally. There was a long silence as the class replayed the words in their heads.

Michael continued. "There is, of course, the opposite principle—chance. For our argument, let's define it. Chance says chaos is the norm. Certainty is impossible because there is no cause-effect relationship to anything. Anything can happen, therefore, nothing can be certain. And if nothing is certain, then anything is possible. If anything is possible, what's honesty? I can say anything I want, because, after all, anything's possible. The drug that wouldn't deliver results in the laboratory might do so if the patient would just *believe* that it would, anything's possible. Who knows, maybe Kat *can* fly, anything's possible. Perhaps Madison *can* run the 200 in half the previous time, anything's possible. And *suddenly*, as a salesperson, if I hold this principle, my ethic is 'there are no limits to what I can say about my product.' It's open season, and my defense is, it's possible."

Heads were shaking from side to side throughout the room. Michael waited for someone to speak. It didn't take long.

"Come on. No one would go that far. Lies and deception are found out," said Bobby.

"True. Few people go that far, and lies and deception are found out," Michael said, repeating Bobby's words methodically. "But if you'll recall, we said principles are at work whether you know it or not. If you don't have the principle of certainty, then you must, even unknowingly, accept the principle of chance. You'll notice I've intentionally used the word 'evasion' instead of 'lying' as the action related to the principle of chance. Evasion concedes that the principle of chance is often a default, because the principle of certainty isn't accepted. Evasion can be ignorance or intentional avoidance. Evasion is often half-truths, or out-of-context explanations, or the shunning of knowledge so that the principle of chance can go unchallenged. Evasion is a *'slipping by unnoticed'*, *'lucking out'*, *'dodging a bullet'*, *'maybe no one will ever know'* approach. At the extreme, you have the intentional liar—they usually end up in jail. But there is a vast group of evaders, both intentional and unintentional, and their evasion takes on degrees. Every drop of evasion is a compromise with honesty. Dishonesty is a matter of degree. You might slightly evade reality, and be slightly dishonest. Honesty is simply adherence to reality, nothing more and nothing less."

With that, Fischer saw an opening. "Whoa. You can't possibly explain everything to a customer. It would take all week. You're saying we should lay out every fact so the customer can judge—it won't work. Persuade people of the chance that the product will do what's promised. That's the job."

Fischer's technique was to redefine the speaker's view. Michael was too smart to let him get away with it. "Are you sure that's what I said?" he asked.

"Complete honesty, that's what you said. It won't work."

"No, Mr. Fischer, what I said was *complete contextual honesty*. Its definition should be reasonably clear. Anything that applies to the 'marriage' of the customer and the product should be considered, weighed and presented. If it's not, it will surface, either in the product failing to deliver, customer dissatisfaction, or more likely—both. The principle of certainty is that you can determine what is important to the customer and what is not. It holds that no matter what, you *can't* evade the reality of the physical world or the lack of knowledge about it, and finally, that *honesty* is nothing more than recognizing these facts. What *won't* work, Tug, is the mind-fog of evasion. What *does* work is concise, surgical application of the facts in the context of the customer's needs."

Michael turned away from Fischer and addressed the entire class once again. "What impact does the action of evasion have emotionally? Bobby was right when he said that few people go to the extreme of evasion. So let's look at the impact of compromising honesty—by evading just a little bit. Our minds are very good at recognizing contradictions with the physical world. The emotional impact is *stress* or *fear*—depending on how severe the consequences of evasion. Let's consider the mountain again. Did anyone feel stress on the mountain?"

Sally just smiled. It was to the point that her trouble on the mountain was practically a badge of honor—a legend to be told and retold.

Ryan answered. "Sure there were lots of moments of stress. Most of it had to do with not 'knowing' what we were doing."

"What do you mean, Ryan?" asked Michael.

"Whenever I feel stress, it seems like it's when I'm not sure of what I'm doing. On the mountain or in anything that I do. And when I really feel stress is when someone else is relying on me—and *I'm* uncertain."

"Is stress good or bad?" asked Michael sincerely.

Laughs.

"It's an important point. Our culture accepts stress as part of life's package. If it's no good, then why don't we eliminate it?"

"Because we can't be cer . . . " Ryan stopped in mid-sentence.

"Certain?" Michael finished it for him. "Ryan, if you don't hold the principle of certainty, you accept chance by default. See how easy it is to let it happen?"

"But I don't understand how to avoid it," he said.

"Get up and walk around, bump into things. Try to walk through walls. What you'll realize is that you *can't* avoid it. The question is whether you'll recognize it as your principle and act accordingly. The principle of certainty rests on the underlying law of cause and effect. It does not insist that you know everything;

you can't. But you can know what you don't know. And you can understand the results of your actions. You can have contextual certainty. And you can decide *not* to put yourself in the position of an action for which you do not know the outcome—when the outcome could be damaging."

Michael paused for a moment, then continued. "And, there are degrees of certainty, given the complexity of the situation. For instance, in the example of stepping over the ledge on the mountain. If there were a ledge below you that would stop your fall, the certainty of falling doesn't change, but the outcome has more variables like, will you land on the ledge or miss it. Now you can make some determinations about what type of a leap would be required to land on the ledge. If you had to leap four feet out from the ledge above in order to land safely on the ledge, you can determine, with a degree of certainty, whether such a leap is possible. Uncertainty doesn't force you into a shell."

"But you haven't eliminated stress yet," said Ryan.

"He's right, Michael," said Tip Bailey, nodding to Michael then turning to address Ryan. "But Ryan, imagine all the stressful circumstances that could be eliminated. All the problems we create and the stress we take on unnecessarily. All of that can be eliminated. Go back to the chart. This is really just a better understanding of honesty. It gives it a foundation, a . . . principle," he said.

With the last sentence Bailey smiled to himself and many in the class shook their heads in a new appreciation for the *principle-action-emotion* chain and the legitimacy of the Sales Esteem philosophy. Many of them removed this sheet from their stack of papers and examined it again.

Tip continued as though he had uncovered buried treasure. "Michael, most of us learn that honesty is just something we *should do.* This idea gives honesty a reason. It makes it obvious. If we don't act on certainty, if we evade it, we get a truckload of stress. If we honor certainty, we eliminate most of the stress."

"But Tip, you're missing the most important aspect. Do you know what it is?"

"I'm not sure."

"Anyone else know?"

Kat Kelly did. "Michael. I think *I* do. Anytime you get rid of something negative, there's a positive flip-side, right? Looking at the paradigm, I see calm as the result of honesty. If I eliminate stress, and find—calmness, I guess—my productivity should increase. Like cleaning sand from the gears, and reoiling them. I should be better emotionally, and because of it, sell more."

"Yes, Kat. But don't miss the importance of understanding that the action must come first, then the emotion. That's the trap that most of today's sales gurus will lead you to—a whitewash designed to make you 'believe' you're calm without doing the things that cause you to be calm. Honesty eliminates stress because it works. You avoid the messes, the unhappy customers, and your own negative assessment of how you operate."

"Yeah, and it seems to me that the last one may be the most important," said Tip.

Michael nodded. "Go back to the slide of our primary values. Happiness contains the values of self-respect, pride and self-esteem," he said.

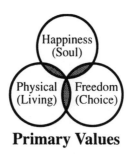

Primary Values

"I think we've hit pay dirt. Did everyone in the room make the same connections?" Michael asked, surveying the room for a moment. "What's the value of this thing called calm?"

"It sounds boring," said Shaw. "Who ever wanted to buy something from a wet noodle?"

"It's a good question," replied Michael. "We all enjoy dynamic people more than we do stoic, or uninteresting people. Would we ever want to be calm?"

Shannon Shelley spoke up. "No. I think salespeople build fires under their prospect. Enthusiasm is what I want from a salesperson."

"I really like that word," said Michael. "Give me some examples of enthusiastic people."

Shannon bobbed her head from side to side. "Uhmm. Let's see, school kids, athletes, artists. You know, generally the young at heart."

"Why did you add that last description?" asked Michael.

"I'm not sure. I guess most of the enthusiastic people I know are younger, less weathered, I suppose," said Shannon.

"Give me some examples of professionals who you see as enthusiastic."

"Michael Jordan after he's tossed in a three-pointer to win the game." It was Bailey who loved his sports analogies.

"Oh Tip, come on. You call that just enthusiasm? He seems a little more excited to me," said Michael.

"Yeah, you're right. It's stronger than enthusiasm."

"Elation?" offered Michael.

"Yeah, that's the word I would use," said Tip.

"Enthusiastic professionals, name 'em," challenged Michael.

"I'm not so sure I want enthusiastic professionals," interrupted Ryan. "Can you imagine discussing surgery with a doctor when your kid's life is at stake and he comes across as enthusiastic. I can see it now: 'Come on Kev, ol' buddy, I think we can pull this surgery thing off, what da ya say? Are you with me?'"

Laughs from the class.

"It's an excellent point," said Michael, putting his hand to his chin in mock confusion. "Someone tell me when they would want an enthusiastic professional?"

Kincaid said, "I think it depends on the type of selling that's being done. I mean, if it's a sales clerk in a toy store, I want enthusiasm. If it's someone who's advising me on my professional sports career, like Tip, hell—I want confidence, not enthusiasm."

"Shannon?" Michael asked, "What do you think?"

"Yeah, I think I understand. Enthusiasm works when the stakes are low; it makes it more enjoyable. It's also okay when you're anticipating a positive outcome to an unpredictable event—like the sales of my clients' books. I can see why athletes, artists, and young people seem enthusiastic—they're less certain of the outcome. But when the importance of the sale increases, the attractiveness of enthusiasm seems to fade. It almost becomes a liability, like Ryan said. A professional should be calm and assured," she said slowly, as though she were thinking out loud.

Others in the room were nodding their agreement. Michael was too. "Any objections to that explanation?" he asked. There were none.

"Are we all in agreement that the professional salesperson, whether recommending, advising, suggesting, or persuading his customers, will benefit more from calm than from enthusiasm?" asked Michael.

More nods.

"But I liked the Michael Jordan thing," said Michael. "What about elation?"

Shannon Shelley said, "That's satisfaction in your performance. It's entirely different. Excitement, or elation, means you like what you do and you've done it well. I want calm until I get the win—then let's celebrate."

More nods.

"All right. I think we all understand. Certainty, honesty, calm versus chance, evasion, stress. Those are the principles and their corresponding results. Let's tie up the final question of certainty, one that Tug raised. Does certainty mean *inaction*? After all, we said we could only reach contextual certainty—like the moon walk? Are we forced to be boring, inactive, ineffectual?" he asked.

Ryan's view of the world was changing. He had struggled with this question and it was coming into clear focus now. He answered, "The things you *don't* know, you should disclose. There's nothing wrong with not knowing, as long as you're honest about it to the customer. I sell bonds. No one has ever predicted with exact precision the prices of bonds, but I know the range of prices, and I know what causes the price to rise and fall. I know with contextual certainty that given a customer's specific needs—if he can hold the bond to maturity—I can tell him the degree of certainty of realizing his investment goals. Anything I don't know, he'll know. If he doesn't like the degree of uncertainty, then it's not for him. But if he understands the parameters, and accepts part of the responsibility, then we're okay."

Shaw didn't like the sound of this. It lacked the persuasion Shaw considered to be central to all good selling. It lacked convincing the customer that the salesperson was far more suited to direct the customer, and that the customer should go willingly. It lacked the flair of the evangelist who could reach out and grab his congregation on faith. It lacked being in control.

"Ryan, if I ever hear you disclose enough to kill a sale, I'll charge you for the trade. If the customer is willing and ready to go, you close," he said.

For a brief moment fire raced through Ryan's face. Michael expected him to respond to Shaw's comment. But he didn't. The color faded from his face and he sat silently. Ryan was raised to respect authority, and Shaw was still his boss. The moment came and went, and had the potential of real damage to Ryan. Michael had to level the playing field for him. He walked over the Shaw's table, stood behind Shaw with his hands placed firmly on his shoulders, and addressed the rest of the class.

"What the rest of you don't know is that Mr. Shaw is so committed to helping his salespeople that he just can't help himself when the opportunity presents itself—even though his management pleads with him to take a break and let Ryan draw what he will from the conference. Thank you, Mr. Shaw, for your concern, but please, your company has given you a week off for your own experience. Mr. Matthews is in good hands." Michael patted Shaw's shoulders, firmly. The message was clear, although only Shaw and Ryan understood the meaning behind it.

Michael continued as he walked back to the front. "You can't be omnipotent. You *will be* paralyzed if you think you must know everything. You can know what is certain—and what is not. And you can know when the difference is important to the customer. Sometimes it will demand you take the time to educate the customer. You want the customer to be part of the decision-making. Your job is to understand the certainty of what the product might possibly achieve, apply it to the customer's circumstances, and then demonstrate the connection, as calmly or enthusiastically as is appropriate. It has big rewards, honesty does. Your soul stays intact and you avoid stress. You're better at what you do. It's really that simple."

Rick Kincaid was very confused. He sat with his arms crossed staring at the desk in front of him, deep in thought. His entire career was about forging a compromise between two perceptions of reality. The labor negotiations always focused on both sides asking for more than they needed or wanted, and then battling through to a compromise. He practiced the art of different perspectives and different realities. He was always the mediator, trying to loosen the resolve of each side in order to find a comfortable middle.

"Michael, I'm sorry, but I just can't buy this. The world is about compromise. Everyone wants more, nobody gets it all. I just couldn't argue certainty to my unions, or take their side and argue certainty to management. It just wouldn't work."

"Yep!" It was Fischer. "You're way off on this one. It works fine in a lab, where you can control the mice, but not in the real world." Fischer smiled and rocked back in his chair, arms crossed above his head which revealed sweat stains under his arms.

"Rick. You've represented auto manufacturers over the years?" asked Michael.

"None of the Big Three, but I do study the casework closely."

"How would you characterize the labor negotiations in the U.S. auto industry over the last decade?"

"Well, brutal at first, the unions had all the cards, then came a dramatic change which returned the advantage to management. Management asked for concessions early, and were rebuffed, so they went on a cost-cutting spree which crippled union membership and ultimately weakened them."

"Are you forgetting the Japanese?"

"They weren't involved in the labor negotiations," he said, bewildered by the question.

"Let's take this in stages. Would it be fair to say that before the seventies, American car makers were far better at building cars than anyone on the planet?"

"Sure."

"How did they do that?"

"Quality, efficiency, value."

"Now jump ahead to the seventies; did the American consumer go stark raving mad and start buying Japanese cars because they were inferior?"

"No, of course not. They bought them because they were better—or I should say, they were a better value. Less costly than comparable American cars."

"How could that have possibly happened? Were we asleep?"

"Cheap labor."

"Define cheap labor for me," said Michael with a grimace on his face.

"Well, relative to what we had to pay workers in this country, the Japanese paid their workers far less."

"But since American labor was so much more productive, it was worth the extra cost, right?"

"No. It wasn't necessarily more productive. The Japanese worker equaled the output of the American workers. That's why it's cheap, comparatively."

"Why was there such an imbalance?"

"Culturally, Japanese workers would accept lower wages."

"Or perhaps, *culturally*, American workers demanded too much? How would we know the difference?"

"I don't know."

"Did American productivity keep pace with increases in labor costs?"

"No. It was flat. During that time wages were going up."

"So. More money for the same work? Do you think that's a measure for determining whether a wage demand is realistic?"

"No. The workers have a right to increase their standard of living."

"Do you think the Japanese disagreed with that?"

"What do you mean?"

"Where are labor prices now, compared with the Japanese, and compared with productivity?"

"Well, they're similar to the Japanese. The measure is to determine the labor content of each car price. Also, American car quality is way up, and so is productivity."

"Why?"

"Competition."

"So the Japanese had something to say about the cultural demands of higher wages, after all?"

"If you want to put it that way."

"Here's how I would like to put it. In a global market, labor cost increases that exceed productivity gains will, with certainty, expose the company to more productive competition. The Japanese exploited the cultural weakness of *compromise*, Mr. Kincaid. The compromise that asserted American workers were not bound to increase their work relative to their pay demands. That compromise defied reality—evading the fact that cost and productivity were important to what rolled off the assembly line. The Japanese, on the other hand, embraced the certainty of all of this, and entered an industry that until then had been closed to them. Please, when you say that the real world is compromise, don't pretend that it's true. Compromise opened the door for overpaid, underperforming, and unmotivated labor. The result was shoddy product, and we got our tails kicked by the *uncompromising* Japanese. Rick, has there been a change to any of this in the last few years?"

"Yeah. American productivity is up, and so is quality. Labor costs, relative to productivity are lower, and are now practically competitive with the Japanese. We've come back."

"Earlier you said that labor had the superior negotiating position, and then lost it to management. Do you see a connection between our recent resurgence and the changing character of labor negotiations?"

"No. I just think our technology caught up."

"You're *certain*?"

Laughs filled the room. Kincaid didn't grasp the reason, but he sensed the group had no sympathy for his position. He felt alone and more confused than ever. "Michael, are you suggesting that there was a time when management should have held their ground and refused the demands of the unions?"

"Rick. I'm sure under productive workers weren't the only cause of the malaise of the auto industry. I can point to instances of tired design and poorly structured organizations with overlaps and redundancies. But all of them were at fault for the same reason—evading reality, and compromising with certainty. To answer your question, yes. Management should have held its ground, and tied any wage increases to productivity gains. The same standards should have been applied to management and to engineering. In the end, just as in all attempts to fool reality, the auto companies were *forced* to increase productivity just to survive. It's not a matter of can we pull it off. It's a matter of will it work. One is a compromise with reality—one is substance.

"Everything that happens is cause and effect oriented. The universe, the world, and people. Understanding causality may be the most important thing a person does. Can anyone guess why?" he asked.

"We can understand that our actions will have results—probably affecting other people as well as ourselves," said Ryan.

"That's the obvious impact, Ryan, but not what I'm looking for. Go a little deeper," urged Michael. "Anyone?"

Madison was still steaming about Kevin's comments at lunch. She sat with her hands folded across her chest.

"Madison?" Michael asked, turning to her.

"What?" she said, jolted back into the discussion.

"Why is causality important?"

"For the reason Ryan gave," she covered.

Michael could see the anger in her face and looked over to Keller who returned his stare with raised eyebrows and a shrug. "Madison?" he asked. "Would you mind helping me in an exercise?"

"No, of course not," she said.

"Come up front for a moment," he said as he jerked his head at Keller to join them.

Madison met Michael at the front of the room and looked suspiciously at Kevin. Michael rolled the white board's towel into a bandanna and tied it in a blindfold over Madison's eyes. "The goal of this game is to reach each of the room's four corners with the help of your navigator. Madison, meet Kevin . . . your navigator," he said with a smile at Kevin.

"Your navigator will take commands, but can't speak back to you," he said.

"Where can I find a relationship like that!" blurted Kat.

"Cute," said Michael. "Other than that, there are no other rules. You may begin at any time."

"Navigator?" said Madison. "How many steps am I from the corner directly to my right?"

Keller didn't answer.

"Okay . . . I get it. Navigator, come close enough that I can put my hand on your shoulder," she said.

Kevin moved up behind and placed both his hands on her hips. Her anger had subsided and she giggled slightly. "I guess that will do," she said. "Point us in the direction of the first corner."

Keller wiggled her back and forth playfully and then shifted her to the left a quarter turn. He waited.

"Navigator, walk us toward the corner . . . " she began.

Kevin pushed her forward and immediately ran into the podium. He held her short to keep her from stumbling.

". . . but *stop* before we run into *something*!" she grunted after the collision. "Very funny. When I say start, walk us around the obstacle we just *ran into* and the towards the corner, but *stop before we run into the next obstacle!*" she said to laughter from the class.

There was nothing else between them and the corner. Kevin shuffled her around the podium and to within six inches of the corner of the room where he stopped. Once there, Madison gave him the next command. "Okay, now move around this obstacle and towards the corner," she said, with a hint of annoyance.

Kevin hesitated so that he could enjoy hearing the fateful command a second time.

"Navigator, I said . . . move around this obstacle and towards the corner."

With the second command, Kevin grabbed her more firmly and pushed forward until her feet banged into the intersecting walls that joined to form the corner. According to plan, she stumbled forward, but under his control, and bumped her nose and forehead slightly against the wall. The class burst into laughter. Madison was a good sport and laughed at herself, determined to conquer the game.

"First corner was a partial success. Now on to the second. The corner to my left," she said. "But this time, navigator, I want you to stop when you come to either an obstacle or the next corner. At an obstacle I want you to twist my hips left and right and then continue around the obstacle and towards the corner. When we reach the corner, leave my damn hips alone so I'll know when we've arrived. You can start now," she said smugly.

Kevin pushed, pulled, slid and bounced her towards the next corner, stopping at the obstacles, twisting her hips as she had commanded, and then moving on. It was playful and by the time they got to the corner, Madison was laughing so hard that tears were streaming down her face. Kevin stopped her at the corner and the group fell silent. She realized Kevin hadn't twisted her hips and she reached out to touch the corner walls. As she did the group let out a cheer. Everyone was laughing. Michael was clapping as well and stopped them before they continued.

"I think you've got it now, Madison. You can take the blindfold off," Michael said. Madison pulled the bandanna down around her neck, mussing her long blond hair in the process. Keller stared in admiration at her beauty. Madison caught his stare and understood it immediately. Their eyes met for just a moment until she let a sly smile interrupt the exchange. It was fast enough for no one else to notice. They returned to their chairs and trying to ignore each other without much luck. Neither one seemed able to go long without a quick glance. Kevin caught himself trying to remember when he was last smitten. It had been a long time since he felt like he did.

"Okay," started Michael. "What did Madison rely on to get her around the room."

"Kevin," said Shannon.

"Before that," said Michael.

"Communication," said Kat.

"Which is what?"

"The transfer of concepts through language," said Madison.

"Very good. And what did the concepts rely on?"

"Causality," said Madison. "I was able to act because I knew the outcome of my actions would be the same every time. Cause and effect."

"You're a scholar, Madison. Causality is the foundation of our ability to reason. Without it, life would be hit or miss. With it, we can have goal-directed action. For humans, that means we use reason to figure out how to move through life without bumping into things, and we rely on cause and effect to do so. It provides us with the most important aspect of survival—contextual certainty. Or in other words, 'in this particular situation, if I do this . . . then this will be the outcome. If I do that . . . then that will be the outcome,'" said Michael.

"This little exercise also helps with another lesson from the mountain. Ryan, earlier you made a comment about seeing the entire mountain. Could you explain?"

"It's simple really, when I said the *whole* mountain, I meant we could imagine the entire trip and anticipate what actions we should take. It seems to me to be one of our unique human abilities—to be able to consider practically our entire life and what effect our actions had, and then to look forward, as far off as our deathbeds, and predict what impact our actions *will* have," said Ryan.

"You used the term perspective, which is close. But let's expand it to include the explanation you just gave us regarding something we have to imagine, the future," said Michael.

"How about *vision?*" said Ryan.

"Perfect. Although it's been overused and is quite worn out, 'vision' is exactly the word we need. Let's go back to the diagram," said Michael, poking the switch of the overhead.

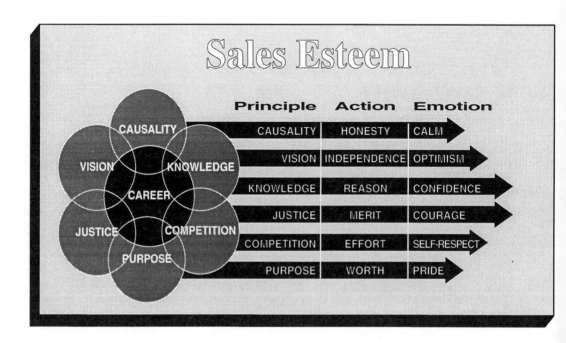

"Vision is our principle. It leads to *independence* as an ethic which results in the emotion of *optimism*." He paused.

"Do we need vision?"

"Aren't we forced to use it, everyday?" asked Kat.

"Explain a little further, Kat, if you would."

"If I understand your explanation, vision is the use of the principles we've formed from our experiences. We use it to help direct us in the present, with some insight into what result our immediate actions will take. We make some mental calculations about our actions based on our past experiences. Cause and effect gives us a chance to predict the future. Even for the everyday tasks we do," said Kat.

"Kevin, can we think fast enough to recall our memories in every situation?" Michael asked, turning to Kevin Keller, who was seated at the table beside the podium.

"We often use memory as a guide, but there's something much better," said Kevin still sitting. "The process Kat described is pretty close, but the mind uses shorthand, 'conceptual shorthand', to make it easier. We take experiences and forge them into categories in order to save space and 'recall time'—almost like compressing information on a computer, only much more complex. Everyone has undoubtedly heard the term 'my whole life passed before my eyes'? Well, we believe that's essentially an all-out, data-dump by the brain searching for relevant information to deal with a life-threatening situation. In that case, literally trillions of bits of information have been organized into concepts, principles, memories, hypotheses, etc. As we've seen, without cause and effect, this type of reflection would be useless.

"The more interesting mental functions are those that predict the future," Kevin continued. "Let me show you what I mean. If everyone will lift their right hand," he said, waiting for the class to follow his directions.

"Now ball your hand into a fist. Right."

"Now take your arm back and thrust it forward into a punching motion." The class was mass of waving arms.

"Each of you predicted the movement of your arm through space. No big deal right? Now, Tip, if you wouldn't mind helping us. Go to the glass window and make the same motion into the glass, if you will. But please give us a narration of it as you move your arm," said Kevin.

Bailey walked to the glass wall and stood four feet from the window, cocked his arm and started to swing when Kevin stopped him. "Closer to the window."

Bailey moved up a couple of steps and stopped, looking back over his shoulder at Keller with an inquisitive look.

"A little further."

He took another step.

"Okay, wind up slowly and tell us about it as you go."

Bailey cocked his arm behind him and started speaking as the slowly uncoiled his closed fist toward the window. "Okay, I'm moving my arm forward, forward, and stop." Bailey pulled up six inches from the glass.

"Why did you *stop*?" Keller asked, with a rhetorical tone.

"Obviously," said Bailey, pointing at the window.

"It's not quite that simple," said Keller, turning to the class. "Tell me what had to happen for him to make the decision to stop?"

Kat answered. "He needed some knowledge about glass," she said.

"What about glass would he need to know?"

"That it breaks on impact."

"Good. Could he have lightly tapped the glass without it breaking?"

"Probably."

"So he needed a concept about the degree of impact that would cause the glass to shatter. And why does he care whether the glass shatters at all?"

"Because he doesn't want to get cut."

"So he needs a concept of sharp, and skin, and blood—and a concept of the necessity of blood for continued life and on and on and on. He must also understand concepts of space and motion. And the concept of an innate object which will remain stationary when you threaten it. If he had swung at Tug, the object would probably have moved in some way. Thanks Tip, you can sit down now," said Kevin, nodding a second thank you to him as he took his seat.

"Tip's actions and their reasons seem rather obvious on the surface, but they are extremely complex overall. The number of conceptual calculations, and the predictions that occur, are truly remarkable. Here's a theory I think you'll find interesting that demonstrates this human quality. Let me ask, has anyone ever experienced déjà vu?"

Hands went up all over the room.

"Yeah, me too. What do you think it is?" asked Kevin.

"Well, some people think they've lived it before," said Shannon Shelley.

"Uh-huh. But you don't."

"No. There's got to be a better explanation."

"I think we dream our déjà vus before they happen." It was Kat.

"Yeah. I've heard that explanation too, only there is no known human ability to perceive a physical event without observing it in the present. In other words, you would need a sixth sense. Such an ability doesn't show up at any other time, and can't be measured with any credible scientific validity," said Kevin.

He continued. "Our theory is that the mind's constant predictive capacity is always making short-term forecasts of every situation. Déjà vu is an *unusually* accurate prediction, just seconds before the event actually occurs—kind of like the perfect guess, although it's not a matter of guessing. Had Tip truly intended to smash his fist through the window, the mind would have made micro-predictions of the entire event, instantly and continuously. Most often, they would be slightly off. But every so often, the predictions would match perfectly, and the short time lapse from predicting the event to experiencing it, leaves the impression of having experienced it before." He paused.

"In any event, Kat is correct about the necessity to use existing knowledge and predict the outcome of every action. We have to do it to survive on a rudimentary basis. I think the point here is that man has the capacity to *envision* much *further* into the future. Right, Michael?"

"Exactly. Vision is the principle of looking both backward and forward. Of recalling our knowledge of cause and effect, and applying it to our actions with the expectation of knowing the likely outcome. Let's go back to Tip's punch at the window. Tip, don't you think it would have been more dramatic to actually punch the window?"

"Sure."

"But you didn't."

"No. I didn't because I knew the glass would break and I might cut my hand."

"How did you know?"

"I know about glass—it breaks. And when it does, the sharp edges are dangerous."

"Have you ever actually punched a glass window before?"

"No."

"So you don't have an actual experience to draw on. You have to imagine or envision the result of the action based on your knowledge of broken glass and tender skin."

"I guess so."

"Kat," Michael said, "You've done rotten commercials before?"

"Please don't remind me," said Kat.

"You wouldn't recommend them to your clients again, even if they fit the product?"

"No, I have a low tolerance for humiliation," she said.

"And the good commercials, you would recommend them again, in the right situation."

"Sure. I have a high tolerance for repeat business," she said with a smile and laughter from the class.

"So you hold the principle of vision?"

"Why, I suppose *I do*," she proclaimed proudly.

"What if the President of the company felt differently about one of your *bad commercials*? What if *he* liked it, but *you* knew it was a flop? What if he liked the idea of reusing commercials to extend their profitability? What if he *asked* you to find a way to use it again? And what if your reputation was on the line every time you made a recommendation?"

"Well, I would . . . uh . . . I would—I would tell him it's a bad idea," she said, caught slightly off guard.

"He thinks it's a good idea," said Michael.

"Then it's his decision."

"What does that mean? It's your commercial. It's your reputation. It's your..."

"It's *his* company and *my* job," Kat interrupted. "Maybe I'm wrong about how good the ad is. Does the customer want it? Maybe I *have* to listen to his opinion," she said.

"Let's say that every bit of evidence you have indicates the ad will fail. And you explain that to him. He disagrees on the basis of extended profitability, after all, there's no new cost, so how can it fail? If it was acceptable once, why not again? His primary motive is to enhance the original production's profitability. Your job is to persuade the customer it will work. After all, selling is persuasion, isn't it?"

"No, not when it's going to fail and you know it," said Kat. "It's a dilemma."

"No, Kat. There are no dilemmas—only choices. You either compromise on your principles or stick to them," said Michael.

Kat looked unhappy for the first time since she had been at the conference. This wasn't easy. She had always had decent managers. She hadn't considered the possibility of the situation Michael had confronted her with. She wasn't sure what she would do. "Do you think that's very realistic?" she asked.

"If you're asking me whether I think the problem would be that blatant, the answer is 'no'. If you're asking whether I think more subtle instances of this kind of thing happen everyday, the answer is a definite 'yes.' What do you think?"

"I'm afraid you're right."

"What are the choices when we're asked by an authority to deviate from our knowledge—our vision?" asked Michael.

"You can go with your own beliefs, or rely on the authority to accept responsibility," said Ryan.

"And if you do the latter, what do you suppose would be the result in the example we drew before?"

"From the company's perspective, success. From Kat's perspective, it would be terribly damaging. Sort of like if you had insisted she try to save Sally yesterday using a frayed rope."

"Oh, good example. But it would be okay, right, since the President would take responsibility for it?"

Most of the class members were shaking their heads in disagreement. Ryan continued. "I'd bet the guy would be nowhere to be found when the problems came up. You'd get saddled with it, Kat."

Jock Shaw saw no problem with authority taking control and didn't like the direction of the conversation. "I don't think things are ever that black and white. The guy has a responsibility to the company. Maybe he's right and Kat's wrong. It's worth a try to run the ad again," he said.

With that, conversation broke out across the room. Michael let it run its course. There were a few heated debates, but most of the comments centered on being put in an awkward situation by management. After a few minutes, Michael raised his hand and asked for their attention.

"So we have two principles, don't we? One holds that someone else's desires, or worse yet, loyalty to a non-living entity like your company, has a sovereign claim to your actions." He paused. "The other principle is vision, which puts you in control of your own destiny. The action is to act independently. We'll refer to it as Independence. In fact, I think it is helpful to view all states of being as actions, psychological actions.

"In the first instance, we use the word abdication because we're talking about your role in the process. You may feel strongly influenced to go along. You may even feel forced to in order to keep your job. Whatever the reason, you abdicate your knowledge and your responsibility. Your action is dependence. This, I am sorry to say, is the more prevalent attitude of sales managers—the attitude that you do whatever it takes to get the job done. And it has a name—loyalty. Can someone give me a clear explanation of corporate loyalty?" Michael asked.

Jock Shaw was one of a handful of sales managers at the conference. But unlike the others, Shaw came to protect his views and not to question them. Authority was the only principle Shaw understood. He had fought hard to acquire his authority and most of it had come from deception and politics. "Come on, who doesn't understand loyalty? It's as simple as following your boss' direction," said Shaw.

"You can do better than that, Jock," said Michael, knowing Shaw would give him the contrarian views he needed for comparison.

"Loyalty is like being part of a team. The company is the team. And the team's goals come first. You have to be willing to sacrifice for the good of the team, personally or professionally. Managers are the coaches. They're responsible for directing the team to reaching its goals."

"Good," said Michael, getting the definition he wanted. "Now, how many of you see your environment that way?"

Two-thirds of the class raised their hands.

"Who decides what the team's goals are?" asked Michael.

"The boss," said Shaw.

"You mean the Big Boss?" Michael widened his eyes. "The Big Cheese? The Chief?"

"Yes, the Big Cheese is the head coach." Shaw was annoyed.

"How does he know what to do?"

"That's—why—he's—the—*boss*," Shaw said as though it was an incontestable reason.

"I see . . . so regardless of whether the boss is right or wrong, the team should submit to his wishes?"

The class wasn't about to accept the suggestion and conversations broke out among individuals at the tables. Few of them agreed with Shaw's comments.

Rick Kincaid said, "The definition of the team is okay so long as the coach can be questioned."

"Now we're getting somewhere. Why do you make that distinction, Rick?"

"Because the boss isn't always right, and a good boss knows it. Authority doesn't have anything to do with control. The root of the word is 'author', which means the originator or master of the subject. Authority in the right definition speaks to merit and knowledge of the situation," said Kincaid.

"Well stated, Rick. So we have no concerns. The boss will step aside when someone with knowledge steps up to make a decision," said Michael.

Nervous laughter of disagreement filled the room. Michael feigned surprise. "What? You don't think it works that way?"

"Not in this millennium," said Kyle.

"Seems like a conflict to me. Do we comply with the boss' wishes or take the opportunity to question him when we believe he's made a mistake?" asked

Michael, pacing at the front of the room. No one answered and this was one of those moments when Michael was not going to help. He waited. "Am I to believe that everyone in this room is going to blindly follow authority regardless of the circumstances?" That got them going.

"Of course not," said Kat. "At some point, you decide if you can put up with it any longer."

"Okay. When do you do that?" asked Michael.

"When your princi . . . " Kat hesitated. "When your principles are at stake," she said, smiling at the connection she made.

"Let's tie this together. Vision as a principle is properly positioned above certainty. It holds certainty as its foundation. Vision as a principle says that you *can know*, and you *can anticipate* the outcome, regardless of whether you're the big boss or the janitor. So long as you have the knowledge, you can insist on authority over *your* actions—no one else's perhaps—but always over *your* actions. This is independence. What it means for the salesperson is the right to turn down any sale, disengage from any activity, or retire from any campaign if the salesperson's vision of the outcome is contradictory to the principles he holds. The antithesis is dependence on authority which ultimately comes down to reliance on that authority. When you do this, you abdicate responsibility for the action to the authority since you acted at the authority's behest. The only problem is *you* were the one to act. Does anyone recognize the contradiction when you are the 'apparent' beneficiary of your actions, yet you pass responsibility for those actions to someone else?"

Madison was staring blankly at the floor. Michael noticed and guessed correctly that she had experienced something germane to the discussion. "Madison, do you want to give it a shot?" he asked softly.

Madison was startled back into the discussion. "Yeah . . . uh . . . sure. I was just thinking about the NCAA championships in my senior year. I had these grueling qualifying heats in the 200 meters and I was wearing down physically. Our anchor-leg on the mile relay team had the flu and I was asked to run the qualifiers for her so she could save her strength. The problem was that I needed all my strength to have a shot at winning the individual 200. I was the favorite but my times were off because I was exhausted. I knew I would have to kill myself to help the team qualify and if I did, I wouldn't have a hope in my specialty. It was just too much. I explained it to the coach. He knew better, but I guess he was hoping for some super-human effort on my part. I told him I didn't need any more motivation, and no matter what, I couldn't pull it off. I guessed correctly that I would let both the team and myself down—and that's what happened."

"What happened, Madison?" Michael asked, pressing her to continue.

"I got continually worse in the heats for both races. Then I missed qualifying for the individual 200. When it was time for the finals in the relay, I had to back away and let the anchor run it, even though my times had been faster than hers by then. We finished fourth and lost the team championship because of the whole mess."

"Wait. The whole plan exploded on your coach?" bellowed Tip Bailey.

"Yeah. Even though he knew better. *I* knew better. It's just like what Michael was saying. I was the authority on whether it should be done, but I let the coach's authority push my better judgment out of the way. The irony was when my teammates treated me as though I let them down—not outwardly—but I could sense their disappointment." Madison spoke about the incident as though she had experienced it the day before, and was still hurting.

"Madison? Did you ever ask him why he made the decision?"

"He said the team always came first, no matter what—which I agree with, but it was a desperate move. Since then, I've asked others if they believed the strategy would have worked—even if I hadn't been so physically exhausted."

"What do you mean, Madison?"

"I've analyzed all the runners' pre-meet times. It was an outrageous gamble to win the championship by a desperate guy who never thought he'd have another shot at it."

"The team *never had a chance to win*," Michael repeated as though uncovering lost evidence from a century-old mystery. "Can I ask a risky question?"

"Sure, why not?"

"Are you certain the anchor runner was sick?"

"Hmm, everyone has wondered the same thing. She won't talk to me and I know what the implications are."

Michael lifted his stare from Madison as though he had just realized the presence of the rest of the class. "I'm sorry for the diversion. But this is really such a perfect example. The fallacy in the way Madison was coached is subtle, but undeniable. Does anyone else see it?"

Kat Kelly was nodding ever so slightly. "He sacrificed her, for his own goals, while all the while criticizing her for being selfish."

"You're very close, Kat. First, let's ask the question. Did Madison have an obligation to do what was best for the team?" asked Michael.

The group was split almost evenly in their response.

"Madison. College track is essentially a team sport, right?"

"That's right."

"And you knew this when you accepted the scholarship, right?"

"Right, and I've never questioned that point," she said.

"Madison had *bargained* to do what was best for the team. That is exactly the same thing each of you have *bargained* for with your companies. You were hired to further the cause of the company's business," he said to draw the analogy for them.

"And the coach was, for all practical purposes, Madison's boss. So far, no big deal. Certainly no ethical problems at this point, only a typical employment arrangement. Where did Madison's coach go wrong?"

"He asked her to sacrifice her own best interest for the good of the company," said Kat.

"No. That isn't the issue here. After all, she was the one who bargained to help the team. If the team had a shot at winning, Madison had a responsibility to follow his request."

A radiant smile came to Kat's face, as though the light bulb of understanding came on—the kind when answers come flooding in. "He asked her to sacrifice for *him!*" she said.

"Yes, Kat, for him," said Michael.

Madison eyes were misty. It had been painful to miss her opportunity to win, but even more painful to be self-indicting. She had blamed herself, even though she was not at fault.

"Michael? . . . How do you tell the difference between the company goals and those of someone like Madison's coach?" asked Kat.

"Would anyone suggest that we return to our principle of vision?" he asked.

Nods of agreement came from throughout the room.

"Fine. Someone explain it to me," insisted Michael.

"Easy," said Ryan. "Vision rests on certainty. Together the two maintain that the individual faced with delivering the action—whether Madison on the track, or any one of us as we sell—has a responsibility to do what we know is right. Otherwise, it's likely to fail, and we can only blame ourselves. If we rely on the coach, or our manager, or anyone else to guide our actions, then we're practically begging them to consider their best interest first. It's only a matter of time before we run across a coach like Madison's. And the only way to protect ourselves from it is to make our own decisions . . . independently."

Jock Shaw was furious. It was an assault on everything he stood for. He rose slightly in his seat as he began barking a response. "That's bullshit, Ryan. What do you think managers are for? We're here to think for *you!* We're here to mold the maverick individualists towards some sense of organization and team play—to be sure the company's goals are realized—and that chaos doesn't consume the entire company."

He turned his glare at Michael. "It's ideas like this that ruin companies. It's people like you who . . . " Shaw stopped when his eyes met Michael's.

"Go on, Jock. You're free to say whatever you wish here."

"You're advocating anarchy. Well, I've got news for you—*it's been tried . . .* remember the Dark Ages?" he yelled as he sat down.

"Jock, if you're going to cite history you should try to get it right," Michael said calmly, in stark contrast to Shaw's outburst. "The Dark Ages were a period of complete repression by the authority of the time. *Individualism* was struck down. Anarchy was the *result of the authority's oppression.* In fact, you can find 'rule-by-unquestioned-authority' at the center of all of man's historically anarchist periods. The Renaissance, on the other hand, was just the opposite—a celebration of the individual—and individual thought. You'll also find that man's brightest moments were marked by individualism—including the founding of this country." The depth of Michael's tone signaled passion for the subject that ran far deeper than was evident on the surface.

Once he had dismissed Shaw's errant statement, he continued. "Ryan's comments were right on the mark. The critical distinction is that Ryan presumes the company's goals are consistent with employee goals." He paused to let the comment sink in.

"If the idea of the individual realizing their goals is contrary to the company realizing its goals, it can only mean one thing . . . the goals must be different," said Michael.

"Of course they're different. There isn't a person I know who thinks employees benefit when the company does. Christ! That would require handing over the company to them," said Shaw.

"Not a *person* you know?" Michael turned to the rest of the class. "Does anyone in the room believe employee and company goals can converge?"

Rick Kincaid was the expert. "Michael," he said. "Most of the people in this room come from Fortune 100 companies. I can tell you personally, that the majority of those companies do their damnedest to align employee and company goals," he stated emphatically.

"Does anyone agree?" asked Michael. "Give me a show of hands."

It was a ridiculous scene—Shaw sat in the middle of a sea of raised arms.

"Jock, you gotta get out more often," deadpanned Michael. Laughter diffused the tension between Shaw and Ryan.

"Let's get this back on track. You have bargained to work for the benefit of the company. You were hired to pursue your self-interest with the understanding that it would contribute to the company. Neither your companies, nor your managers, believe they can control your actions every moment of every day. Without congruent goals, we *would* have anarchy. The responsibility, however, for determining when to resist making mistakes in the name of the good of the company rests with the individual . . . *especially when it comes to selling*. And as odd as it may seem to most outsiders, I think you will agree that the salesperson is in an unusually advantageous position to be independent. You are the catalysts of action. You are the ignition point. If you decide not to turn the switch on—nothing else happens. No matter how much of an argument it would cause outside this room, the fact of the matter is that your role is potentially the most *ethical*—or unethical—in the company. You decide if the company's product or service applies to every customer you contact. And with that opportunity comes both power and responsibility. If you abuse it in the name of the good of the company—you'll suffer ultimately. If you use it for your own rational self-interest, *you* benefit and subsequently, *your* company benefits.

"The principle of *vision* holds that you must act with *independence*, and when you do, the emotional result is *optimism*. Its antithesis is the principle of omniscience of the authority, and therefore, dependence on that authority. Its guiding principle is abdication of responsibility and control. The result is *anxiety*. The moment you transfer control of your actions to someone, or something else, the only possible emotional result is anxiety.

"Can anyone in the room tell me that they feel less anxious when their careers are in the hands of someone else?" Michael asked rhetorically. "Can anyone in the room tell me they feel less anxious when they rely on someone else's knowledge and direction? Can anyone tell me they feel less anxious when they submit to a dependence of an authority?"

No one answered. Even Tug Fischer, who was hoping for any chance to disrupt the discussion, believed it was more comfortable to control his own actions.

"Can someone estimate the impact on sales productivity when the emotional result is anxiety?" he asked.

Madison glanced around the room, answering symbolically for everyone there. "Michael, it's another example of good and bad principles at work, isn't it? One works and the other doesn't. One leads to a positive emotional state, the other to a tragic state. We're either more effective at what we do and therefore more productive, or we end up with weighty emotions that no one can carry for very long. It comes down to choosing between the things that cause a healthy human condition or a 'rotting-one.' It's the comparison of an athlete to a fat, beer-guzzling, old man. The healthy one will always outperform the other, always." She finished with a glance around to check for agreement. Practically everyone was nodding.

Michael paused to let Madison's comments settle in. Nothing was more effective than the class forging forward and learning on their own. He sat against the table at the front and lifted himself into a sitting position—feet dangling over the side. "Wonderful. And with that we are now ready to discuss the idea of 'rational self-interest'.

"Your career is the focal point—it's the equivalent of your professional life. All that you do is geared to enhance your career. It's rational to do so, and anything that damages your career is just the opposite. You have tools for protecting and enhancing your career. The first is the principle of *certainty*. It's real simple—you can't *alter* the physical world—you can't *change reality*. Embracing reality leads you to rely on the certainty of 'cause and effect', and gives you the luxury of being honest with yourself and others, because to be anything else ultimately fails in the real world.

"The second tool is vision. You can anticipate the effect of your actions and recognize their causes. You can place yourself into the equation and realize that *your* actions influence the outcome, and by assuming control of your actions, through independence, realize that it is the only sure-fire way to protect your career.

"*Rational self-interest* means assuming responsibility—and using vision and certainty to fiercely protect your career no matter *what the circumstances*, no matter *what the short-term gains*, no matter *how strong the influence of authority*—no matter *what!*"

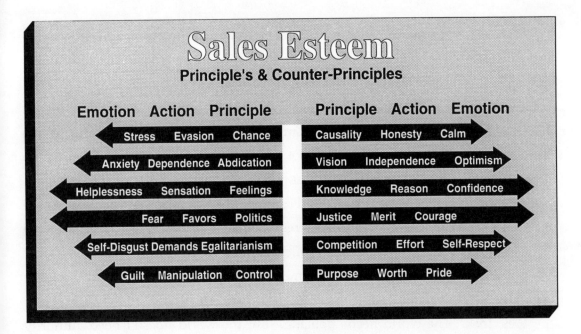

"Here is the diagram of the two opposing principles, their associated actions and the emotion that results," said Michael as he brought up another slide.

Ryan's smile could have lit up a dark room. Kat was sitting at an angle that provided a view of his face and couldn't help but notice. She felt a strange surge of adrenaline. Shannon and Kyle shared a glance and nodded at each other. Tip Bailey put his hand to his chin and bobbed his head up and down. Jock Shaw was looking out the window, dejectedly. And Tug Fischer stared blankly at Michael's feet, arms crossed, thoroughly disgusted.

Kat spoke first. "Michael, you realize that if this idea gets out, you may put an entire profession out of work?"

Michael smiled. "I think I know what you're hinting at, but to be sure, why don't you share it with us."

"Every regulator, every compliance officer, every board-of-whatever, believes the opposite. They see salespeople as short-term operators who willingly risk it all for a few extra bucks every month. They think we're too stupid to consider the impact of our actions and that we'll take whatever bait is thrown out in the form of compensation. They think we are lead around by the nose in a chase of quotas, sales goals, money and prestige. When I think about it, it's really rather insulting."

"Yes, Kat, it's insulting. I can tell you that there are many people who agree with the idea of rational self-interest, but hide the feelings because our culture says anything that is motivated by self-interest has to be damaging to others. The complete opposite is true. Self-interest in our personal relationships means fostering the relationship so that it continues. Self-interest as it relates to the company means fulfilling the promise of contributing based on shared values, so that we can continue to make contributions to the overall good of the company. Self-interest in selling means assuring customers benefit from our actions, so we can continue to sell. Rational self-interest asserts that we protect the things we value, through vision of our actions." Michael paused.

Shaw was still angry. "The moment you remove management and the regulators, you'll have chaos. The world needs policemen."

"Yes, Jock. The world needs policing. But the world doesn't need authority dictating action. Individuals need to determine that—it's called freedom. What the world *needs* are principles that reward the right actions and deliver justice to the wrong actions. So long as our society will allow justice, you can be certain the individual will do the right thing. Those that don't are knowingly criminal. That's what the policemen are for. Although it takes time, bad principles, even if they are not criminal, always—and I emphasize always—end up in failure. The overwhelming majority of people—in a society that insists on consequences for actions—always choose the right principles. It's the nature of human existence."

"But if you don't . . . " Shaw started but was cut off by Tug Fischer.

"Shut up, Jock," said Fischer.

Shaw went silent. Michael paused as he thought of the ironic humor of Fischer's authoritative control over Shaw. He laughed to himself.

"Please don't misunderstand the idea of independence. You can't become an island. It doesn't mean that you forsake the guidance of those who are capable of advising you. It doesn't mean you must discover everything on your own. The world needs leaders. Our progress is a continuous chain of transferred knowledge. Independence holds that you think on your own while taking advantage of all the knowledge available, all the intelligent guidance within your reach, and typically, with the aid of a leader of some type." He paused.

"Does anyone in the room still have a true, *child-like* hero?" he asked, emphasizing the word 'child-like'.

The room was filled with shrugs—except for Tip Bailey, who shifted uncomfortably in his chair. Michael continued. "The romantics I've known would be distraught, but the fact is, we normally replace childhood heroes. Anyone ever notice?"

Tip Bailey had been an ardent sports star worshiper as a kid. He had been a better-than-average athlete when he was growing up, but too small to play most organized sports. He idolized most of the stars of his day and his passion for sports was key in his decision to become an agent. He worshipped the great athletic stars of the past and present still today. His sports star clients were no different. They were from another planet as far as he was concerned. The role of sports agent had never felt that comfortable to him, although it had thrown him into the sporting world in the only manner left open to him. He felt terribly uncomfortable surrounded by adults who had abandoned their heroes while he clung to his. The senior partner at Tip's firm had rightly diagnosed it as the source of his "sales frustration." It was the reason his firm sent him to the conference.

Bobby Green answered Michael's question. "Sure, adults get cynical. Kids don't have the ego to be embarrassed about having heroes."

Bailey liked the sound of that.

"It's not that simple, Bobby. Do you have heroes?" asked Michael.

"Well, not in the way you mean. But there are people I admire a lot," said Bobby.

"That's precisely the distinction I want to make. You don't consider yourself a cynic—*do* you?"

"No."

"So what are we missing?" asked Michael.

Bailey was frustrated. "You're suggesting that as adults we admire the immortals instead of idolizing them. Is that it?" he asked.

"There is a significant difference between admire and idolize. But you're on track," said Michael.

"Yeah," Bobby agreed. "Heroes are mystical . . . unexplainable . . . unbelievable. For kids, heroes are either physically or mentally on an entirely different plane—one a kid can't conceive yet. But when we grow up, we catch up. The gap is narrowed and instead of holding them in awe, we admire the level of achievement."

"That's an excellent explanation," said Michael. "Now someone tell me. Where do leaders fit into all of this?"

"What kind of leader are you referring to, Michael?" asked Rick Kincaid.

"Is there more than one kind?" said Michael.

"Sure. Those who demand to be followed, and those who are followed willingly."

"Ahhh. I think you're being far too generous in describing the first as a leader. I would prefer to think of them in the same terms as the authority position from our earlier discussion. Wouldn't you?"

Kincaid nodded agreement. Others in the room did as well.

"Real leaders are adult heroes, aren't they, Michael?" asked Ryan.

"I like to think of it that way, Ryan. What do you suppose adults admire about these hero-leaders?"

"Knowledge . . . achievement . . . purpose," he said as though it was more than obvious.

"Things we could all attain, or come close to attaining?" asked Michael rhetorically.

"Sure. They're the best at something, because of a likely reason—like one of the three I mentioned," said Ryan.

Michael returned to the podium at the front of the room. "Independence does not exclude either being a leader, or following a leader. Independence is the objective determination of who the leaders are, and why they should be believed, admired, or followed. Independence is the process of seeking the greatest level of knowledge, skill or vision. We all have much to learn.

"Among all the character traits of a leader, the one you will find most frequently, is that of independent thought. Leaders aren't omniscient and don't care to pretend to be. True leaders, as Rick said, don't typically crave to be followed. The best among them insist on independence among those who would follow them. Leadership and independence generally go hand in hand. We aren't islands. We all have leaders. Even leaders have leaders. Independence strips away the false leaders, and encourages us all to find the best people to fit that role."

The late afternoon sun sank low enough to shine in through the wall of windows with a blaze of reddish-orange. The room started to glow. It was nearly five o'clock and practically everyone was surprised at the late hour. They had been captivated by their discussion and lost track of the time. The flood of sunshine crossed half the room and glinted off Michael's eyes.

"I'm not sure I can resist the drama of the sunshine pouring in at this moment," he said. "You've had a full day. You've ventured into ideas and examples that are neither easy to grasp nor ignore. The culmination is the idea of rational self-interest, which is built on honesty, independence, certainty and vision. The rewards are staggering. You've gotten a glimpse today. Wait until you put them to work with purpose. I like the glow of rational self-interest. Interest in doing the right thing because it works. And wrapping the idea of the right thing around your *self*. Claiming the right to benefit from your actions, protecting your career with the tools you have available, and realizing that the payoff is a healthy emotional state. One that leads to greater productivity, greater sales, greater rewards, one that leads to Sales Esteem."

With the last statement, the full red disk of the sun was shining through the windows and the room was aglow with its light. Michael paused. "See you in the morning."

9
The Trap

The fire you kindle for your enemy often burns
yourself more than him.

—*Chinese proverb*

"Look just to the right of the creek. Do you see it? Just beyond those trees," asked Fischer, handing a pair of field-glasses to Shaw.

Shaw was breathing quickly. His reply was just as fast. "Yeah, yeah, yeah, but I can't see how it's fastened onto the bridge."

"Shhh! Here they come," huffed Fischer.

Kevin was first to cross the bridge. He turned his head and looked backward over his shoulder as he ran, shouting something to the runner behind him that was too muffled to be heard from where Fischer and Shaw hid. They crouched in the ravine fifty feet below the bridge that Kevin and the others were crossing on their morning run. The bridge thundered a drumroll from his steps as he crossed, sending a rattle of vibrations down through the caissons that supported it.

"There, right there," hissed Fischer. "See the beam shake as he crosses it?"

"Uh-huh."

The creek ran along the bottom of a fault-line, eroding it further, and carving out an unusually deep crevice. The walls of the ravine were gently sloped to a point where they became flat rock walls and fell twenty feet to the riverbed below. The spring floods had deposited large boulders in the riverbed, making the floor of the ravine a solid landscape of rock floor and walls. The two support caissons measured twenty feet in length and were set across from each other on each side of the creek. They bolted into a cement footing.

Fischer and Shaw could hear a second voice returning Kevin's shout. It was Madison. Her voice had a higher pitch and was easier to make out. "Bet I beat you today!" she yelled back as she crossed. The bridge and its supports rattled again.

"If . . . one of the columns . . . slipped off its foundation . . . " said Fischer.

"Wait a second. I don't want to hurt anyone!" Shaw said defiantly.

"I thought you said you'd like to see a little accident?"

"Yeah, but I didn't mean . . ."

"Relax," Fischer cut him off. "No one's going to get anything more than a broken arm. Even if it collapsed completely, whoever was on the bridge would be thrown onto that flat grassy spot over there. There's no way they could fall all the way to the bottom," said Fischer.

"You sure?"

"Yeah, yeah . . . I studied engineering in school," lied Fischer. "Anyway, look for yourself."

Shaw looked through the glasses, studying the bridge, the hillside, the caisson, and then back to the bridge. He shook his head up and down and whispered, "When do we do it?"

"Tomorrow morning. Cevanté will have a hard time being so damned certain about an accident on his precious little path. With any luck it will be your boy, Ryan."

"Wait, I don't want to hurt him, Tug," protested Shaw.

"You want to shake some sense into him, right?"

"Are you sure this will work?"

"Shaw, I'm going to start believing you're a real chicken-shit if you don't shut up."

"Let's get out of here," said Shaw.

Madison could see Kevin sweeping around the trees thirty feet ahead of her. She had narrowed his lead considerably and knew she could probably overtake him with a final surge up the hill. She chose instead to enjoy the run and save beating Kevin for another day. The air was thick with the surge of gulf air that had moved north overnight. The sounds of the forest were all around her. She glanced from side to side to enjoy her surroundings while she pressed on at a furious pace.

The path whipped back and forth through the trees, and she bounced up and down with it like a leaf in rushing water. The uphill climb finished the run and she exited the forest into the clearing, expecting to see Kevin huddled over and heaving with deep breaths.

A curled smile came to the corners of her mouth when she saw him. He sat on a rock bench in the clearing with his legs crossed reading the morning newspaper. He couldn't have been there more than fifteen seconds, but was pretending to have been waiting for fifteen minutes.

"Have a nice run?" he asked.

"You can take a breath now. I don't want you to pass out trying to make up to me."

Keller gasped loudly, and caught his breath. "Come on. Let's talk about it," he said. "It's really not that big of a deal. I thought we were starting to understand each other."

"I'll get over it," said Madison.

"Listen, did you want me to lie to you? You can't really expect me to risk my life for someone I barely know," said Kevin.

"No, I guess not. What I was hoping for was a sign that you might feel the way I do."

"Madison, it's been such a short time that we've known each other, but there's something drawing us together, I know that. I want desperately to see where it will lead." Keller's gaze moved from Madison to a hilltop on the horizon, and back again. "Whatever is going on between us, it's going to take more than three days. I'd be lying to you if I said I would be willing to give my life for you before I knew I was in love. I want it to be honest from the start."

"*Are you* . . . falling in love with me?" her voice ending in a hopeful question.

"Yes. At least in the way you mean."

She looked down shyly. "Me, too."

Ryan popped through the trees at the end of path, gasping heavily, and interrupting their conversation.

"Uhhh. Yeah. Better get going, huh?" Kevin asked, standing and lifting his hand to his head, rubbing it brusquely in a sure sign of embarrassment at Ryan's discovery.

Ryan's smile was unmistakably knowing. Madison didn't care who discovered them. She laughed at Kevin's embarrassment and said. "Yeah. Someone else may see us."

Back on the path, Bobby and Sally Holiday were within fifty feet of each other. It had taken Bobby much longer to catch her, and he was frustrated. He was pushing himself harder and was at her heels within another hundred yards. "Hi, huh, huh, Sally," he panted. "How's your run?"

"Great, Bobby! Took you a little longer to catch me today," she said, with less difficulty.

"I didn't think you were keeping track," he said.

"The whole class is."

"Right. See you later," he said and made a move to get around her. She was running faster than he thought, forcing him to make a sudden move to avoid a tree stump on the side of the path. As he cut back in front of Sally, her toe caught the back of his calf and sent her tumbling to the ground. Bobby turned to watch Sally slide across the path on her chest and forearms. Bobby stopped instantly to help, but to his complete surprise, she bounced up in a single motion and continued running—right by him as he stood watching. He turned and chased her, even more frustrated. He was running as fast as he possibly could and caught her within fifty feet.

"Are you okay?" he asked sincerely.

"Yeah, fine. Thanks."

They were finished before he could say anything, exiting the forest and slowing to a walk to catch their breath. "I'm really sorry, Sally," he said.

"Don't worry about it. I'm okay . . . really."

The class streamed across the finish one-by-one, each a little stronger than the day before. They showered and gathered for breakfast. Bobby guessed that rumor of his 'tackle' on the path would have spread by the time he got to the cafeteria. It hadn't. Not a word. He admired Sally's toughness.

The Central Texas weather was nearly perfect and was attracting water-lovers to the lake that sprawled below the conference center. It was a picture-postcard day, but the class members were more interested in what lay in store for them in class. Michael and Kevin entered the room as the group took their seats.

Michael stood at the tote board at the front, ready to record running times. "Good morning. Welcome to spring in Texas. Sally, how'd we do today?" he said, looking back over his shoulder.

"Nineteen, thirty-five," she said proudly.

Michael turned back to face her. "Sally! You've cut your time by a fourth. What's going *on?*"

"Sorry, I guess I just love to run through the forest. It seems like it's getting easier to do," she demurred.

"Eeez-zzz-er?" said Michael to emphasize the point.

"Well, you know. It's hard, but I like to do it, so it doesn't seem so hard. I'm sorry, I know that doesn't sound too intelligent, but I'm not sure how to explain it."

"No problem. I think you understand it far better than you know," he said.

"Bobby. Your time?"

"Uh . . . 18:31:03," he said sheepishly.

Michael jotted the times down.

"And Madison?"

"Sixteen."

"Sixteen, what?"

"Even," she said.

"You ran a sixteen even today?"

"Yes."

"You can check-out at noon. I'll arrange for a taxi to take you to the airport." Michael said, with a straight face. Madison giggled.

"I suppose I have to reveal the path record now?" he said as though it would have to be pried out of him. Madison was shaking her head in agreement. Michael scribbled the new times on the tote board, adding a new column for the course record.

	Bobby	Sally	Madison
Run 1:	18:15:06	26: ?	18:10 ?
Run 2:	18:09:11	22:33	16:55
Run 3:	18:31:03	19:35	16:00
Record:	-	-	15:38

"Bobby! What happened to you, today?" he asked, swinging around toward the group.

"Uh, I got tangled up a little with Sally," he offered.

Michael looked over at Sally. "What does that *mean?*"

"We kind of bumped into each other," said Sally.

"Uh-huh. Sally, you know there is no pushing on the playground?"

Bobby didn't think it was very funny.

"Bobby, do you think you'll improve beyond eighteen flat?" asked Michael.

"I don't know."

"Sally will be at eighteen-and-a-half tomorrow," challenged Michael.

"That still won't beat my best time," said Bobby.

"Oh . . . so you're competing against Sally's time. I kind of expected you to be shooting to improve your time."

"But you said . . ." complained Bobby before trailing off.

"No. I've never suggested that Sally's times would be faster than yours. Sally, are you competing against Bobby?" he asked.

"Oh, heavens no! It just feels good to go faster. I guess I'm competing with myself," she said.

"Wait a second. Is this about improving our personal times?" protested Bobby.

"All we've done is observed, Bobby. The purpose for running faster or slower is probably different for each of us."

"What do you mean?"

"We'll discuss it after our final run. Right now, we're headed for the university to hear an address by an alumnus of the Sales Esteem conference. Please, everyone. No notebooks, just bring yourself. Be down at the bus in ten minutes." Michael spun around and headed out of the door. The group filed out after him. Ten minutes later they were boarded and on their way to the university's auditorium amphitheater.

10

The Legitimacy of Selling

There's a man in the world who is never turned
down, wherever he chances to stray; he gets the
glad hand in the populous town, or out where
farmers make hay; he's greeted with pleasure on
deserts of sand, and deep in the aisles of the
woods; wherever he goes there's a welcoming
hand—he's the man who delivers the goods.

—*Walt Whitman*

Callie McCoy stood on the amphitheater stage behind large curtains that were
fastened to the ceiling far above. She caught a glimpse of Michael and the class as
they filed down the aisle and took the seats reserved for them at the front. She shot
a quick wave of her hand to Michael and went back to her preparations. Across
the front of the curtains was a large banner that announced the event. It read
"Capitalist Quorum." The amphitheater could seat five thousand people and was
filling up quickly. The audience was a cross-section of American businessmen and
women. It was the event of the year for the sponsoring organization, The Thomas
Jefferson America's Foundation, and Callie McCoy was the hottest property on the
speaking circuit. She had risen from anonymity to the national spotlight on the
heels of a best-selling book that chronicled the rotting of America's economic and
political institutions. A weekly television show had followed the book, causing
somewhat of a grassroots following to develop. It was difficult to find a special
interest group who didn't identify with Callie McCoy. Her message crossed racial

and cultural lines and was delivered in such a compelling manner, that even her enemies conceded many of her key points. Politicians feared her. Middle America loved her.

When Callie came on stage, a roar of applause greeted her. She stepped forward to the front row and shook a few hands, smiling as though she were at a social function. She had the elegance and charm reserved for socialites, yet was renowned for her frank humor. The applause continued until she returned to the podium to speak. Forty-five hundred people waited in excited tension for her to speak. No introduction was necessary and would only dampen the theatrical style she so dearly loved.

"Well, I'll be damned," she shouted. "Four thousand angry capitalists looking to set the record straight . . . ."

It was her television show introduction, which many recognized and repeated with her. Callie's mantra was celebrating business, and battling anyone critical of capitalism, free enterprise, or profit motives. She had become the lone defender of business in a country that was once recognized as the birthplace of twentieth-century business. It was an absurdity to Callie that no one had occupied the spot before her. And it was her passion to speak out against business' practitioners who acquiesced to the critics of capitalism—those who accepted the label of 'evil-but-necessary' profiteers.

Callie's infectious smile seemed to be ignited by the enthusiasm of the adoring crowd. "I am truly honored to be with you today. I feel as though I am among family here. But I have a message for my family—a message for each of you," she said sincerely.

"You must . . . *reclaim* your dignity."

The crowd settled in. This would be vintage McCoy. Michael surveyed the class members with a quick sweeping glance. Most were familiar with Callie's philosophy and style and looked as anxious as the rest of the audience. A few seemed to be especially thrilled at being so close to a national celebrity.

"Our culture asks its champions to be humble . . . and champions usually are. Our culture asks its leaders to do more . . . and leaders do. Our culture asks its best to do better . . . and the best seek new heights," her voice resonated like a tight drum.

"But it's not the call from society that they respond to. It's the call they get from within. Unfortunately, no one has explained this to those making the demands." She paused and swept her glance across the entire audience.

"We live in a country that once admired its best. And made no claims in its admiration. We live in a country that once made a connection between brains, effort, and guts and the resulting success and happiness. We live in a country where the intellectual disease of envy and jealousy was once recognized for what it is . . . poison . . . easily spread and equally destructive. We live in a country that could once point to its past with pride in the achievement of the individual. Among the many things that made the formulation of the American entrepreneurial spirit the most brilliant, shining moment in all the world's history—is the adulation of the individual and his or her achievements.

"I am terribly saddened to say that those descriptions of America—are no longer true. Today, our society seeks to tear down its winners in order to fabricate a hollow self-esteem for the masses. There are, of course, those who need to be pulled down. The cheaters and the frauds who occupy a higher plateau for a moment. They are the exceptions—the freaks—that we must all work to rid ourselves of. But they are a minority significant only in providing headlines for a sensational attack. Today, we seek out the infinitesimally small number of criminals so they can be used as poison for the rest." Her voice was clear and precise.

The auditorium belonged to Callie McCoy. They hung on her every word. She touched them where few could—at their core—their belief in themselves.

"A Capitalist Quorum," she said, smiling warmly and shaking her head slowly up and down, as though she was contemplating the meaning. "A Capitalist Quorum is the celebration of the individual. Our founding fathers knew what each of you know deep down in your souls—unlocking the rights, freedoms, power and creativity of the individual was the natural, human thing to do. America once reveled in the triumphs it brought about, but no longer. Worse—society has begun to stake a claim on the individual. Fewer rights, fewer freedoms, more restrictions and a debt to be paid by those who achieve to those who don't. In short, hatred of the individual and his or her achievement, and the intellectual assassination of this uniquely American idea.

"Capitalism is the natural outgrowth of our fundamental political rights—those envisioned by the men who penned the Constitution and Bill of Rights. Government did not create capitalism, as we're seldom dissuaded from believing. At best, government has stayed out of capitalism's way. Capitalism, at its very base, is individualism. It is the free exchange between individuals—free from the claims of a king, or a mob of kings, or a mob of serfs. Today, individualism is under an all-out siege. Even as the most ruthless of mob-driven politicos—the Russians—are rediscovering the wonder of the individual, your country is seeking every possible way to destroy the individual. Yes! Your country is doing all that's possible to weave the individual into a single mass.

"If you are unable to distinguish that the destruction of the individual for the benefit of the mob is the same as what has occurred in every socialist country over the last forty years, you've missed one of history's most essential lessons." There was no criticism in her voice, only a challenge to understand.

"I'll restate my message. *You* must reclaim your dignity. Psychologists will tell you that ego is critical to your emotional health. Yet, *you* have *allowed* society to convince you that it's immoral to recognize your self-worth. The role you play in the success of your business is clear, yet *you* demean your importance in the name of *humility*. You cling to the idea of the power of the *individual*, while creating another *committee* to appease the group. You admire performance, yet submit to demands that you *respect* the *average* performer. *If* you are unable to defend the essence of what made *you* successful, who do you suppose will take up the charge in your place?

"It took thousands of years for the world to discover the importance of the individual. We can't expect it to thrive unless it's maintained. If you think you have no obligation to your own convictions, they will quickly disappear. They must be fostered, coddled, refined, improved, supported and instilled in your actions. They won't go into hibernation waiting for you to use them when convenient. They'll rot if not cared for. That, my friends, is at the root of attack on the individual—the attack on you. You haven't tended your garden. And it's time to weed and replant the seeds of respect for the individual and the achievements they heap on the rest of humanity. It's time to dust off our American birthright and get it back to work. And it has to begin with those who are responsible for its preservation. *You* are its caretakers. Stand up proudly and proclaim your self-worth. Stand up and assert your right to the benefits of what you have worked so hard to create." Callie's performance had whipsawed them through a brutal wakeup call and a call to arms. She hadn't expected it but one by one, people in the crowd rose to their feet—standing symbolically to restake their claim.

"Stand up tall and insist on the recognition of your achievement. Stand up and demand that those who depend on your brilliance, hard work and convictions, while stripping you of the crumbs they can beg for, hold you in esteem. Stand up and proclaim the injustice of the criticism of the very values they wish to extort from you. Claim them as your own." Most of the crowd had risen to their feet.

She gathered herself to close. "You are the last chance to salvage the ideas that brought America to the precipice of utopia. Don't let her down. Don't forsake the battle waged for you by your fathers and their fathers. Fight for your values in every arena—at every opportunity. And never, ever, give up," she closed.

The crowd exploded into thunderous applause. Callie raised an open hand to wave a thank you, and stood as the applause continued for several minutes. She finally gave a large sweep of her hand and disappeared behind the curtains. Michael motioned to the group to stay in their seats. They were tightly packed in the first two rows of the auditorium and spoke feverishly among themselves about Callie's speech. Ushers moved up and down the aisles, hustling people out, but ignored the Sales Esteem group. Michael and Kevin sat on the stage with their feet dangling off the edge talking quietly. The group was gripped in a discussion about Callie's speech. She was controversial and dynamic, and had delivered a message that would be discussed by the auditorium's crowd for weeks. Fifteen minutes passed and the auditorium was nearly empty except for the class members. The stage lights still burned brightly, and the class began to suspect something else was in store for them.

Callie McCoy pushed her way through the opening in the curtains and slid to a sitting position beside Michael. She had changed to casual clothes, but still held the aura of a celebrity. The class went quiet. Michael and Callie gave each other a warm embrace and Kevin reached over to grasp her hand. All three dropped off the elevated stage onto the aisle in front. Callie pulled a chair down from the stage and sat down knee-to-knee with the class members in the front row. Michael and

Kevin drifted to the back. Callie motioned to those seated at the ends of each row to pull their chairs into a semicircle around her. "Let's get close enough to get to know each other," she said. They complied eagerly.

"Four years ago my life changed when Michael Cevanté spoke about legitimacy at the Sales Esteem conference I was attending. Before that time, as strange as this may sound, I could *not* speak in public." She stopped to let them consider her comment.

"I had classic stage fright—only worse. I couldn't speak to *any* group without being nervous. I was paralyzed on a stage, and even stuttered when asked to introduce myself at a meeting," she said.

The facial expressions of the group took on every type of disbelief possible. Callie was as accomplished at public speaking as anyone they had ever seen. And her stage presence signaled nothing if not poise, confidence and composure.

Callie rolled her gaze from one end of the group to the other. "Before I understood the importance of legitimacy, I was practically useless."

Kat Kelly adored Callie, and her message. She was the essence of the strong, ambitious and intelligent women: Kat's role model. She was startled by Callie's comments. "Callie? You were at the Sales Esteem conference to learn about legitimacy?" asked Kat.

"No, I was here because I was selling radio spots at the time. But my sales career took off when I discovered Sales Esteem, and it wasn't long before I got a break and began my broadcasting career. I consider what I do now to be selling. My product is slightly less tangible than most, but my job is persuasion. I sell *ideas*," she stated firmly.

"Michael will unveil the idea of selling's legitimacy later. My intention is to frame its importance for you. I spoke to four thousand people today without a single moment of being unnerved. Even now I marvel at the two extremes. Before my work with Michael, I would have gone catatonic in front of four thousand people. Now, I'm too calm and sometimes I worry that I'll make leisurely mistakes. My emotional state before was fear . . . hell, . . . it was absolute terror. The terror of being in the spotlight regarding something I didn't feel *legitimate* in discussing. Now, I understand how desperately people want to hear what I have to say. They are willing to exchange their hard-earned money to listen. An incredible leap of faith? Hardly! I discovered my *legitimacy*. I discovered that I was *real*. I discovered that the thoughts I have make sense, they work, and are of value to others. I learned that purpose and legitimacy go hand in hand. Once I found my legitimacy, I found my purpose." She paused and sipped a glass of water.

"Deep down—way down—at our most inner self, we tend to be terribly honest with ourselves. It's my belief that maintaining this honesty is the anchor of our sanity. At that level, the level of the soul, we know the truth. We know all about honesty. We don't make contradictions with ourselves, because the risk is literally, insanity. At the level of the soul, we've got a pretty firm grip on reality. That's where I want to take you today. I want you to go all the way down. It is the only source of legitimacy," Callie said, pausing to catch a glimpse of their reaction. There were more than a few dry throats in the auditorium.

"You see . . . we often make compromises with the things we're unable to control, and so the world goes. But we can't make compromises at this level. Fortunately, your soul is, and always will be, yours to control. The key to legitimacy for me was to discover and understand, at this level, why I was of value. Why I had something 'worthwhile' to offer others. And to *dispel* the possibility that the primary focus of my life, my career, was parasitic, and that I had nothing of value to offer other than being in the way.

"Our culture disdains the concept of selling, yet admires persuasion. I cannot tell you how many times I have come across an honest salesperson doing his best to describe his profession as *anything* other than selling. Each of you have seen the same. Perhaps you've done your share of rationalizing your profession. Why the contradiction? It's simple—a lack of understanding of the legitimacy of selling. They don't understand 'why' they're important, and they fail to make a connection for the service they provide. Hard to believe? Then tell me why the overwhelming majority of sales workshops, clinics, and seminars are built on the theme that 'you're okay.' Tell me why auditoriums like this one are filled to capacity with evangelical 'soothes' leading the throng in chants of 'feel good' hexes. Entire sales philosophies built on *blunting* the pain of rejection, subverting the distasteful act of selling, forcing the mind into a numbness to avoid the 'difficulty' of selling?" She paused as though she was waiting for an answer that she knew would never come.

"There can be just two explanations. The practitioners of 'mind-over-reality' technique are terrified to face the truth, deep down in the soul, where they fear discovering that they are, indeed, parasites. Or, they're not intelligent enough to assess their worth, and use mind games to treat the symptoms of their guilt instead of reason to assess the cause. Legitimacy has nothing to do with either of these. Legitimacy is knowledge of what you do, why you do it and why it has value. In short, it's the assessment of your worth. And it must be based on substance. Sales Esteem is the philosophy of selling that contributes at every turn to the idea of selling legitimacy. It's substance that counts. And it's legitimacy that will move you from wishing, and hoping and pretending to reach your potential, and move you into actually realizing it. It's the end result of looking at what you do and then testing it against your soul for the ultimate review of honesty—honesty with yourself. When you have discovered the substance . . . and the reason . . . and the legitimacy of what you do . . . you will be ready to achieve your full potential— with no dishonesty and no contradictions," she finished in a flurry.

Callie stopped and looked at Michael. "Can I stay?" she asked.

"I'd be honored," said Michael. He came forward and pushed himself up into a sitting position on the table. Callie joined him.

"*Untouched* is how I would describe the treatment most sales organizations give legitimacy," started Michael.

"Off-limits!" said Callie, adding a theatrical tone.

"Yeah . . . the organization might discover all sorts of things they'd rather not know," parlayed Michael. "What I have never understood, Callie, is why someone would pursue something without ever questioning the reason. Without ever asking why?"

He pushed himself off the tabletop and paced back and forth feverishly. "I want to know! What does a salesperson do? What legitimate *purpose* do you serve? Are salespeople *necessary*? Why are one in every ten workers salespeople? For what reason?" He stopped and stared at them earnestly. "Who needs *you*?"

An outside observer would have been shocked. The group was among the country's sales elite. Hundreds of thousands of training dollars had been spent on the people in the room. The best sales minds in the country directed their selling.

They were successful in their careers. They were intelligent, educated and experienced professionals. And still the question was raised . . . who needs *you*?

"The company needs us," said Bobby.

"Why, Bobby? Miss Kelly here is an advertising executive. Maybe your company could replace you with a 30-second television spot," said Michael.

"It's not that simple," said Kyle. "There are lots of ways to communicate to customers. Mass media, direct mail, or through a sales channel. It's a matter of touching the customer in as many ways as possible," he said.

"That's a start. How many of you see marketing and selling as having the same goal of moving product, but operating with entirely different methods?" he asked.

Half the class raised a hand. The others shook their head in disagreement. Madison spoke up. "It's all the same. Selling is a branch of marketing. Marketing is the broad function, and selling is an extension. They're not only related but connected," she said.

"A show of hands from those who agree," said Michael, raising his hand. Most of the group agreed. "Marketing is simply a global term to describe any—and all—efforts to get the product to the customer. The closure of the marketing cycle is the sale. The sale is the transaction—the exchange of the product from the company to the customer. If marketing is the function of getting the product to the customer, then selling is the company's last act of marketing. They're inextricably tied together." He paused to allow objections.

"So, does the marketing department need you because you're the final link before the transaction?" he continued.

"No," said Ryan. "If the company could move the product without us, they would. Like a catalog, or a shelf, or a commercial."

"Is there anyone suffering under the illusion that the company would resist getting rid of you if there was a more efficient way to deliver the product?" asked Michael with the desired frankness.

There was no disagreement. Michael was aggressive and challenging and they found it invigorating.

"So why are you still working?" he pressed.

"Because we add value," said Madison.

Michael spun towards her. "Oh, nooo!. Someone said it. Value? You add *value*? Be careful, now. We're bordering on a substantive discussion of selling. Are you sure you want to go any farther?" he asked.

Madison went on, slightly annoyed. "Michael, salespeople are the best way to communicate. We're tools—walking, talking, breathing tools for the company. That's of value," she said.

"Madison, you're only partly correct. Tell me what you mean by communicate."

"Explain the product to the customer," she said.

"That sounds like a monologue to me," said Michael.

Kyle interrupted. "It's not just communicating. It's persuasive communication. It's action-oriented communication," he said.

"I like the term action-oriented communication. But I'm still not clear on the *nature* of the communication. Is it one-sided? Is it educational? What's the purpose?" asked Michael.

"The purpose is obvious," said Ryan. "It's intended to persuade the customer to buy."

"Hmm, let's see. Persuasive communication with the goal of delivering the product?"

"Right."

"And if the customer has no use for the product?"

"Then you create the need," blurted Shaw.

"Ahhh. I see. So you *make* the customer *believe* he needs what you have to sell?"

"No! You educate him as to why he should want it!" snapped Shaw.

"What if the customer knows exactly what he wants? What if the customer is more highly educated than you are about what he wants . . .and you don't have it?" challenged Michael.

"You've got to be kidding. Are you suggesting that you let the customer decide what they need? Everyone knows that salespeople create the need," said Shaw angrily.

Michael laughed lightly and addressed the group. "How many of you *know* that salespeople create the need?" he asked. The group was staring at Shaw as though he had been asleep for the last dozen years. No one came to his defense.

"It's a matter of finding the right product for the right customer," said Ryan.

"That's not realistic," said Kat. "No one has a product that perfectly fits every customer."

"That's absolutely correct, Kat. So, how does the product tie in?" asked Michael.

"Well you have some choices. You can try to jam your product down everyone's throat and let them blow you off when it doesn't fit . . . not very appealing, but probably the most frequently taken approach," she continued.

"Yes, from my experience," said Michael.

"Or you can change your product slightly to fit various customers."

"That's also a frequent choice, isn't it?" asked Michael.

"Or you can search for that magic little moment when you find the customer who is perfect for the product . . ."

"Or?" asked Michael.

"Or . . . or . . . I don't know. Is there another?" she said, still composed.

"Anyone?" asked Michael to the group. "It's the most important from the Sales Esteem perspective." He waited but got no answers.

"Let's talk about product and the customer's perception of the product. Someone tell me how the customer views the product," he continued.

"Mostly they're unaware," said Ryan.

"Well, sometimes. What do you suppose they're unaware of?"

"The product's complexity. Engineering, the support systems, customer service programs, everything that goes into the product that the customer doesn't see," said Ryan.

"Okay, that's probably true, but who cares?"

"The customer should," insisted Ryan.

"Perhaps . . . but we haven't defined what's important to the customer yet. I would agree if the customer was buying the underlying attributes. In your business, for example, the research, the surveillance, repricing and management of the bonds you sell is the main event. The bonds themselves are actually nothing more than the entire package that I just described wrapped up nicely and made tangible by the piece of paper referred to as the bond, correct?" asked Michael.

"Exactly," said Ryan. "There's nothing but service and the movement of money."

"But for something like air travel, the customer is reasonably knowledgeable about the product. And consider all the products available out there. Some are complex and poorly understood by customer, some are more thoroughly understood by the customer than the salesperson, from time to time. So where does that leave us?" asked Michael.

"Selling your product based on its appeal to specific customers, and the perception you can create about it," said Tug Fischer.

"There we go again, wanting to create things that didn't exist before," said Michael. "I'd like to tell you about a recent experience and ask for your analysis. An art gallery in our area raises money every year for the purpose of showcasing local talent. The fundraising is a big event, complete with a full week of outdoor art reviews, wine tasting, and an auction of donated items. Each year, a single work of art, from one of the gallery's local artists, is selected as the event's centerpiece. It's recreated as a poster and sold during the week leading up to the auction. The price of the poster this year was fifteen dollars. And for that price, the buyer got a rather accurate—no, let me put that another way—a *nearly* indistinguishable reproduction of the original. On the day of the auction the poster's price was reduced to five dollars in order to sell the remaining inventory. But the best was yet to come. The original artwork was the last piece to be auctioned. Its final bid was fifteen. . . . *thousand.*" He paused. "Now, give me a definition of the product, and tell me its real price?

"The last buyer, the one who bid on the original, wasn't buying art at all. He was buying something entirely different," said Ryan.

"Yes, that's right, Ryan. What do you think he was buying?"

"Prestige, probably."

"Maybe he saw it as a donation," said Sally.

"It could be either," said Michael. "But what does that tell us?"

"That some fools are more easily separated from their money than others," said Fischer.

"Uh-huh. Tug, tell us, would you, what kind of a car you drive?" said Michael.

"A Porsche," said Fischer.

"Do you like it?"

"Yes. *I like it.*" He was annoyed.

"Is your mother still living?" asked Michael sincerely.

"Yes."

"And what kind of car does she drive?"

"A Honda."

"Why not a Porsche?"

"That's a dumb question," said Fischer, looking over the top of his glasses which had slipped to the end of his nose.

"She doesn't believe in fools being separated from their money?" asked Michael with a grin.

"Very funny," smirked Fischer.

"So what was she buying?"

"Cheap, economical, reliable transportation," allowed Fischer.

"And you?" asked Michael.

Kat answered for him. "He's the same guy who paid a hundred times too much for the painting?" she said, garnering laughs from the group.

Fischer glared at Kat and growled his answer to Michael. "I bought 'quality' transportation. There's a significant difference."

"Yes, there is. But not in the manner you think. Can we all agree that a product is 'of value' to the buyer?" he asked, waiting for the expected nodding agreement. "Then how do we define the product's value?" he continued.

"Each product has an intrinsic value waiting to be discovered by the buyer," said Kyle.

"That's very eloquent, Kyle, even romantic-sounding, but it's not accurate," said Michael.

"I don't understand. Every product must have a value on its own. Isn't that intrinsic?"

"Not quite. Intrinsic means standing on its own, without regard to its environment or the circumstance," said Michael.

"Then no product has intrinsic value—if it has to be considered within that context," said Kyle.

"In what other way would you try to value it?" asserted Michael. "A product's value relies completely on its utilization. A daisy holds no value to a blind man, a glass of fine wine is dangerous for an alcoholic, a jet plane is useless to a downtown commuter. The only reasonable definition of a product's value is in its utilization." Michael paused before asking, "And take a wild guess at who is the primary catalyst in determining the product's application?"

Smiles on their faces signaled they knew the answer. Michael continued. "The product, any product, has only *potential* value depending on the manner in which it will be used. All of you can think of ways in which your products can be misused and as a result, have absolutely no value for the customer. What do you suppose happens when there is a mismatch between perceived and actual benefit?" asked Michael.

"An illegitimate sale," blurted Ryan.

"Right. Do you all agree?" asked Michael.

"No. I don't," said Fischer. "We've all seen circumstances where the customer didn't have a clue about the benefit they could realize from the product, until they were educated by the salesman."

"Tug, don't confuse the act of introduction or orientation with creating a need that didn't exist before. Selling often involves the introduction of a new benefit that was previously unknown to the customer, but it is always, and I emphasize always, tied to an existing need. Even something as high-tech as virtual reality will have commercial applications only when it is applied to meeting or enhancing an existing need. It's a subtle distinction, I realize, but an important one. The idea that a need can be 'created' is the philosophical equivalent of the idea that 'anything is possible if you just believe strongly enough.' Introducing a solution to the customer's needs, whether it's a century-old solution like paper delivery or a pioneering solution like downloaded electronic news over a home computer, automatically sorted according to the customer's personal interests, still meets a need—information," he said.

Michael jumped to his feet and shuffled through a file folder that was at the table at the front. The auditorium had a built-in audio visual station at the podium complete with a slide projector and a retractable screen. Michael pressed a button and the screen dropped slowly into position from the scaffolding above. He popped a slide into the tray and flicked on the projector. It was a photograph of a steel rod, half out of the water, half in the water. The viewer could see the whole bar, but at the point where the bar entered the water, it bent off at an extreme angle, giving the impression that the bar was bent by the water and calling into question the ability to perceive objects accurately.

"I'm sure some of you have seen something like this before. Can someone explain this for me?" he asked.

Madison was tired of doing the scientific stuff but by now the class was relying on her as the resident expert. She glanced around and noticed several looks of expectation. "Okay, okay. The bar is straight but the refraction of the light is different through the denser medium of the water. In other words, our eyes pick up the light after it bounces off the rod and goes through one of the two mediums, air or water. Since the light waves travel at different speeds through the two, our perception of it changes. That's why it looks as though it's bent," she said.

"But the rod is straight?" said Michael.

"Yes."

"If I was ignorant about light dynamics, would it be possible to persuade me that you could bend steel by inserting it into the water, after all, seeing is believing?" he asked.

"Chances are that you're familiar with other optical illusions—like rainbows— and you wouldn't buy it, but I suppose in some circumstances, I would agree."

"An interesting choice of words, that I wouldn't buy it." smiled Michael. "What we have done here is to change the perception of what is actually there. The bar never bends—it's the medium that changes, distorting our 'highly-trusted' perception. A similar event is the legend of the ancients who understood planetary movement and could predict solar eclipses, which were perceived as pure 'magic' by the populace. And one of my favorite examples of this is the story of the young boy who told of listening to the radio with his father as they would ride together in the car. The father, in order to impress his son, would wave his hand over the radio just as he was passing under a bridge, or tunnel, or some obstruction, and command the radio to 'be silent.' The boy, having no understanding of radio-wave reception, would marvel at his father's magical powers." He paused.

"In each case, perception is 'bent' in order to persuade."

Tug Fischer saw an opening. "Wait! What about the perception of the art that the idiot in your story bought for fifteen grand? His perception didn't match what others thought of the painting, but he's probably at home in his study admiring the thing right now, thinking how wonderful it is."

"Wrong again, Tug. Setting aside the fact that he probably paid for prestige, his perception does not change the painting. A rose is a rose. But *his* valuation of everything that was wrapped up in buying the painting—the beauty of the art itself, the prestige of being the highest bidder, perhaps even his attempt to support a cause—was worth the money he paid. Given different circumstances, it's unlikely he would have paid as much," he said.

"So where does that leave us? We've touched on three aspects of selling legitimacy . . . the company's view of our role, the product, and the interaction with the customer. Those make up the three perspectives of whether or not you have a legitimate role. Let's look it this diagram," he said, searching through a few old slides until he came to the one he wanted. It flashed on the screen.

"We are concerned about three perspectives: The company's, the customer's and yours."

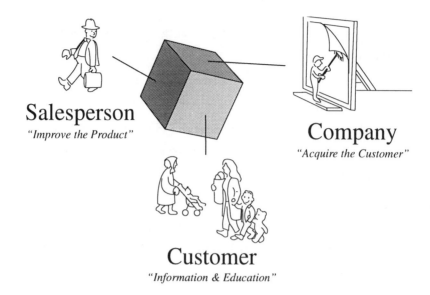

Salesperson
"Improve the Product"

Company
"Acquire the Customer"

Customer
"Information & Education"

Three Perspectives of the Sales Function

"In general terms, the customer is seeking information or education from the salesperson. The company's view of selling starts with the emphasis on the identification and acquisition of the customer. If a professional salesforce isn't the most effective method for landing customers, the company will seek other methods. And finally, your perspective generally begins with the perspective of the degree of additional value you can bring to the entire equation," said Michael.

"Like the rest of the Sales Esteem philosophy, legitimacy relies on substance—a reason. You cannot 'wish' to be legitimate. You cannot 'hope' to be legitimate. You cannot 'believe' you are legitimate. You can only be legitimate on the basis of real world issues. Callie McCoy is a living example of the energy released by discovering honest legitimacy. That's what we're shooting for." Michael paused and looked around the room, stopping to look at each of them to make eye contact.

"There are three aspects of the legitimacy of selling," he said, and punched up the next slide.

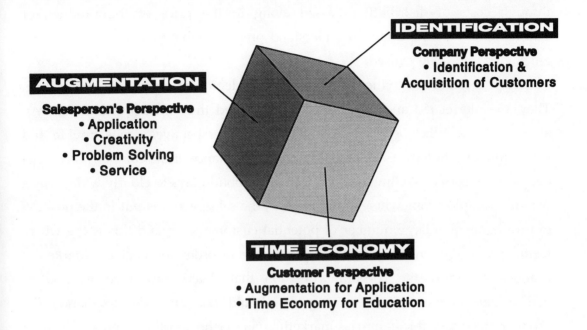

"As you can see, the first is one I refer to as augmentation. This is the role of the salesperson as the artist in applying a product's benefits to particular customer needs. It is *as* important, *if not more important,* than the product itself. Order of importance—salesperson first, product second. In simple terms, augmentation is a question of what value you bring to the equation . . . does the product sell itself . . . or is your involvement critical? If the answer is yes to the first, you have no legitimate role." He paused.

"The second aspect is the perspective of the company and the manner in which it views your role in selling the product. This is more clear-cut because someone else has already made a decision about your legitimacy or you wouldn't be in the position to begin with. But there are some interesting questions that relate to the legitimacy of your company's business, or product, and how your company expects you to sell the product.

"And finally . . . and I think most important of the three . . . is the perspective of the customer. Sales Esteem takes a scientific view of the function of selling. That view is called the Time Economy Model.™ It is the foundation for the 'purpose of selling.' Since the customer is ultimately paying for your involvement—either through costs of distribution passed along in the price of the product, or commissions—it's important to understand precisely what you do for those who are paying you." He paused.

"Each is important to the overall view of the legitimacy of your role in selling. They are interrelated and when effectively applied they work in harmony. An absence or a conflict between two of the three perspectives spells trouble and brings into question the issue of legitimacy. For instance, if the company's channel decision is incorrect—selling hedged, derivative bond plays to elderly widows as a playful example—somewhere along the line, the salesperson is put in the position of turning away a large number of potential customers; or, and this is the where legitimacy weighs in, misleading the customer in order to survive. Marketing channel is simply the corporate decision that determines what method of persuasive communication the company should take in order to market the product. Beer sells through mass-marketing via macho sporting events. Cleaning products through mass-marketing via soap operas. Did you ever wonder where the term 'soap opera' came from? Investments and jet airplanes are sold through highly trained individuals. Some companies choose to market through a different channel even though it's not the ideal channel. Mutual funds are a good example. Two channels are used, brokers who augment the product and earn a commission, and direct from the manufacture—or no-loads. The no-loads are seeking customers who don't need, or at least don't think they need, the advice of the broker. The no-loads choose a channel that eliminates augmentation, although they seek customers out by spending millions in a different channel—newspapers and magazine ads. The company chooses the method of contact with the customer that it believes will be most effective. For those of you in direct sales, your companies have already chosen. So here are the questions of legitimacy you must ask. First, what is your role? Is it augmentation? Next, is there an adequate number of potential customers, given the compensation per customer, to allow you to turn down a reasonable number of your contacts who aren't suited to the product. In other words, how often can you tell the customer the product, as well as its augmentation, is not right for the contact?" Michael paused. It was one of his favorite parts of the conference because it practically guaranteed howls from a handful of the group.

"Stop! Wait! Hold on! No . . . stinking . . . way . . . am I ever going to turn business away," said Jock Shaw.

"Jock, that's very eloquently stated. Unfortunately, you can't just grab a word like 'business' and use it in any circumstance you choose. It's an 'end-justifies-the-means' mistake. The word business means something, something just and fair. It's a concept that is built upon many other concepts, one of which is mutual benefit with the customer," said Michael.

"I don't understand."

"What's your definition of business?" asked Michael.

"Any sale."

"Do you ever have repeat customers?"

"Sure."

"Do the dissatisfied customers buy again?"

"Usually not. So what?"

"So some sales are bad business?"

"No, at least you made money the first time."

"Uh-huh. Jock?" asked Michael with a slight amount of frustration. "What's the most difficult and most time-consuming part of selling?"

"Uh . . . probably prospecting," he shrugged.

"Is it the most costly?"

"I guess so."

"Is it the most costly from a motivation standpoint?" asked Michael.

"I don't know. I guess."

"Jock's guessing," said Michael, turning to the rest of the group. "Do the rest of you agree that prospecting—the process of identifying a qualified prospect, contacting that prospect, gaining the prospect's confidence, and ultimately earning his trust—is the most costly part of selling from both a time and a personal motivation perspective?" he asked.

Most of the group nodded. A few voiced their agreement. All agreed with Michael's point. "Okay, Jock. The rest of the group believe it's costly to land a new customer. Do you agree?" he asked.

"Yeah. Sure."

"Would it be a stretch to suggest that you would sell more if the majority of your customers were repeat buyers?" asked Michael.

"No," said Shaw.

"So a single sale is not a great return on the costs associated with prospecting?"

"Perhaps not. But I would still rather get the one sale."

"Do satisfied customers ever refer new customers to your salesmen, Jock?"

"Sure."

"Do dissatisfied customers ever refer new customers, Jock?"

"Probably not."

"Do dissatisfied customers demand more customer service?"

"Unless they leave first."

"Would you still argue that it's good business to try to repeat the most expensive aspect of your business, the most time-consuming, the least likely to pay additional dividends, and the most costly to service—all because you didn't have the courage to tell the customer you couldn't help? You've stolen the concept of business, when in fact, you're recommending business, failing business, the kind of business that any businessman would try to avoid. The point is, turning down bad business is the opposite—it's smart business," said Michael.

"As complex as that might sound, it is actually quite straight-forward. Let's look at the next diagram," he said, turning to the screen and bringing up the next slide.

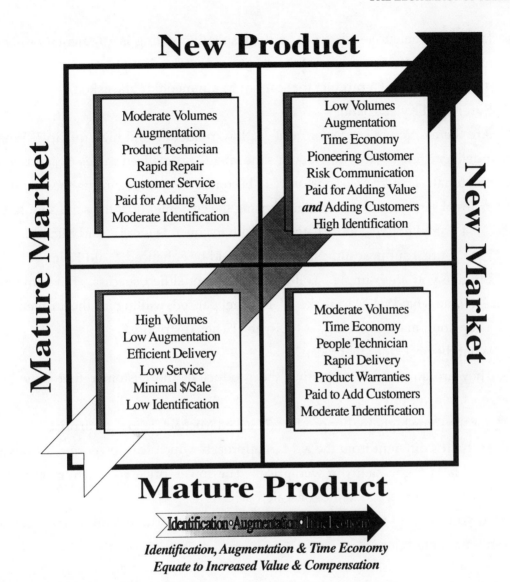

New Product

Moderate Volumes
Augmentation
Product Technician
Rapid Repair
Customer Service
Paid for Adding Value
Moderate Identification

Low Volumes
Augmentation
Time Economy
Pioneering Customer
Risk Communication
Paid for Adding Value
and Adding Customers
High Identification

Mature Market

New Market

High Volumes
Low Augmentation
Efficient Delivery
Low Service
Minimal $/Sale
Low Identification

Moderate Volumes
Time Economy
People Technician
Rapid Delivery
Product Warranties
Paid to Add Customers
Moderate Indentification

Mature Product

Identification•Augmentation•Time Economy

*Identification, Augmentation & Time Economy
Equate to Increased Value & Compensation*

"In essence, different channel decisions are based on the customer's need for 'time compression,' and the product's ability to be augmented. Inherent in all marketing is the function of awareness—communicating the product's availability. As you move towards each quadrant, the channel becomes more apparent. Let's dissect the ideas of augmentation and time economy and I think the entire picture will become more clear. Let's start with your role—augmentation. This is *not* a new concept. Theodore Levitt is generally thought of as the father of marketing augmentation, or at least its formal identification. Augmentation is explicitly that, adding something to the product, whether it is advice, recommendations, service, assistance, convenience—whatever. All consultative selling is augmentation, and all products can be augmented." Michael paused. "This last point is an important one. Can you think of a product that cannot be augmented?" he asked.

"Sure," said Kyle. "Sand."

"Are there different grades of sand . . . low, moderate and high quality? What about delivery time? And how about sand mixes, specialized mixes of sand with other material? Is there an opportunity to become an expert regarding the chemical properties of sand and play a role in advising the customer how the sand should be used . . . I don't know . . . the greatest strength in concrete work," said Michael.

"I see. Sure, I suppose almost anything could be enhanced," said Kyle.

"I'll give you an example. Wal-Mart is an unqualified success. But someone please tell me what Wal-Mart makes?" Michael paused, waiting for the answer.

"They don't make anything," said Ryan. "They distribute."

"What the heck does that mean?"

"They are so efficient in getting the product to the customer that they can charge a far lower price."

"For the same high quality products?" asked Michael, feigning surprise.

"Yeah. It's different from the K-Mart approach, which was lower quality, lower price. This is high quality, lower price. The lower price comes from efficient inventory control and economies of scale," said Kyle.

"So you mean to tell me that an entire company, worth several billion dollars, doesn't make anything?"

"Right."

"Augmentation," said Michael.

"Kat. Ever have a client who wanted to create an ad campaign that was destined to be a disaster?" he asked.

"Sure, from time to time," she answered.

"What happened?"

"We talk 'em out of it."

"On what basis?"

"That it won't work and they would waste their money."

"So you advise them on the content, strategy, style, message, theme, etc. of their advertising."

"That's generally what we do anyway. Sometimes we have to be more assertive than usual."

"And how do you distinguish your company from the competition?"

"Our strategy, experience, style, creativity and know-how."

"That's the product?"

"Mostly. We put film in a can, you know, the ads themselves. We put print media together. We do radio. But the real product is the intangible, the creative."

"Augmentation?" asked Michael, rhetorically.

"Yep," said Kat.

"Ryan? What do you sell?" asked Michael.

"Not bonds," laughed Ryan.

"The research, strategy, pricing, delivery all are more important than the bonds themselves. They're pretty much the same."

"Augmentation?" asked Michael.

"Yes."

"If you took away augmentation, what would you have?"

"Nothing," blurted Kat.

"So tell me. What's more important: the tangible product, or the augmentation?" he asked, not expecting a voiced response. "The concept of augmentation says *you*, the salesperson, are the most important aspect of the product. If this is true, you have the substance of legitimacy," he said. "If your focus is on the value you add to the sale of the product, then you distinguish yourself from the other product providers. Product distinctions are minuscule. What is distinctive is the value added by the marketing segment, the selling group. The more value you bring, the higher the value of the 'total product,' regardless of any comparison you make in competing products. If you're unable to add anything extra, and all you can show is the product itself, then you've eliminated any opportunity to make yourself part of the product. You've forced yourself into the role of an order-taker and you are at the mercy of the limits of your product." He paused.

"Michael, I have a real problem with the idea of augmentation." It was Bobby Green. "My business is price competitive with very little added value or augmentation. By your definition, I'm less legitimate because I sell primarily on price," he said.

"It's a fair question, Bobby. May I answer it with another question?" said Michael.

"Sure."

"What happens when you can't compete on price?"

"Well, it's never quite that easy. Usually a lower price means less quality."

"Do you ever explain that to the customer?"

"Yeah. And it usually works."

"When does it fail?"

"When the competing product has the same quality *and* a lower price, or quality is *not* of importance to the customer."

"Do you see any contradictions between that and what we have discussed?"

"No, I'm okay with that part, but I don't understand the legitimacy stuff."

"Would you feel legitimate in asking the customer to buy a more expensive component—regardless of its price, or the importance your customer places on quality?"

"No. In fact, I guess I've actually benefited from telling them when I thought they should buy somewhere else."

"Explain that for us?" asked Michael.

"Well, those customers trust me for being straight with them. I guess I have credibility. I guess they think I'm . . . legitimate."

"Excellent. There is an opportunity to augment any product. The more you add, and the better you are at the enhancements that you bring to the product, the greater your legitimacy in asking for the business," said Michael.

"But legitimacy isn't automatic—just as Callie said. For instance, what if Bobby's response had been to ask his customer to buy his more expensive part on the basis that they were friends?"

"What's wrong with that? People buy all the time from their friends. That's one of the tools of a good salesperson," said Jock Shaw.

"That's exactly the kind of salesperson I never want to be," said Kat.

"You'd never work for *me*," said Shaw.

"You got that right."

Michael stopped them. "Okay, okay. Jock, I think you might want to try a slightly different recruiting technique. Kat. I couldn't agree more with what you said. Unfortunately, short-sighted customers and illegitimate salespeople often try to replace the idea of augmentation with a surrogate, like personal gifts or bribes. But like the other bad principles, it always results in failure. Frauds don't last, and customers who prefer the imitation to the real thing usually get what they deserve—inferior quality and an extra martini."

"Wake up," said Shaw. "That's the way business is done in this country. People expect martinis, and nice trips and other perks. Wining and dining is as old as free enterprise," he said.

Shaw was becoming the whipping boy of the class. The others muttered at his comment, some laughed. "Before we criticize Jock's view too harshly . . . ," said Michael, "we need to recognize the truth in what he's saying. All of us have seen the glad-handing vendor at some point in our career. Favors, gifts, entertainment—you name it—is the literal opposite of sales legitimacy. No question that there is some legitimate entertaining, a kind of thank-you for the business, but it's easy to draw a distinguishing line. When the gifts, thank-yous and celebrations outweigh the value you bring to the relationship, it's not legitimate. As to Jock's comments, all I can suggest is that you recognize the purpose of the Sales Esteem philosophy. It is not a recasting of the way things have always been. It's not putting a new face on old practices. It's an entirely fresh approach to selling that eliminates the traditions of the past that make you squirm. If you are here to discover a new philosophy, then clinging to past traditions is a complete contradiction," he said.

"Michael . . . ," said Kat thoughtfully, "I used to hate prospecting when I started in this business. But now it's something I actually enjoy . . . ," her voice trailed off as she contemplated its segue with the current topic.

"What was the difference, Kat?"

"The difference is legitimacy, I suppose. Like Callie, I realized I was more than okay . . . I was good, and deserving, and worthy."

"What do you think, Callie?" asked Michael.

"She's got it," said Callie with a broad smile.

"Legitimacy as it relates to the marketing channel is a question of whether the company is asking you to sell with good principles or bad. It comes back to the principle of independence—and abdication. If the company's product, or its marketing channel, is poorly designed and unappealing, you're forced to make decisions about your ethics and putting food on the table. That's why I use the simple test of whether there are enough potential customers, given the compensation plan, to turn down a reasonable number of prospects. If the answer to these questions is 'yes,' then the company—and you as the company's representative—are Legitimate."

He paused and turned to Ryan. Michael knew he was struggling with the legitimacy of his profession. "Ryan, what do you think?" he asked.

"It changes the whole equation for me. I used to look at my role as though I was a sponge just soaking up a few drops that were left behind when the customer needed the product. Now, I'm not so sure the customer would ever have discovered the product, or the value they receive without me. And I'm not sure whether they would have the knowledge or expertise to use the product in the right way. I mean . . . it makes me feel as though I might be the *most* important part of the process," he said.

"Please, everyone. A round of applause for Mr. Matthews. It reminds me of a discovery made four years ago. How about you, Callie? Remind you of anyone you know?" asked Michael.

Callie smiled at Michael and answered. "Ryan. I'm the person he's referring to, and you're absolutely right about your importance in the process. I don't want to take anything from the brilliance of the designer of the product, or the vision of the individual who brought it to the market, but as we have discussed, the manner in which a product is used is paramount, and the salesperson is the catalyst in making that determination."

"Okay. The third aspect of legitimacy is the perspective of the customer. We're going to look at this as an engineer would, from the standpoint of function. We're asking the question, What worthwhile role does the profession of selling play from the customer's perspective? We're going to throw out all the cynical answers—and you've heard them all . . . 'your role is the pretty face behind the product—a kind of walking brochure.' Ohhh, I hate that one," he said with a theatrical grimace.

"We're going to completely reject the idea that selling is a numbers game, that your job is to pitch the product at everyone who will take the time to listen and see what sticks. Any definition that puts the salesperson *'in the way'*, with no other purpose than as window-dressing . . . or as a human billboard . . . or as a manipulator—is out," he said.

He pushed the buttons on the projector's remote control to load the next slide.

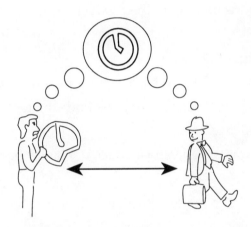

"This slide shows the basic *but flawed* idea that most people have of sales. The guy on the left has a broken bicycle wheel. He wants a new one. The salesperson thinks that's just fine and will be glad to sell him the replacement. How would you describe this process?" asked Michael.

Kat rubbed her chin as she answered. "What's wrong with *that* perception of selling? The customer has a need and you fill it."

"I didn't say it was necessarily wrong. I said it was *flawed*."

"What's the difference?" said Kat.

"In some circumstances, this might be exactly the right thing to do. But how would we know?" said Michael. "Can someone supply me with a description of this process?"

"Order-taking," said Ryan.

"Any disagreement?"

He continued. "What assumptions are required about the knowledge of the customer?"

Kat answered, "He knows what he wants."

"Right. And what does the salesperson bring to the table?"

"He has the product."

"So he's 'in the way'?"

"No. He's the guy with the ball. And if the customer wants to play, he needs the ball," said Kat.

"So the salesman adds nothing to the product. His only function is that he has it in his possession?"

"I suppose that's right," she said.

"Why pay someone for that? Why not put a picture of the wheel in a catalog and let the customer thumb through it until he finds the tire he wants. It's gotta be less expensive," said Michael.

"Maybe the guy wants a personal touch. Maybe he wants to work with people," she said.

"There's no doubt that a market exists where customers would prefer a warm body to a catalog. But people are expensive. It will remain a niche market with the majority of 'informed customers' preferring the low-cost method of buying their replacement. What would you choose to do—go down to your neighborhood bike store and pay twenty-five percent more, or order the same item over the phone with overnight delivery?" he asked, and clicked the projector forward to the next slide. But maybe there's more to be discovered. Let's see how the customer came to the salesperson in the first place."

"Well now, isn't this fascinating," said Michael. "The customer is dreaming about love, crashes and needs to replace his *mode of transportation*. Does that offer any clues?" he asked.

"Maybe there's more to the story than just replacing the wheel," said Kyle. "How would we ever know?"

"Because the product is not the main event," said Ryan excitedly. "The utilization of the product is more important."

"Bingo," said Michael, punching up the next slide. "If the salesperson asked the customer what the intended use of the product was, he would likely discover that there is more than a single option for the customer to consider."

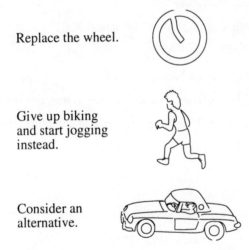

Replace the wheel.

Give up biking
and start jogging
instead.

Consider an
alternative.

"Why should the customer consider anything other than a replacement?" asked Michael.

"Maybe he rides his bike for exercise," said Kyle.

"Maybe he rides his bike to impress the girls," said Madison wryly.

"Excellent. Exercise might lead him to consider jogging instead. And perhaps the salesperson will find that what he really wants is romance, the mode of transportation isn't as important as finding the girl," said Michael. "How would we know if we do nothing more than take an order?"

"You wouldn't know," said Madison. "You'd just pitch your product and ask for the sale."

"And suppose you have the most expensive wheels in town. What exactly are you going to say?" asked Michael.

"You're stuck. Unless you discover that the customer wants to impress the girl and he agrees that quality is one way to do it," she replied.

"So suddenly we're adding value by seeking the intended use of the product. Suppose the first instance in which replacement is the main goal—all he really wants to do is ride his bike—no romance, no exercise. And our wheels are the most expensive, highest quality wheels available. Let's also say that the customer is a college student who lives on a budget—or more accurately, needs to conserve beer money—and wants the least expensive wheel he can find. How are we going to make the sale?" asked Michael.

"Coercion would work about now," laughed Kat.

"What would you do?"

"Send him on his way," said Kat.

"The next slide is the full rendition of the Time Economy Model.™ It's the functional view of augmented selling—from the customer's perspective, he said, bringing up the next slide.

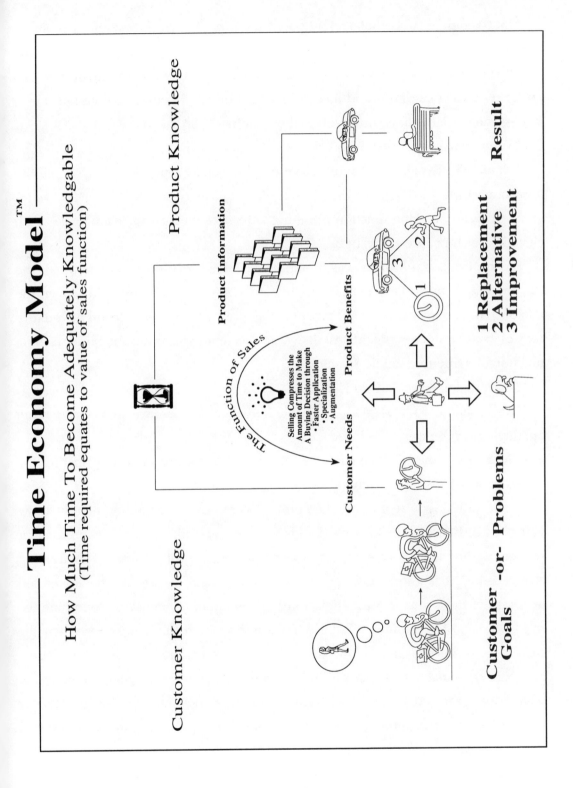

Time Economy Model™

How Much Time To Become Adequately Knowledgable
(Time required equates to value of sales function)

Customer Knowledge

Product Knowledge

Product Information

Product Benefits

Customer Needs

The Function of Sales

Selling Compresses the
Amount of Time to Make
A Buying Decision through
• Faster Application
• Specialization
• Augmentation

1 Replacement
2 Alternative
3 Improvement

Result

Customer -or- Problems
Goals

"Its basic premise is that you augment the process, which is obvious enough, but is not enough by itself. It has to be essential to the process given the circumstance, and there must be a payoff." Michael paused for a moment to let his group of sales stars digest and analyze the statement. "Under what circumstance is it essential and what is the payoff to the customer?" he asked.

"Time, obviously," said Ryan.

"Obviously, Ryan—that's why we've titled it Time Economy. Can you see the consequences?"

"I think so . . . . the function of selling is to save the customer time?" he said, elevating his tone into a question.

"Ahh. Time," said Michael as though it carried a romantic connotation. "If the customer had an endless supply of time to research products, to discover the intricacy of the manufacturing process, the product's material content, quality control, benefit, its component cost, its value and finally its application, what single function of marketing would remain?"

"Advertising!" proclaimed Kat.

"Kat's selling as we speak," chuckled Michael. "Can we describe it more broadly as 'awareness'?" he asked.

"Sure," said Shaw. "The customer still needs to be prodded into making the decision. Most customers don't know what's good for them."

"Jock, I think you're missing the point. Awareness means letting people know you're in business to meet a need they may have, and you have a product or service to do so. Awareness is always necessary—regardless of marketing channel—but it is rarely the selling method. When we are at the lower left quadrant of the Strategic Marketing Matrix,™ Awareness may serve to initiate the sale—catalogs, for example. But it serves as the selling method only when the customer is thoroughly knowledgeable, and therefore requires no 'time-compression'—*and* when there is little or no potential for augmentation. How often does the customer find himself in the position of being broadly knowledgeable about the product, and competing products, and the myriad methods for applying and using the various products?" he asked.

"When the product is a commodity," said Bobby.

"Absolutely. And as you've demonstrated, Bobby, there are opportunities to augment commodity sales as well. But how frequently are customers in a commodity buying position? Consider for a moment the complexity of buying a home—neighborhoods, schools, taxes, transportation and resale values. It takes time. But it's not limited to such important decisions. Go into Sears and decide about a VCR camcorder, or television, or an electric razor. If no one shows up to explain the choices and applications, what happens? We haven't even scratched the surface . . . insurance, investments, vacations, entertainment, books, movies, boats, colleges . . . oh, and by the way, you need to go to work today," he smiled. "Without you—the salesperson—as the expert regarding the product's application, the customer would simply have no time. You compress time for customers. You bring knowledge about the product, its competitors, and its application together with the customer's needs. You divert a customer from making the wrong choice—that's the dog at the bottom of the diagram—and steer them towards making a decision that meets their application needs. The time savings is practically incomprehensible." He paused.

"Michael, excuse me. But this is a big deal as far as I'm concerned," said Ryan. "I've never been exposed to the view of selling from the customer's standpoint. I used to feel like I was a necessary evil from the customer's perspective, but now I wonder if maybe I should be charging more."

"I hope you agree that it's a fascinating approach to the customer's viewpoint. In essence, you sell time. You're time efficient and therefore time economical from the customer's perspective. Without getting too dramatic about it . . . time may be one of the most precious concepts a person can transfer," said Michael.

"I'm not sure I agree. It seems like emotion plays a much larger role here," said Shannon. "I mean, it's so technical . . . and black and white . . . and scientific. Isn't there an emotional aspect?" she asked.

"She's right," said Fischer. "People buy because of two emotions—greed and fear. How do you account for that?"

"Integrate all that we have said to this point, Shannon," said Michael, directing his answer to her instead of Fischer. "We've not eliminated customer emotion from the equation. In fact, the example of the art buyer could be viewed as completely emotional. The fact is, some purchases are emotional, others are rational. Some rational people buy things for emotional reasons, and some emotional people buy things logically. It's not your role to change people. Your role is to identify the 'application' of the product regardless of its decision-making basis. The responsibility that you hold when you subscribe to the idea of legitimacy is that you refuse to be the catalyst of a poor decision on the basis of creating false emotion, or for that matter, pressing for an emotional art buyer to consider the rational investment value of a work of art when their intended use is as an emotional value. Your role is to discover what the customer seeks. The difference, from an emotional perspective, is who is the source of emotion—you or the customer," he said.

"So where does it fit in? I mean, I sell with enthusiasm."

"Given what we've said over the last forty minutes, where do *you* think it fits in?" he asked.

Shannon was silent for a moment as she considered the question. Michael waited. "Well," she said. "I guess enthusiasm can always be applied to the role that I play—the augmentation aspect. I suppose I can always be *up*, as it pertains to what I do," she said.

"Now *that* really sounded enthusiastic," Michael said sarcastically to a handful of laughs. "Passion is not excluded anywhere from this model. It's a perfectly wrong stereotype that those who follow a process or a method, lack passion. Passion implies intense satisfaction *with the process.* How many times are you passionate about something you know *nothing* about?" He paused before saying slowly, *"Passion relies on knowledge."* He let that sink in.

"How many times are you passionate about things that fail? . . . *Passion relies on success."* He smiled now.

"How many things are you passionate about that just happen, regardless of your involvement?. . . *Passion relies on effort and energy. . .*

"How many things are you passionate about that end up mediocre, average or second-best? *Passion relies on excellence.*

"Passion is not a substitute for substance, although there are those who would like you to believe that precision kills passion. They want to dispel precision so they're not bound to results. The truth is, they substitute raw emotion for passion, but call it passion as a disguise. It's not. Passion is about depth that is invisible

without the sight of process, knowledge, success, effort, energy and excellence."
He paused.

"It's all far too rigid. You've left no room for style," said Fischer.

"Just the opposite is true, Tug. The more thoroughly you understand something, the more it can be stylized. Style is perspective, not difference. Look at the distinctions of business jet designs. The sleek Citation jets are my favorite, but aerodynamically they possess the essentials of every other aircraft to ever fly. Style is tremendously important because it delivers knowledge in the form in which the individual discovered it. The further you reach down to the principles, the fewer you will find and the result is far more fluidity in style, perspective, and creativity," Michael finished, silencing Fischer's complaining. "We'll have an opportunity to discuss the emotion of selling this afternoon. For now, I want to wrap up our discussion of legitimacy. An understanding and delivery of substance in the sales process is the core—the foundation—and the absolute essential of legitimacy. You must start there before you can arrive at the emotional result of self-respect." He paused.

"Callie, does that agree with your experiences?" asked Michael.

"Completely. I didn't understand the value of what I had to offer. The result was a lack of confidence. It's hard to stand under a spotlight without confidence. But it wasn't enough to 'believe' that I had something to offer, I needed to truly have something of substance—of value. When I discovered that point, it was easy to justify not only what I did on a daily basis, but the commissions I earned as a result. Finally, I could put my career into perspective and be proud of my work. Now, I sell ideas to people who find them reflective of their values. I exchange the value of my ideas for the value they have to offer—money. I'm proud of that and the understanding of legitimacy is at its root," said Callie.

"But Callie, come on, how can it be honest and legitimate if you do it for *money*?" said Michael. "We've all been taught that the money is an immoral goal. If you do it for the money, you're crass and uncaring, or so today's culture says. You're supposed to do it for the money, but only up to a point. Then you're supposed to feel guilty. Otherwise, you're selfish, greedy, and uncaring!"

Callie smiled. "Funny, isn't it, how the minds of men can warp things so far out of perspective?" she asked.

Ryan answered. "It depends on whether you have it?" he chuckled.

There were nervous laughs throughout the room.

"Have what?" asked Michael.

"Money!"

"I'm not sure I understand, Ryan. If some people have money and others don't, where does it come from? Are we born with it? Does money find us? What *is* money, anyway?" It was Michael's probing tone that signaled the group they should buckle-up for another roller-coaster ride.

"If I were to read a cross-section of today's writings, I would get every perspective of money imaginable. Good, bad—you name it. I would begin to believe that money is alive, that it is something of substance, with a life of its own. That it is fickle and elusive, and chooses arbitrarily the individuals it destroys or helps," said Michael. "Could someone sort it out for me? What is money?"

"It's a ridiculous question," said Fischer. "We all know what money is!"

"But I'm not sure we spend much time thinking about its connection to selling, and I am quite certain that we fail to attach the appropriate meaning to money as it relates to our legitimacy. So Tug, help me out a little here. Give me the textbook definition of money."

"It's a medium of exchange. And a store of value. Econ 101," he snapped.

"What exactly does that mean, Tug?"

"It means . . . it's a way that we. . . trade . . . our services for someone else's."

"Do you have a twenty on you?" asked Michael.

Fischer reached into his front pocket and pulled out a money clip that was rather thick. He licked his thumb, grasped a bill and snapped it out of the clip.

"Here. I have a one dollar bill. You have money and I have money. You said trade. Will you trade your money for mine?"

Fischer was annoyed. He tilted his head and pursed his lips, but didn't answer.

"So your money is different than mine?" prompted Michael.

"Yes. It's *more* money than yours."

"It looks the same to me, other than those numbers. The same size. The same color. The quality of the paper looks the same. You don't seem to have more paper than me."

"Yeah, yeah . . . I know. Okay. It's paper. It's only a representation of value," he conceded.

"Whew, sometimes it's the little things that are the most difficult. So money doesn't have intrinsic value?" he said, turning away from Fischer and addressing the group. "Someone help me out with this idea of representation. What exactly does that mean?"

Ryan had studied Wall Street's capital markets inside and out and figured he knew exactly what money was. "Money is like a raw material. It's the way we repackage labor, or assets, or products so it can be moved around from one place to another."

"Good, Ryan. Money stores value and we transport it in that way. *You* move money, and your perspective is an appropriate one, but we need to go deeper. What value does it represent?"

"I suppose work . . . effort . . . *labor*," said Ryan.

"Yes. Is there more?"

"I don't know what you mean."

"Does money represent creativity?" asked Michael.

"I still don't know what you mean."

"You work hard, right? So does Bill Gates. Why does he have more money than you?"

"Good question," grinned Ryan good-naturedly.

"And what about the guy in the mailroom; he works hard, too. But you make more money. Is that just?" he pressed.

"I don't think of it as an injustice. It's a matter of education and knowledge," said Ryan.

Michael spun to face Rick without giving Ryan a chance to answer. He wanted to include other group members in the discussion. "Rick, you're an expert on this type of thing. Is it injustice that Ryan makes more than a mailroom clerk?"

"No, not really. Ryan's world is different from the clerk's. He gets paid more because he has more stress," said Kincaid.

"Shannon . . . and Tip. You make more money than a school teacher. Why?" quizzed Michael.

They looked at each other pensively. Shannon answered. "I'm not sure a . . . teacher . . . could . . . well, they just don't . . ." She stopped short so that she could avoid a controversy. "I guess there are just fewer agents and it comes down to supply and demand," she said half-heartedly.

"Kyle, you make more money than a nurse. How come?" Michael folded his arms and leaned back against the desk.

"I've never really thought about it," said Kyle.

"Well, let's think about it together. Nurses are more highly trained in medicine, right? They certainly understand the pharmaceuticals you sell. They work long hours under difficult situations. They are exposed to trauma so they have a great deal of stress, and they add emotional support and caring to the equation. Is it an injustice that you are more highly paid than a nurse?" said Michael, with the emotionless tone of a prosecuting attorney.

"Michael, I don't know. I guess the only way to answer is that they do what they're good at. And I do what I'm good at. Someone believes I'm worth more."

Michael gasped theatrically. "Somebody finally said it. Could it *be* that money is a representation of *worth!* A reflection of *value!* An interpretation of creativity, knowledge, skill, intelligence, and ability!" He paused and looked around the room to make eye contact with several in the group in order to emphasize the statement.

"Could it be that Bill Gates has more to offer than Ryan, and Ryan more to offer than the clerk in the mailroom? Dare we suggest that someone values Kyle's knowledge, skill, ingenuity, drive and effort more than society values the contribution of a nurse!" The volume of Michael's voice rose. "Ryan, you said it was a difference of knowledge—true. Shannon, you muttered something about supply and demand—partly. Rick, your explanation was stress—maybe. But at the root—at the source—money represents value. It isn't precise, but it's darn close. People value Bill Gates' skills more than Ryan's. And they value Ryan's skills more than the clerk in the mailroom. And yes, Kyle, as much as the altruist deplores the idea, people value you more than they do a nurse. How do I know? Because they are willing to pay you more. And when they pay you, they do it with their most precious possession. They pay you with the representation of the thing they hold dearest—their own value.

"Money is a reflection of the individual and the action that created the value for which it is exchanged. It can't be anything but a representation. Money is not good or bad. It's value created and stored. Bad actions don't create bad money. Bad actions are bad actions and money is money. Value is the only thing that creates money over the long term. It's a simple equation. Principles that work create value. The value created is exchanged for its representation—money which can be exchanged for value in the future. Poor principles don't work, not for long. Value isn't created. Money is not exchanged. The transfer of money is directly reflective of your legitimacy. The more you make over time, which is the crucible of effective principles, the more legitimate you are. They go hand in hand." he said, pausing, and signaling Callie.

Callie added the conclusion. "Legitimacy is a critical part of Sales Esteem and is reflected in the fair exchange of value—one that comes from the individual's efforts to enhance the product. Without a respect for your profession, it's virtually impossible to respect your role in that profession. If you understand the importance of the profession and your opportunity to make it even more valuable to the buyer, respect for your work increases your energy by multiples—it's a basic premise of Sales Esteem," she said.

"Thank you, Callie. I'm grateful for your time," he said, initiating applause from the group. Callie bowed gracefully and hugged Michael . The group filed by her one after another, some collecting an autograph, others like Kat, just wanting to savor the moment. So far the guest list had been quite impressive. And no one expected that Michael could top Callie McCoy.

11

Dreams

Talent fills the glass halfway. Aspirations make it overflow. Courage comes from knowing we can climb the ladder to our dreams, and that our ladder is planted firmly on solid ground.

—Michael Cevanté

The bus glided along the road back to the conference center. They has stopped to eat lunch along the way, and were still buzzing about the morning's activities when they pulled into the circular drive in front of the Summit.. As Kyle stepped from the bus' steps, he noticed a sleek black Mercedes pull into the parking lot and recognized the driver instantly. He stood by the side of the bus dumbfounded as Billy Williams stepped out of the car. Kyle Mitchell had many sports heroes, but just one idol. And he had just stepped out into the parking lot. Michael noticed Kyle gawking at the man and his black Mercedes and strolled to his side. "Do you know who that is, Kyle?" Michael asked.

"Are you kidding? That's Billy Williams. The one and only, Dream Williams, as he was called by the media." Kyle drifted back into a daze.

"Yeah. I didn't think he would come," Michael said with a curious tone. He walked towards the man and met him as he was entering the Summit lobby. Michael extended his hand. "I didn't expect to see you."

"Yeah . . . I didn't think I was coming till I got your note. You're lucky I was smart enough to understand it. It wasn't easy, you know," said Dream.

"Yes, I know. But if it were easy, you wouldn't be here . . . would you?"

"No, my friend, you got that right. Only, I'm here now. I'm taking a chance, you know?"

"Yes. But I believe it will be worth it—wouldn't you agree?"

"Yeah . . . I guess that's right. What do we do now?" said Dream.

"This way . . . and . . . by the way—thanks for having the courage to come," said Michael.

"Better wait and see if I get it right."

Dream Williams broke into professional basketball when he was eighteen. A high school diploma had been the least of his concerns. Since his rookie season he had taken the NBA by storm and now, he *was* basketball. In his eight years he had become a perennial All-Star selection, had gathered five MVP trophies, two championship rings, and his most cherished achievement—a college degree. Dream Williams was also HIV positive.

Everyone in the sporting world was stunned when he made the announcement. But Dream Williams was more than just basketball. He was a statesman of the game. His charismatic charm was engaging and he used it to break down racial and social barriers alike. He was a diplomat carrying a message of hope, and personified what both blacks and whites hoped for: the union of two diverse American cultures. Dream Williams had it all. And even in the darkest hours of his affliction, his infectious smile generated enough energy to light up a city. His work, his charm, his hope was now turned toward the dreaded disease—not in the ordinary way of public demands and political maneuvers—but through a campaign of talking to kids, giving them a chance to understand their role in preventing the disease. Speaking to adults was not his first choice.

Michael had tried to contact him for several months, and was turned down each time. They met accidentally at a book signing. Dream agreed to meet with Michael over dinner and listened patiently to Michael's requests for him to speak. Dream refused, scheduling his precious time with the many children's groups that wanted him to speak instead. Michael hadn't expected Dream, and wasn't certain what he would say to the group now that he was there. But he would make time for him, certain that he would have something extraordinary to share.

The group had returned to the conference room and were waiting for the next session, newly alight about the strength they had found in the ideas of Callie's legitimacy discussion. Michael and Dream walked into the room and a hush fell over the group. Dream was instantly recognized by everyone. They were as stunned as Kyle. Michael stood at the front and made the introduction. Dream followed him to the front of the room, waving a hand and smiling broadly to calm the applause. "Thank you, thank you all, very much . . . thank you. Thank you," he said.

Dream stood at the podium. He had a presence that could be felt. His speaking engagements were frequently part of the nightly news, and always carried the somber message of AIDS understanding and prevention. Abstinence was his typical message, but not today. Today, Dream Williams was going to stand by his convictions. By now he was an accomplished speaker, but retained a genuine demeanor of a happy kid who was able to earn a fortune doing something he loved. His character never seemed to fade.

"I didn't like Michael Cevanté the first time we met . . . or the second. In fact, I've spent just two hours with him and they weren't enjoyable at all." He paused and looked at Michael as though to reinforce how serious he was about his comments. Michael smiled slightly and nodded his head in understanding.

"You see, Michael Cevanté is the first person to spotlight the cause of my disease, and it wasn't comfortable because the spotlight was shining squarely on me. I didn't want to *see* him again, or *hear* from him, or *think* of him ever again. I didn't return his calls. I wanted him to go away," said Dream. He paused and looked out over the group. They were perfectly silent.

"Then . . . he sends me a handwritten note! And written on the note were just two lines: *You have the chance to move the knowledge of an entire culture forward, but first you have to make an acquaintance with reason and emotion—and decide for yourself which comes first.*

"*MAN!* I crumpled it up and tossed it into the trash can." The smile reappeared, but with a cynical twist. "Can you imagine that. What a thing to say. I just laughed at it. But I couldn't stop thinking about its meaning. That night, about two in the morning, with those words echoing in my mind, I got up, spilled the trash out of the can and onto the floor, and stared at the crumpled-up paper. I just looked at it. I stared at the darn thing like it had some magic power over me. Finally I picked it up and unraveled it. The words seemed different. I didn't sleep that night." He looked over at Michael again. "You owe me one night's sleep!" he said, pointing a long finger in Michael's direction.

"Deal," said Michael.

Dream continued. "But I began to understand. And now here I am. After two weeks of thinking about Michael Cevanté's words, here I am to tell you the way it is for me, Dream Williams."

They were on the edge of their seats.

"I *feel*. I feel emotions all over. I wouldn't want to be alive without them. My life is about emotions. All my life—I've chased 'em, yearned for 'em, grabbed 'em. Michael saw my life that way, too. But he saw something I never did—until now. Michael Cevanté, on a cold evening in Baltimore, paid me the highest compliment anyone ever will. He told me I had always earned my emotion. He asked me to remember a single moment in life when I hadn't worked for the emotions I harbored. He challenged me to grasp the relationship between values and emotions, and asked me to point to a moment when my emotions weren't the result of my values.

"He was almost right. You see, when I was a kid, there was no one to pick me up when I fell. There was no one to show me the right direction. There was no one to share my dreams with. I didn't dream like most kids do. My dreams all had one thing in common—I knew no one was going to help make them come true. I knew it was up to me, and me alone. I knew wanting it wasn't enough. I knew I had to *do* something before I could *feel* something. I realized emotions are results. Feelings didn't win ball games at my high school, and they sure don't win 'em in the pros. Effort wins ball games—emotions come later. Desire is an expectation of gaining your values, and the emotion that comes when you do. Enthusiasm is only a mind set that signals you believe you can be your best, and reach your goals. The thrills, and the joy, and the elation, and the self-respect, and the pride—all come when you get there." He paused, looking toward the ceiling in an introspective pose.

"There were a lot of people who thought differently where I grew up. I saw them *'feel'* euphoric on drugs. I saw them break store windows and *'feel'* as though they owned TVs. I saw proud, poor people walk into welfare offices and *'feel'* the value of a paycheck, only to walk out without their pride. I saw punks with knives *'feel'* like leaders. And I heard plenty of talk about the *'feelings'* on the street—feelings of hatred—and anger—that always led to the *'feel'* of cold steel bars. I saw gang leaders *'feel'* authority through rituals, only to end up bleeding in the streets. I saw people who never earned their feelings pretending they were real, and then watching reality come stomping down on them. *I knew feelings had to be earned.* And it lead me out of that world.

"I never felt first. I *did* first. And I figured out the things to do that made me feel good. Winning felt good, so I worked my tail off to win. It had nothing to do with feeling first—it had everything to do with winning first. Then came the feelings. Drugs were just the opposite, they made you feel good first, for no reason. There's a price to pay for that. So I never did drugs. I worked hard at school cause 'feeling' like I was smart wasn't going to make me smart. I worked hard at my job after practice, cause *'feeling'* warm soup in your stomach before you've eaten isn't the same as eating it and feeling full." He paused.

"Michael knew where I came from. He told me he knew that somewhere along the way I had figured out the logic of doing first instead of *'feeling'* first. Michael was almost right. You see, my whole life, I didn't let emotions make up my mind for me—until I let my feelings fool me about love." Dream's voice started to crack. "I was all wrong about love. Love is substance first and feeling after. Intimacy is the celebration of love—not the path to love. Love grants you the right to be intimate—and the joy of intimacy."

Tears were streaming down Dream's cheeks. Michael rubbed his eyes to stop the same thing from happening to him. "I chased the feeling and forgot how my whole life was built on getting the real thing first and being immersed in the joy of the emotion it brought. It was the one time I messed it up in my entire life, and . . . it . . . cost me my . . . life." Dream looked down at the podium and tried to gather himself. There was a long, uncomfortable silence. It was the first time many of them had ever experienced a moment of pure remorse, without condemnation.

"The message I used to take to kids is to be careful. From this point forward my message to kids is to seek love honestly, without rushing into love caused by feelings. To think about what they're doing and then decide if they've really found love. To think about the people they spend time with. To find the emotion, to celebrate life and all the rewards it has to offer—all the emotional rewards—but do it honestly. Don't fake it by wishing, or *'feeling.'* Do the real things first and the real emotions will come. And the chances are you won't make the bad decisions. The chances are you will choose the right things—and the right people—and find the right emotions—the real emotions of love.

"I'm sorry I'm crying. I guess it's because of regret and understanding, and a desire to pass on something for someone else to use. Michael said I could move our culture's understanding by talking about reason and emotion. I think he's right. Kids of America, look out, here I come."

The smile burst through the tears. Dream wiped what remained of them aside and bounced slightly on his toes. He raised his right hand into a wave. "Thank you," he said.

The group stood when Dream was finished. It was certainly not what they had expected, it was more. Dream had always been an inspiration, but never more than at that moment. They applauded for Dream not as adoring fans, but in admiration of his human spirit. There were quite a few dry throats in the room. Dream left the podium and walked toward Michael. They stood face to face at the door—without words. Dream's look said it all. Dream stared into Michael's eyes for a long moment, finally nodding. Michael returned the nod. Dream's large hand reached out and grasped Michael's, he pulled him close and they embraced as brothers would. When they parted, Dream whispered, "Thanks," and walked through the door. Michael found himself in a moment of silence. Dream had both moved him and touched him at a deep level. Michael turned back to the group and said. "I can't imagine what I would say after that. What do you say we move out to the deck and break for a half-hour. It might be nice to just gaze out over the lake and think for awhile."

There was no discussion. They moved slowly out onto the deck and chatted quietly among themselves. It was a beautiful spring day and the gentle breeze blew across the face of the cliff as they stared out over the valley below.

12

Reason and Emotion

The great man is he who does
not lose his child's heart.
—*Mencius*

Forty minutes later, they gathered back in the room. Michael was reading a letter from Hallie who was still struggling with the lottery winnings. She wrote:

> *Dad, it has all the makings of a dilemma—but you've always insisted there are no dilemmas. It has given me the perfect chance to demonstrate character, but I just can't see why character is valuable right now. You and Grandpa instilled in me principles that are hard to live by. I don't really want to give the money to Grandma and work a second job. What is it that I'm missing? Why shouldn't we just take what comes and not worry ourselves with reasons, and causes, and consequences? So long as we take just the good things, and avoid the bad, does it really matter?*
>
> *—Love Hallie*

Michael smiled to himself. He thought about the alternative discussions he would have with Hallie depending on her decision. Either way, the lessons she would learn were going to be terribly important to her for the rest of her life. Michael knew the evaluation alone would be the key. He would rather she was spared the rigors of deciding, but it was old hat for her by now. The Cevantés had spent seventeen years letting Hallie discover her own course through life—guiding her, fencing off any seriously damaging threat, letting her fall down when her decisions were poor, picking her up and letting her discover the cause without lectures, rules or commands. She also discovered the power of her good decisions, always reminded by them that they were hers to be proud of. The same things were happening now.

When he looked up from the letter the group was almost settled. He pushed himself to a sitting position at his favorite spot in the room, the table top.

"At our first meeting . . . I made harsh comments about contemporary sales motivation. This is the point when I give you the rationale for that criticism and let you decide for yourself," said Michael. "All week we have discussed the nature of emotions as the payoff for good principles and their corresponding actions. Traditionally, selling and emotion have gone hand in hand—an inseparable pair. But as I said at the first of the week, emotion is mistreated and misunderstood, especially when it comes to motivation. Let's start by defining the term 'emotion' and then put some of our concepts about emotion to the test and see if they can be defended. First, can someone summarize Dream's message about emotions?"

"I still don't understand why we can't just control our emotions—but be careful about the ones we select," said Sally.

"You missed the point, Sally," said Kat. Her response was reinforced by a dozen nodding heads. "There's nothing wrong with emotions. We want the good ones. It just depends on whether they are a *result or a trigger*," she said.

"I like the word trigger for this point. Go on, Kat," said Michael.

"Emotions don't just exist out there on their own. They're an end result. They come from actions—just like our paradigm. It's a kind of an . . . if-then equation. There are good emotions from good actions—like the exhilaration of closing a big deal, or being named the top producer for the month. And bad emotions like stress and guilt are also end-products, only they have a different cause," she said.

Ryan was sitting forward in his seat. All the answers he was hoping for from the conference were falling into place. He nearly cut Kat off to add, "The fraud comes in if you try to induce an emotion when there's no cause. Emotions are an effect, always with a cause. If there is no cause, then the emotion is fake and bound to fail," he said.

"Ahhh . . . bull!" said Fischer, shaking his head in disgust. There are contradictions to your theory *everywhere*. I know more emotionally driven, successful people than you've had clients, if I'm guessing right. There are some things that benefit more from pure 'zing,' than from thinking. And one heck of a lot of selling is 'zing,'" he said.

"Yeah, I'll bet there's a lot of 'zing' in your deals, Tug. My experience tells me that emotion gets you trouble," shot back Ryan.

"Like anger," said Michael with a smile. Pushing himself off the table top with a short thrust forward and taking two steps to break the visual plane between Fischer and Ryan. Fischer's glare turned away from Ryan and toward Michael.

"You're wrong twice, Tug. Mr. Matthews here has plenty of clients, and regardless of whether people use their emotions as a guide or not . . . they are forced into some mental action before they react. There *is* no 'zing' without some conscious thought first," said Michael.

He flipped the switch to the overhead projector. Up came a photograph of a group of thatched-roof huts near a bubbling jungle stream, surrounded by tropical vegetation. The picture captured a brilliant red sun poking in and out from the trees. In front of the huts was a large grassy meadow, about the width of a football field. Smoke drifted from several of the huts. A bridge crossed the stream and lead to a planted field to the right of the village.

"What emotions are evoked with this picture?" he asked.

"It's peaceful," said Kat.

"Would your emotions change if I told you this was a North Vietnamese village about to be attacked during the war in Southeast Asia?" asked Michael.

"Of course," she said.

"What changed?"

"I know what an attack will do to the village—to the people there."

"That's the perspective of an educated professional and mother to two children?"

"Right."

"What if you were the sergeant leading the attack?" Michael pushed the remote control and summoned the next slide; a photo of a platoon of posing American GIs came to the screen. "Would you feel differently if you knew these men were relying on you?"

"Sure, now I'm concerned about *their* lives," said Kat.

Michael punched the projector's control panel to load the next slide. A man with a red bandanna and a Kalashnakov rifle crouched behind one of the huts, eyes fixed toward the field in front of the village, rifle drawn and held in both hands at his side. Behind him was a woman and a child. The woman's arms were wrapped around the child and her face was clenched in terror.

"Same peaceful setting. Different emotions. Kat, do you think a military strategist, a political scientist, a Red Cross medic, a platoon sergeant, and a mother of two would feel different emotions at this moment—even though the events are identical?" asked Michael.

"Extremely different," she said.

"Yeah, what does the mother feel?"

"Fear. Horror."

"The sergeant?" he asked.

"A threat. The enemy."

"The medic?"

"This sounds funny, but my first thought is that he would feel anticipation or, maybe apprehension is a better description," she said.

"The military strategist?"

"Probably cold-hearted calculation about the enemy."

"Yes, probably. If you were the mother of an American GI, isn't that what you'd want him to feel?" said Michael.

"Yes."

"And the political scientist?"

"I'd rather not think about what he would feel. Genocide, or ethnic cleansing, or something disgusting," she said, curling the corner of her mouth up.

"I guess that would depend on your political perspectives. How would Thomas Jefferson view the conflict between socialism and democracy? How would he feel about America as the world's policeman? How would he view a murderer like Pol Pot, who was killing untold numbers of his own people?" asked Michael, not expecting an answer. He punched up the next slide. It was a picture of a run-of-the-mill convenience store perched on a corner in a sleepy suburb. The photo's perspective was almost exactly like that of the village. The store and village occupied the central focus of the picture, foliage framed them both. Streets replaced fields and meadows but were similarly positioned.

"Compare your value assessment of the village and the store. Does the store evoke any special emotions?" asked Michael.

"Inconvenience," giggled Kat. Others in the room laughed with her.

"Not peacefulness like the village scene?"

"Not at all. Those stores are robbed so often, if you asked which of the two were more 'threatening,' I would pick the store," said Kat.

"Funny you should mention that." Michael poked the remote control and up came the next slide. It was a photo of a SWAT team. "These guys have been summoned to the store. You're their commander."

Up came the next slide. Now it was obvious to the class. Each slide corresponded to its earlier counterpart. The village and the store. The platoon and the S.W.A.T. team. Now there was a photo of a man and his hostages crouching behind a row of potato chips and pretzels. In his hand was a .38 revolver. His other hand clasped to the wrist of a young women and her infant child. Her face showing a similar terror to the earlier photograph of the mother and child of the village.

"Different circumstances. Different settings. Similar threats. Very, very different emotions. The military strategist would probably yawn. The medic and police captain would probably have very similar feelings, the mother surprisingly would probably feel more hope than terror in the second situation, but in both cases extreme fear. And the political scientist would be feeling remorse at society's woes, instead of the earlier version where he was an advocate of an entire culture's political views and their obligation to enforce those views," said Michael.

"No matter what your feelings, you had to think about it first. Feelings are nothing more than a measure of whether your values correspond or conflict with the circumstance. Emotions always—even if it is instantaneous—emotions always follow thought," said Michael. He turned to Fischer. "Tug? Do you agree?"

"Yeah. Sure. I don't know why it matters, though," said Fischer.

Michael punched up the next slide. Up came the Sales Esteem paradigm.

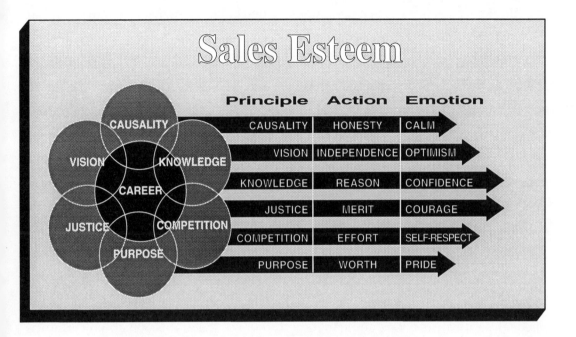

Principle	Action	Emotion
CAUSALITY	HONESTY	CALM
VISION	INDEPENDENCE	OPTIMISM
KNOWLEDGE	REASON	CONFIDENCE
JUSTICE	MERIT	COURAGE
COMPETITION	EFFORT	SELF-RESPECT
PURPOSE	WORTH	PRIDE

"Tug? The 'zing' salespeople in your example. Is it fair to assume they thought about their actions and then used emotion to energize them?"

"Call it whatever you wish. They live on the power of emotion," said Fischer.

"Yes, Tug. *So do I.* The key is what underlies the emotion. Does it have a basis—a reason? Emotion is enormously powerful. It should be a result, a reward. I think we can all agree on that now. So let's discuss the practice of using emotion as a motivator—for both yourselves and the customer. In the Sales Esteem paradigm, the two counter principles are being *Guided-by-knowledge* and being *Guided-by-feelings*. The first holds that reason is the only legitimate catalyst for action and reason is based on knowledge. The second dismisses the need to think, pushing feelings to the forefront. It's the hunch sale. It's vague, fuzzy, foggy and unclear. It's almost always the unique domain of the expert who's *feeling* it. *And it requires trumped-up emotions to convince people of its merit.* It won't stand on its own, therefore it needs the fraud of reversing the cause and effect of emotions. In truth it's an insult to the honesty of deserved emotions.

"But let's consider the principle-to-emotion chain. Knowledge . . . to . . . reason . . . to . . . confidence. Confidence, for our purposes, is the feeling that you have a basis for asking the customer to buy, that you have thought about the product's ability to deliver on its promise, that you have considered its suitability for the customer, and that you can anticipate the outcome with a high degree of accuracy. It's the feeling that you 'know' what you're doing, you 'know' the consequences, you 'know' your actions are conducted legitimately. You 'know' that although honest mistakes *will be made*, you've used your best ability to be right. You 'know' that there are no secrets lost in the fog of emotion. The choices are clear. The customer views them with your help and becomes a partner in a 'reasoned' decision. This is confidence, this is knowing.

"Of course there is the opposite principle where knowing doesn't matter. Knowing gets in the way. Who can really be certain of anything, anyway?" Michael said, pausing for a smile to remind them of the discussion about certainty.

"When feelings count, it means emotional antics. Provoking fear or greed on the part of the customer. Feelings tell the user that 'if you want it badly enough, it will happen.' Feelings are maybes. Feelings are blind. Feelings ultimately end up in the emotion of *helplessness*," he said.

Emotion	Action	Principle		Principle	Action	Emotion
Stress	Evasion	Chance		Causality	Honesty	Calm
Anxiety	Dependence	Abdication		Vision	Independence	Optimism
Helplessness	Sensation	Feelings		Knowledge	Reason	Confidence
Fear	Favors	Politics		Justice	Merit	Courage
Self-Disgust	Demands	Egalitarianism		Competition	Effort	Self-Respect
Guilt	Manipulation	Control		Purpose	Worth	Pride

Sales Esteem
Principle's & Counter-Principles

"Who can tell us why?" he asked.

"Because smart customers—and most ultimately will be smart—want reasons," said Ryan. "And when they get 'trust me' instead, they head for the exits. How can you feel confident when that's your skill—to try to fool people into acting for unclear reasons?"

"You can't," said Madison. "You just end up wondering why people don't trust you. Or don't like you. You get cynical. You feel powerless. I've always had the advantage of people who trusted me because I was a national champion, an expert. But I've never once relied solely on that trust. I've always insisted that they analyze the product on their own, with my help. I've always insisted that they have a 'reason' to buy that is more fundamental than the fact they are buying from *me*," she said.

"Madison, do you think the paradigm fits your view here?" asked Michael.

"It would be *sooo* easy for me to smile pretty, talk about things the retailers couldn't possibly know about shoes . . . design appeal . . . *how they 'feel'* when *I'm* running in them . . . things they would trust me to know because I was the track star, the expert, things that could be baseless, but which they would never realize. The moment one of my shoes didn't sell well, they would have to question whether I was an expert or a con artist. Frankly, I don't want to rely on emotions to put that question on the customer's lips," said Madison.

Tug Fischer was looking over the top of his glasses which had drifted down to the end of his pudgy nose. "Has anyone in the 'Sales Esteem' mentality stopped to think about the number of sales you blow because of this lame approach to sales?" he asked.

Michael smiled. "This is the most important question we've had so far'" he said, surprising Fischer with his answer once again. "Let me see if I can restate it, with Tug's help, so we have a clear perspective of its assumptions and implications." Michael raced to the white board. "Madison! Give me a definition of energy," he said.

"Uh. . . the shortest definition is 'motion.' All energy starts with expansion and ultimately ends in pushing an object from one point to another."

"Does human action require energy?"

"Of course."

"We call it motivation?" he asked.

"Right."

"Is it a conscious attribute?"

"I don't know what you mean," said Madison.

"Psychological or automatic?" asked Michael.

"Everyone knows it's psychological, Michael."

"Does it have an opposite psychological 'state-of-mind'?" he asked.

"Well if motivation is human energy, and energy is motion . . . its opposite would be 'idle'?"

Ryan interrupted. "What about the negative side of emotion?"

"Precisely, Ryan. We'd be making a mistake in presuming that the bottom of the motivational range is limited to zero," said Michael.

"Yeah . . . exactly. Fear, hate, frustration. Destructive feelings," said Ryan.

"Can they motivate you to take action?" he asked.

There were nodding heads throughout the room.

Michael continued. "At the introduction, I made comments about the energy of selling. About directing energy effectively. About efficiency of the use of energy and motivation. This is the essential discovery in explaining why you increase sales through Sales Esteem principles. This is the science behind selling more *because* you sell ethically. The increased productivity promised by Sales Esteem comes from directed energy which takes the form of motivation. The right principles lead to the right emotions. The right emotions are the energy for effort. Not only are poor principles ineffective, but they generate poor emotions which have limited energy. Misdirected energy is like a broken steam pipe at a power plant. It's wasted and can never be recovered. In the introduction I asked you to visualize four people trying to push a boulder around by each taking an opposing side. Lots of energy, but misdirected and contradictory. Sales Esteem points your energy in the right direction. It allows you to avoid waste by eliminating the contradictions. But there's more to it. Not only are the actions inefficient and clumsy, the resulting realization that you're not getting anywhere saps your motivation, claims energy. In the same way, momentum adds to your energy, pushes you harder and farther," he said, his voice strong and clear.

"Tug, your question was whether we have calculated the impact of lost sales caused by objectivity. The answer is an emphatic 'yes.' Closing every sale is a ludicrous idea. If you believe your product is for *everyone*, you should chat with your competitors. It's analogous to a doctor who performs surgery on every patient—needed or not. Or the policeman who collars every citizen, and fabricates a crime to be punished—guilty or not. It's an absolute impossibility without coercion. When attempted, it's a waste of energy. You can close some of those sales, but that will probably be the only positive moment. How many of your unhappy customers are struggling to find value in their purchase? How expensive is continued service to a dissatisfied customer? How costly is it to work to land a customer who ends up leaving in disgust and pointing a finger of blame at you? Compare that situation with the customer who truly needed what they bought from you. How many of them are unhappy? How many of them will buy again and send their friends? Which is a more effective use of your energy? Imagine the efficiency of acquiring the *right* customers and turning the *wrong* ones away. The time you spend with the wrong customer, Tug, the sales you don't think should be lost, can be spent seeking the right customers. And it's not a simple one-for-one exchange. Focused energy has a magnifying effect. In other words, it's *not* an exchange of an hour saved on a rejected customer equals an hour available to replace him The hour you spend closing the wrong customer results in more hours of service work later on, without the benefit of referrals or second sales. He takes more of your time and provides less leverage in landing more customers. If you dismiss the wrong customer, and spend the time finding the right customer, you now reap the benefit of fewer self-created problems, more second sales and more referrals. It's the difference between pushing a boulder uphill or down. One conserves energy and one expends more energy than the result is worth." He paused.

"But even more powerful is the psychological impact of focused energy as compared with wasted energy. We call human energy motivation, and it is terribly misunderstood. Let's return to the discussion we started at the introduction. Michael flipped on the overhead.

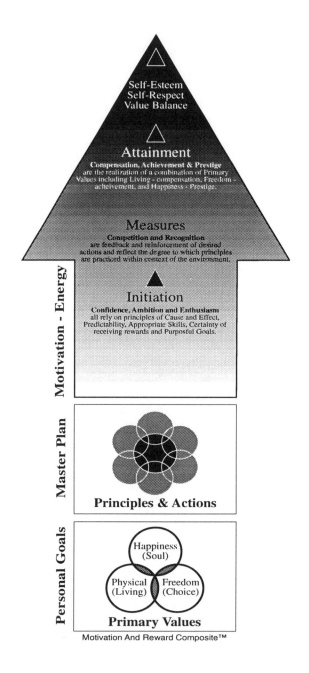

Motivation And Reward Composite™

We've discussed primary values and the principles used to realize those values. The values . . . the plan to obtain them . . . and then the energy to drive us should be obvious by now. The source, and power, and focus of the energy is what will determine the degree of your success. Motivation is frequently misunderstood," he said as he began scribbling on the white board.

"The first is in what I call a 'lump-'em-all-together' syndrome. This is the mistake of assuming that all motivators play the same role, as though it were a 'pick-your-flavor' issue that varied depending on the individual. For instance, who among you is motivated by competition?" he asked.

Everyone raised their hand, some because they believed they were 'supposed' to be motivated by competition.

"Really?" said Michael. "Can someone explain that to me?"

"I love to win," said Kyle.

"And winning is . . . ?"

"Achieving one of the values, I suppose. But it's more than that. I enjoy the struggle."

"Good, but this a treacherous ground. Why do you enjoy the struggle?"

"Well . . . I guess because I can compare myself to someone else."

"So it's important to have some idea of how well you're doing in pursuing values, especially compared to others who are pursuing the same values?" asked Michael.

"Well, sure," said Kyle sheepishly.

"Why?"

"I don't know."

"Think about it for a while," said Michael, leaving the subject for the moment by turning to the rest of the group and asking. "How many of you think of yourselves as inherently motivated, as 'chargers', as ambitious?" he asked.

There were fewer thoughtlessly-raised hands, knowing they may be asked to defend their answer. Neither Madison or Kat needed to think twice—they knew immediately. Madison's went up. Kat's stayed in her lap as she said, "Michael, to tell you the truth . . ." she said, pausing.

"When would you do otherwise?" said Michael.

Kat smiled, recognizing the careless use of phrase. "To be frank . . . ," she restated, ". . . I think of myself as being an optimistic, 'up' person. But sometimes I have to reach down and grab my motivation. I'm not in a constant state of energy. And competition isn't something I savor. I know it exists and I know that I have to deal with it, but would I rather not? You better believe it," she said.

Madison had taken a quick liking to Kat and was bothered by her comments. "Kat?" she asked. "What gets you going, then?"

"The money," laughed Kat.

Madison didn't bother with the polite laughter offered by the others. "Yes, of course. I think we can all agree that we work for money, but isn't there something else?" she said.

"No, Madison. There isn't," replied Kat flatly.

"I don't believe it. You said yesterday that you wouldn't recycle ads that weren't right for a new customer just to satisfy your manager's profit goals. Sorry, Kat, but it's a contradiction you can't hide from," said Madison.

"What do you mean hide from?" insisted Kat.

"Pride in your work."

"Of course I have pride in my work."

"My point exactly. You're motivated to put out good work," said Madison, with a tone as though she were protecting the integrity of a friend.

"Don't you think they go hand in hand, Madison?" asked Kat.

Madison nodded but didn't reply. Michael was smiling. "Kat has made an enormously important point. Kat? What's your definition of pride?" he asked as though he knew the answer before she said it.

"To put out the best possible product, to do my best work," she said with conviction.

"You made two comments before. The second was regarding competition," he said, pausing to get her acknowledgment.

"You may not realize it but competition is the only way you'll ever know if you're putting out your best work. It's the only benchmark you can use to measure. You can compete with yourself but you can't know how you stack up globally. Pride is excelling relative to standards—whether they are low, average, world-class," he said, waiting as Kat smiled and nodded.

"Yes, you're right. When competition gives me that—I don't mind it at all," she said.

"Your first comment regarded reaching down to find your motivation. Just when does that happen? Can you distinguish the circumstances?"

"Well. . . I guess it's mostly when I can't find the admirers of my work, or when I'm unable to communicate my message. I guess it's when my work is rejected," she said.

"What's the antithesis of being down when your work is not recognized, Kat?"

"Being motivated by the opposite, when it *is* recognized," she said in a tone of complete agreement as though Michael was still speaking.

"Finally, the point you made about pride and money being all wrapped together . . . you've made some critical connections. Now, integrate that with the motives of competition as a measure . . . and the motive of recognition of the quality of your work with pride and money. What do you get?" he asked.

"One big motivation mess," she laughed. "It all seems to be related."

"Yes. Which takes us back to Kyle. Have you decided whether you're motivated by competing, winning, or passing someone else on the way to achieving your values?"

"I think I get it. Competition isn't what motivates me. Gaining values is the motivator. Competition just tells me how well I'm doing in my pursuit," said Kyle.

"So we have a bag full of motivation—money, pride, competition, winning. What we want to determine is whether there are different motivators for each person, or whether they are all linked. Sales Esteem holds that they are part of a process of motivation—one that has a chronological order, and a process that is dependent on its sequential parts. The first is to initiate the energy. I'll get us started."

He restarted the slide projector and brought up a familiar slide.

Michael turned to the group. "Let's build the list."

Ryan spoke first. "Desire and Drive," he said.

"Determination," said Kat.

"Enthusiasm," said Madison.

"Excitement."

"Anticipation."

Michael wrote furiously to keep up with their rapid-fire answers.

Initiation of Values
- Desire
- Drive
- Determination
- Enthusiasm
- Excitement
- Anticipation

"These are the 'get-you-going' motivators . . . I think the most important. They're the energy that allows you to put your shoulder against the boulder and start pushing. They're the motivators that are most fragile as well. They're available the first time anything is attempted on the basis of hope. But if the principles and actions fail—or worse, are unethical, the next time you call on the initiation motivators, they'll likely fade."

"You're contradicting yourself," stated Fischer. "You said emotions are a result—but they are the catalyst here."

"Really. Can you tell me which of them has no purpose? How can we have an emotion of desire without something to want for? What is drive if it has no destination? What is enthusiasm?" he asked.

"It's still a starting point. It's an attitude."

"Remember our photograph of the convenience store and the hostage held inside. Do you suppose the S.W.A.T. team in front is enthusiastic about the circumstance? Change the context. Substitute the redemption of a winning lottery ticket for the hostage situation with an off-duty policeman the lucky winner. Emotions are results. Initiation motivators are an emotional result to the anticipated outcome of effort," said Michael, choosing not to waste time on Fischer's mistakes.

"Now begins our sequence of motivation. We've applied energy to the actions through initiation. Now things start to happen, and what is the next motivator?"

"Here's where competition fits in, right?" asked Kyle excitedly.

"Yes, that's right, but it's not limited simply to competition. We'll use a broader category to name the motivators in this category."

He went back to the white board and added it to the list.

Measurement

"Before we begin our flirtation with the complex issue of competition, let's start at the basics of measures. What's required for any type of measure?" asked Michael.

"Standards, goals, time—sometimes all of them," said Madison.

"Why are they necessary? Can't we just put on blinders and keep the effort and energy turned on."

"Perhaps for short periods of time. But human cognition seeks starts and finishes. It helps us in our mental categorization. No matter what we do, we generally have a pretty good road map for checking our progress. It's probably because we need periodic rest to survive," said Madison.

"What type of measures are there in selling?"

"Goal setting and review. Quotas. And competition."

"I refer to this as the achievement level. Our primary values are seldom realized all at once—or even in a compact time period. Whether it's planting wheat or selling, our values are typically achieved in piecemeal fashion along the way and we need feedback to be certain we are getting there. Not only that, but we need benchmarks: low standards, average standards, and high standards to determine to what degree we're putting forth the necessary amount of effort. In its purest form—and believe me, it has been bastardized frequently—but in its purest form, this measurement is what we call competition. For some people, the thrill of competing is a turn-on. But look at what's required. You must have a targeted value as the goal of the competition, you need the skill, knowledge, purpose, etc. in order to compete for the value, and you have to have confidence that your pursuit of it will be treated justly.

"Competition is a measure of the pursuit of values. Cynics treat it as though it were a dirty and undesirable human trait that leaves losers wounded or broken. Accomplishment, achievement and competition all measure progress toward the acquisition of a value. It's okay to enjoy competition, it's an affirmation of realizing values. The overall emotional result is *self-respect*.

"Notice once again that these emotions are results, effects not causes.

"And now we are nearing our goals." He brought up the next slide. "Attainment," he said and turned around. "We discussed money this morning. Would you agree that money, as the representation and exchange of value, should fall into this category?"

Shaking heads gave him his answer as he went back to the white board.

Measurement
- Recognition
- Competition

"What else would you add?" he asked.

"These should tie in with the primary values at the bottom, right?" asked Madison.

"They have to."

"Then money is the attainment of living values," she said.

"Right. But don't forget that money is just a representation of value—your value. So it can also be symbolic of certain happiness values, like self-esteem. While I don't believe you measure people by the money they have, per se, if it was gained because of the value they brought to others who were willing to pay for that value, then it has significant self-esteem value."

"What about other happiness values?" she asked.

"What about them?"

"Most seem to be connected to the individual's view of themselves . Would this be the place for motivators like recognition. . . . and admiration?" she asked.

"Exactly," said Michael. "Recognition signals that the values being pursued—and the manner in which they are being pursued, are important or 'worthy.' This tells the individual that others realize their worth in achieving the values."

Ryan jumped in. "What about prestige, influence and respect?"

"Respect from others, yes. Self-respect on the other hand falls into our next category, and is far more important. What do you suppose that final category is?" asked Michael, scribbling on the white board as he spoke.

Attainment
- Achievement
- Compensation
- Admiration
- Respect
- Prestige
- Influence

"What can you have after you've reached your values?" asked Shannon Shelley.

"You tell me."

"I don't know."

"It has to do with our premise that emotions are the barometer of our actions and their results. If we are going to complete the motivational scale, shouldn't we include an end-point—the ultimate emotional destination?"

"Self-esteem," Ryan practically cried out. "The top of the arrow is self-esteem. It's like reaching the top of the mountain and looking back at the path you took. It's seeing everything from the pinnacle. Kind of an all-encompassing view of what you hold important, how you pursue your dreams, how you treat people and yourself, how you go about living. And you end up with the whole thing; all of the emotions—satisfaction, pride, and happiness. Self-esteem." Ryan's voice was broken with emotion but strong and full of purpose.

Michael walked over to Ryan and sat on the desk in front of him. His hand rested gently on his shoulder as he spoke to the rest of the group. The gesture was so personal that Ryan could practically feel Michael's pleasure at his breakthrough.

"It's a wonderful thing when the clouds clear and you realize that you knew the answer, but had forgotten along the way," said Michael. "I would imagine you feel a little lighter right now, Mr. Matthews."

"Like I could float away, Michael. Thank you!" It was said with a genuine richness that left no doubt about its sincerity.

"The final emotional aspect is that of the all-encompassing view of your efforts, and of yourself— self-esteem," said Michael.

There was a long silence as Michael gripped Ryan's shoulder and rose to return to the front of the room. Fischer and Shaw exchanged a cynical look. Fischer shook his head, but didn't have the courage to speak. Shaw felt detached and resented it. His worst fears were coming true. Ryan had discovered something that Shaw couldn't understand. He was lost in anger and frustration. His only thought was about what could be done to pull Ryan back into his web when they got back home.

Michael surveyed the room and found just what he expected. There was a look of depth on the faces of the group—as though they were discovering unknown expanses of hope and excitement. All except Fischer and Shaw. He moved toward the two of them and continued speaking.

"There is, of course, the antithesis of the Sales Esteem theory and its motivational equivalents." Michael poked at the control panel on the slide projector and brought up the next slide. "We all, essentially, pursue the same primary values, however, the methods we use—our principles—may be different."

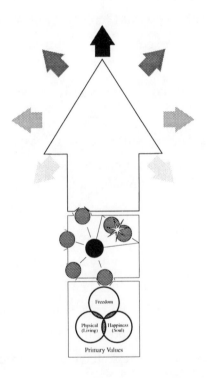

"Instead of hanging together, these principles begin to bang into each other— they contradict or collide. When that happens, the energy being applied to them can't possibly be efficient. This is the explanation of why the 'wrong' customers consume more energy than they are worth. Like pushing the boulder from all sides, contradictory principles push our efforts around in different directions— often in self-defeating directions that waste energy.

"Cause and effect rules this paradigm. Positive emotions, the kind that lead to extraordinary levels of effort, don't arrive without cause. The Sales Esteem

Motivation Theory states that human energy is initiated on the basis of expected success. You simply can't have a consistent model of success unless you subscribe to the principle of certainty. The result is enthusiasm, excitement and drive because you anticipate the realization of your primary values. This may be the most important aspect of motivation. It's the initiation, the catalyst, the starting point. It's believing you can be successful and expending the energy on the activities that will cause that success. Can anyone mount an argument that the same emotions would come from the principle of 'chance'?" he asked.

Ryan still held the look of discovery. "No," he said. "If chance means random success, without cause, all you would have is 'hope'—blind luck."

"But Ryan, people get excited and enthusiastic about the lottery?" asked Michael.

Ryan's smile turned down so suddenly it brought a quick chuckle from Michael.

"Emotions are easy. Being enthusiastic is easy. Drive is a different matter altogether. The superficial emotions can be conjured up without cost—and without gain. It's the effective emotions like drive and determination that are both costly and valuable. Do you see the difference?" asked Michael.

"I sure do!" interrupted Kat. "You know, Michael, it seems to me that most sales motivators traffic in the cheap motivators," she said.

"Can you explain the difference?"

"Every other sales seminar I have ever been to relies on . . . . what's the right word . . . hype. They're all 'feel-good' fluff fests that get the audience to chant 'I-think-I-can' slogans. None of them have ever proposed motivators that cost something," she said.

"Excellent, Kat. And what do you suppose the price is?"

"Principles are the price—and you get what you pay for. Who wants hope when I can get drive and determination," she said.

"Let's move on. Can you give me the cheap and the 'real' version of Recognition Motivators?"

Madison answered. "Sure. If chance, or emotion or worse, deception got you the rewards, they take on a practically meaningless value . . . unless . . . ," she stopped.

"Unless what?" Michael pressed.

"Unless you're corrupt," she finished.

"Why did you hesitate?" he insisted.

"Because corruption has the opposite definition of integrity. Integrity is the holding together of principles—corruption is their disintegration," she said.

"Do you like the conceptual soundness?"

"It's elegant."

"Thank you," he said with pride. "If our measures—competition and recognition—as well as our attainment motivators of compensation, achievement and prestige, are fair, then they act as affirming motivators and propel us on to the next effort. If, however, they come to us without cause (because of chance or worse, they're granted as favors, or worse yet, they are the result of a corrupt ethic), how difficult is it to regain the Initiation Motivators when it's time to begin the cycle again?"

"It's the reason people abandon sales careers, Michael," said Ryan. "I was dangerously close."

"Yes, Ryan. It is the reason. Not only does it have the impact of reducing our energy, but when the initiation motivators are gone, it's a near-impossibility to go on. My personal opinion is that deep down, we're all brutally honest with ourselves. It's how we maintain our sanity. And when we attempt to fake things we have deep, subconscious conflicts that nag, and then ultimately, tear at our souls," he said.

"On the other hand, real emotions—earned motivators—that come from sincere and earned recognition and success magnify our energy."

There were nods throughout the room. "And finally . . . the last motivator. One I believe is the key to all the productivity gains to be found in Sales Esteem— the cumulative view—Self-Esteem. It's the knowledge that your principles were sound, that they had integrity and did not fall apart when tested, that you pursued them with the right emotions—earned emotions based on your knowledge—and that you provided value with a purpose, for which you were fairly compensated. It's the all-encompassing view that says you did the right things the right way. And you can do them again, and again, and again. That is the key to unparalleled sales success. Finding that motivation that never runs dry, that keeps you going no matter what the circumstance." Michael pressed the control to bring up the next slide.

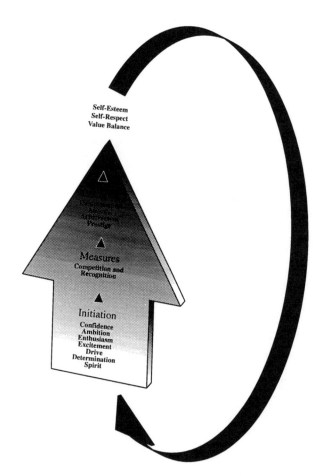

Motivation Cycle

"The motivation cycle is simple. If your principles are correct, your actions work. Good principles give you confidence and courage. Success along the way feeds your values, and finally the Happiness Values—the view of yourself—which is far more powerful than money, or anything tangible, propels you to continue your actions. At that point, depending on how good your principles are, comes an unlimited supply of energy to do more, work harder, achieve more." He paused.

"The arrow expands and grows. Your motivation expands and grows. It's unlimited," he said, pressing the remote to bring up the next slide.

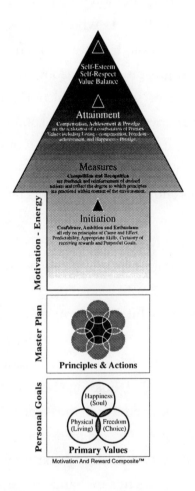

This was a critical point when the foundation of Sales Esteem could be viewed and integrated. This was the apex of grasping Sales Esteem. He paced back and forth waiting for questions. Typically, this was a moment of silence at the conference. There was a lot to consider. He waited for quite some time, even though the class didn't notice. All were deep in thought—all except Fischer and Shaw. They fumed quietly. The line was clearly drawn. They hadn't listened to much of what was said, preferring to avoid it. Both sat, contemplating the bridge, and the run, and their anticipation of watching another disaster occur. It would be their only victory of the week, but they didn't think of it in those terms. It started as a diversion, but had become payback. The bridge, the run—confidence shaken, trust destroyed—chaos. It was all they had left.

Ryan Matthews wasn't deep in thought either. He was far beyond that, having spent months asking the questions to which he now held the answers. It was as though he had been falling through space through a dark empty void, searching for answers, reaching and grasping for reasons, and unable to cling to anything. Where there was once chaos and contradictions, he now saw clean lines of integrated logic. Newly discovered ideas were coming together in one harmonious philosophy. He felt a surge of energy—psychological energy he had never experienced. Then came a memory of his son Casey, climbing a fence in the back yard and looking over his shoulder to capture his father's proud smile. The smile that had come across his face cried out to his father in the desire to gain his pride. The same kind of pride that Ryan desired to see in his son's face when Ryan was the focus. It was his favorite memory of Casey and it occurred to him that he hadn't held the memory for months—not since his agony had begun. Tears welled up in Ryan's eyes as he realized its significance. He no longer felt ashamed in his son's eyes. He felt proud again. Now his mind's eye saw the two of them at the park, he lofting Casey high into the air, Casey laughing with joy, the two of them; Ryan with his arms fully extended, holding Casey to the heights of his love for the boy, spinning around in circles and lost in the essence of life. A tear streaked across his face, but the smile remained. He had made the journey and found his soul.

Michael noticed the tears and realized what he was witnessing. They caught each other's stare. In that moment's exchange there was a mutual understanding of the values each held, and the gifts given and received. Michael's nod confirmed Ryan's long climb out of the darkness.

He pressed the remote control to bring up the next slide. "Which gets us to this point," he said.

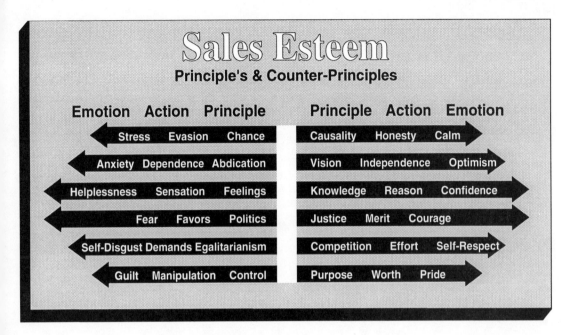

"The principle of being *guided-by-knowledge* leads to the action of *reason* and the emotion of *confidence*. Its opposite is to be *guided-by-feelings*, which can lead to actions motivated by *sensations* and ending eventually in feelings of *helplessness*.

Up came the next slide. "Here's the Sales Esteem paradigm," said Michael.

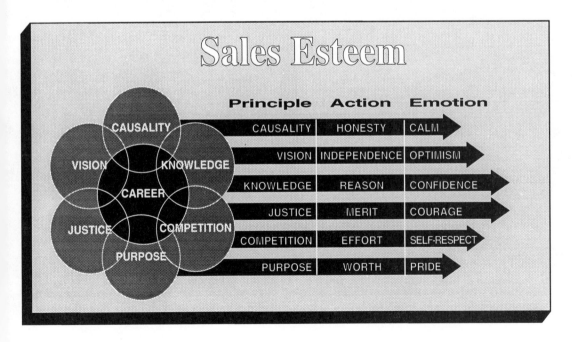

"We'll begin again tomorrow morning on the path," Michael said, jarring them from their deep thoughts. "Madison, we have a special guest tomorrow morning who has heard about your record breaking timetable on the path and would like to join us for the run. You probably recognize the name Kendra McKinney," he said coyly.

"You're joking," said Madison.

"I'm not. Seems she remembers when you used to stumble around the track in college," Michael said, grinning.

"Kendra's coming here?" Madison asked in genuine surprise.

"She hasn't challenged you to run on the path—yet. I'll leave that up to the two of you. See everyone else in the morning," he said.

13
Compromise

Take the course opposite to custom and
you will almost always do well.
—*Jean Jacques Rousseau*

As the class left the room, Rick Kincaid lingered to talk with Michael. The room emptied as Michael was gathering his papers.

"Michael, can I talk to you for a few minutes?" he asked.

"Sure, Rick. What's on your mind?"

"I'm not sure how to explain it, but I think it's a terrible mistake that I'm here," he said. He expected Michael to react strongly, but it didn't happen.

"Would you like to talk about it?" asked Michael.

"Is it unusual to have non-salespeople like me at the conference?" asked Kincaid.

"No, Rick, we have had people from all walks of life here. Anyone who considers themselves to be involved in persuasion of some form can find something of value here," Michael said.

"Well, I feel out of place," he snapped.

"Sit down for a moment, Rick." Michael moved to a table near the windows. "If you feel out of place, there must be a reason. Do you know why?"

"Yes."

"You don't need to explain it to me. You're free to leave the conference at anytime—we'll return your tuition," said Michael with an encouraging tone.

"Yes, I think that's the best thing to do," Kincaid stuttered slightly. He looked slightly dazed as he got up to leave.

Michael rose with him and patted him gently on the back. "Good luck," he said.

Kincaid walked through the door as Michael returned to the task of cleaning up the slide projector. A moment later Kincaid came back in, this time in a rush.

"Life isn't black and white," said Kincaid, just short of a shout. "It just doesn't work that way."

Michael spun around and said softly with the voice as gentle as a grandfather's, "What do you mean, Rick?"

"You expect me to change everything I am for your principles. You expect me to start from scratch," he accused.

"Rick, I have no interest in tearing your world down. It's not our mission. No one has insisted you accept a single word uttered here. It isn't easy to change your principles. You've had them for a very long time."

Kincaid paced back and forth, his forefinger and thumb rubbing his forehead. "Michael, I feel trapped in the middle. You make it an "either/or" issue. It's not. There's always room in the middle."

"The world can be a funny place, Rick. People choose sides. There's the 'mind-over-reality' group, or the 'mind-according-to-reality' group. The 'mind-over' group wants to massage reality. The 'mind-according' group wants to use reality as a rock foundation. The clashes are everywhere. Socialism versus capitalism. Lawless versus lawful. Subjective versus objective. Feelings versus reason. There are black and white lines. There are absolutes. Compromise insults the staunchest of either camp. You're trying to get the two of them to agree. I think you're in a terribly difficult position."

"I don't think I understand. You make it sound irreconcilable."

"Rick, your basic premise is that people can work together so long as there is a give and take. Am I mistaken?" asked Michael.

"No."

"And your approach is to discover weaknesses in each side's convictions to find that common ground, yes or no?"

"It's called a compromise."

"Yes, a compromise of the principles held by each group. Instead of finding the common ground, you distill it down to those things that neither group will compromise on. Instead of driving them towards principles that benefit them both, you drive them farther apart. You create conflict instead of eliminating it. You shear off all the surrounding issues, as minor inconveniences, and strike right to the area of the greatest conflict. For instance, job security. It's definitely a 'mind-over-reality' issue. Job security doesn't exist on its own. It's an intellectual fabrication. The question is whether the whole of the organization can deliver something of value to the buyer in a competitive marketplace. If not, the company is *incapable* of a promise of job security. It can be tried and will eventually run the company into bankruptcy, but it's likely the company will break promises first. Instead of a 'call-to-arms' for the company to produce at a competitive price, the false promise of job security lulls them to sleep," said Michael.

"All you're saying is that labor should roll over for management. We'll be back to the era of human bondage if that's the case," argued Rick.

"Rick, I don't think you really believe that. Employers don't want slave labor. The reality of any business is that you have a group of individuals whose only reason to come together is the concept of the division of labor. Division of labor has a single goal—productivity. The organization exists solely for the purpose of enhancing productivity. The moment productivity becomes a secondary concern, the organization begins to unravel. Increasing pay on the basis of the number of years on the job does nothing to increase productivity. It's a 'mind-over- reality' issue. How do you compromise on fictitious ideas like that? The best you can hope for is to be *partly* wrong, and bleed the company to death more slowly," he said.

"Rick, can you imagine the value you would bring to your labor negotiations if your approach was to keep both parties from straying from the common ground that brought them together in the first place?"

"There is no common ground. It's a war. Two sides, and one always loses a little more than the other."

"There's not an ounce of truth in that statement. Why do you think they got together to begin with? I have had arbitrators, negotiators and mediators at the conference before, and they have all had a difficult time drawing black and whites. Our society says be a moderate, everyone is entitled to their opinion, do whatever you feel, freedom of thought. But the reality of our little world is that there *are* absolutes—opinions are tested, doing whatever you feel often dumps you in the human refuse bin of drug users or those waiting on death row. The world isn't a compromise. Averages don't happen. Those in your profession who have grasped this have become the leaders in the field," he said.

"I can't change. I don't want to change. They need me for what I do, and that's to resolve disputes. If there is no dispute, then there is no need for me. I think you live in an ivory tower. You need to get your feet back on the ground." Kincaid stood to leave.

"Rick, an organization is a social construct. If you believe people seek to exploit others by their nature, I can see how you believe there must be a continuous dispute. But look around you. The successful organizations don't thrive because the individual is exploited. They thrive because the individual is uninhibited. If your livelihood is built upon the idea that exploitation and the resulting conflict is unavoidable, then your solutions will only lead to more of the same. You're a Band-Aid instead of a cure. Where do your principles fall into all of this? It may be more honest to take a side, even if it's the wrong side, than to blow in the wind without a moral base."

"Michael. I don't care about your principles if that's how you define them. I need these people to need me. I need them to be in disarray. It's what I do for a living." He was leaning forward against the desk, his hands clenching the edge.

"I think I should leave the conference," said Kincaid. He expected that this would persuade Michael to take a mitigating view and encourage him to stay.

Michael laughed slightly at the irony. "Yes, Rick. Somewhat of a contradiction to stay here when you've stated you have no interest in our principles, isn't it? We'll refund your tuition and pay for your return trip. Good luck, I hope you find an answer." Michael stood to shake his hand.

Kincaid looked surprised. "Afraid I'll raise questions you can't answer in front of the group?" he asked.

Michael smiled again. "No, in case you haven't noticed, I like an antagonist in class. I'm not interested in taking your money when there's nothing that I can do for you." He reached for Rick's hand and shook it firmly. "Good luck, Rick," he said again with a tone of finality. Rick paused and stared at Michael for a moment. Michael nodded his head and released Rick's hand. He seemed to waiver and didn't notice Michael picking up a stack of books. Michael shoved the books under his arm and headed for the door. Kincaid was sitting now, not realizing that he had slumped into the chair nearby. Michael turned at the door. "Get the lights on the way out, will you?" he asked.

Kincaid just nodded and looked out at the spectacular view of the lake below. He had a strange feeling that he might never see such a sight again—the view might be as grand, but the circumstances would never be the same. He rose and walked slowly to the door and paused there, turning around for one last look at the conference room. He realized he was leaving behind something he couldn't fully understand or forget. He felt empty and lost—and suddenly sad.

The room was still. The sun was on its last retreat as he stood in the doorway. It dipped below the horizon with a final burst of red and was gone. The shadows of the room changed, transforming it into a cold box of steel and glass. Rick had made the same transformation—from the hope of daylight to the dark and cold of a disagreeing world. He flipped the light switch off and left the room even darker, and wondering when he would see the light again.

14
The Bridge

There are few things more inspiring
than a great fight and the two
wary competitors standing at the end,
a winner and a loser—both victorious.
—Michael Cevanté

The bolt squeaked once and then jammed. Fischer pushed a screwdriver into the half-empty hole and used a rock to punch it the rest of the way out. It popped out the end and bounced down to the stream below, clattering softly on the way down. Using the rock, he banged the base of the pier, knocking it off the edge of its concrete footing and onto a two-by-four stud he had wedged into place against the footing. The bridge shook as its supporting beam was moved. Shaw crouched in the brush, fearful that Fischer would bring the bridge down on top of them. The bridge shook again. Shaw shuddered.

"You're sure it'll just scare 'em," asked Shaw.

"Shut up and look for yourself. When the bridge collapses, whoever's on it will fall a few feet to the ridge right there," said Fischer, pointing to the hillside. "The rest of 'em will be stuck on the other side. Let's get out of here."

They scurried up the hillside and disappeared into the trees. Two hundred feet up the hillside the group had gathered for their last run. Kevin and Madison were sitting together and stretching. Their casual conversation was betrayed by their thoughts of the time they had spent together at the conference. Madison didn't want it to end. Keller wasn't sure he could stand the thought of not seeing her again.

"I want you to move to Phoenix so we can be together," he said.

"What's wrong with Portland?" she smiled back.

Keller started to speak, but was interrupted by Michael's hand on his shoulder. "Excuse me, but I think a quick reunion is in order," Michael said.

Kendra McKinney stood beside Michael with a grin as wide as a child's. "Hello, Madison. You look wonderful. Are you slowing down at all?"

Madison jumped to her feet. "Never," she said as they embraced.

"Michael tells me you're trying to set some record on his 'obstacle course' today."

"I think he's more excited about it than I am," she said coyly.

"Uh-huh," said Michael. "And I'm the one that has you running it twice a day instead of once like everyone else?"

Madison gave up nothing but a smile in response. "I've followed your career. You've been through a lot. Congratulations," she said to Kendra.

"Thank you. That's very kind," she replied. "Do you mind if I run with you?"

Madison flashed a look at Michael, pursed her lips and said. "*He* did this, *didn't* he?"

"Of course. He thinks you can better his record. I think he's tired of holding it."

"I don't believe that for a moment," she laughed. "Just take it easy on me if you don't mind."

The group had gathered around them as they spoke. Michael waved them a little closer. "Please, everyone. Let me make an informal introduction. Please welcome Kendra McKinney, silver-medalist from the Barcelona Olympics and world-record holder in the women's 400 meters. I told her Madison was having fun beating up on the path record, and she wanted to come out and play too," he chuckled.

"Later, she's going to join us for our discussion. But first, we're going to let the two of them run side-by-side, if that's okay with you, Madison?" he asked, turning towards Madison.

Madison nodded. "Is this supposed to humble me, or make me want to go faster?" she asked.

"My guess is that you'll go faster. What do you think?"

"Are you kidding?" she replied.

"Kendra, when you're finished stretching, we'll go." He looked down at the ground where she had plopped to start her stretch. "I've already sent Bobby and Sally. Sally couldn't wait any longer," he said laughing. "Kendra, we'll start you first with Madison starting ten seconds behind. Try not to leave her in the dust," he smiled at Madison.

"Very funny."

"Kevin and I will be right behind you to make sure you two don't push and shove while on the playground."

"Uh-huh."

"Isn't this fun?" teased Michael.

Madison rolled her eyes at him in feigned disgust.

Kendra popped up to her feet and added a few more hamstring stretches. "What's the distance?" she asked.

"About three miles," he said.

"Madison can't run that far, can she?" she said grinning, and enjoying the routine Michael had begun. They walked to the point where the path entered the trees and paused there. Kendra extended her open hand. It was met by Madison's. Their fingers locked gently for a moment. Their eyes came together and they shared the joy of the challenge. They squeezed each other's hand softly and separated.

It was a genuinely touching moment that wouldn't last for long. There was too much fun to be had. Kendra's joyful look turned playful. "Ready?" she asked, waiting for a nod from Madison. She waited just a moment for the nod to come and then bolted into a sprint, like a school-aged kid grabbing the advantage with a surprise start. Madison took off after her immediately and let go a scream like the she would on a roller-coaster ride. Michael and Kevin looked at each other and started laughing, then realized they would have a tough time keeping up and with a theatrical look of panic on their faces, chased Madison and Kendra into the forest.

Kendra glided along the path. Madison kept pace, making certain not to let her put any distance between them. The pace was startling. Michael and Kevin were struggling to keep up. The steamy hot air seemed to thin out as the two women rushed through it. Kendra's near-perfect technique was a beautiful display of sheer skill, honed by years of training. Her effortless movements propelled her up and down the winding trail. She ducked and dodged the tree limbs with mechanical precision. Madison mirrored her moves, but with considerably more effort required. Her physical skill was no match for Kendra's, but they both knew the power of competition and the effort it could unleash. Madison was in her own personal heaven. Her pure joy of running was raised another level by the chance to run beside a track goddess. It was a test of her love of running as much as her physical ability.

They crossed the halfway mark, separated by no more than twenty feet. Kendra was running smoothly and getting stronger. Madison was pressing hard and starting to tire. Michael and Kevin were a hundred yards back, running as fast as possible and laughing out loud at the absurdity of how easily the two women were devouring the path.

Where the path crossed the stream, Kendra would soar over its entire width, her powerful hurdling style making a mockery of the low lying obstacles. Madison witnessed a few of the hurdles and attempted to mimic them, stumbling slightly from time to time when she failed to cover the full distance. The successful attempts brought a smile to her face and injected a new shot of energy into her entire body. She noticed she was gaining ground. She focused on every step, feeling the strength in her legs push her forward, momentarily exhilarated with each new step. She could feel her momentum increase, even while she was beginning to feel the strain of the extreme exertion. She closed the gap to ten feet— close enough for Kendra to hear her heavy breathing. Kendra pushed harder, but didn't add any distance to her lead.

They were practically side by side, Kendra yet to kick in her final effort and Madison at the peak of her ability, both physically and mentally. The competition blurred into a shared celebration of performing at a peak, under challenging circumstances, against a worthy opponent. Kendra, out of her element, but possessing superior physical skill and Madison, a skilled runner *in her element*, had the advantage of passion—the intangible they both knew made champions out of 'lesser gods'. Madison darted ahead momentarily and then lost her lead when Kendra hurdled over eight feet of river bed and right past her. They traded positions again, Kendra strong and in control, Madison pushed to the edge and nearly expended.

They were within a mile of the finish, climbing up out of the ravine and heading for the ridge that lead the path to the bridge. Bobby and Sally had started side by side two minutes before Kendra and stayed that way when they crossed the bridge. Its timbers shuddered under the weight. The support beam slid a half an inch but caught the edge of the wood stud Fischer had left behind, stopping it from sliding completely from its concrete base. The bridge held.

With a thump, Kendra's foot caught a limb, sending her sprawling to the ground. She gained her feet, one knee bloodied, and scrambled to get running again. She was fifty feet back and would need all she could gather to cut the gap. Madison had heard Kendra go down, hesitated as she considered stopping to help, and then continued. Kendra's speed was even more impressive than before. They were within a half mile of the bridge when Kendra had closed the gap. Madison was nearly spent, but pressed harder still. Kendra moved side-by-side with her and the two allowed their eyes to stray from the path to catch the gaze of the other. For a moment there was a look between them that they would never experience again. The race they engaged was carefree and of little importance, but the joy of competition at this level was ecstasy. A smile crossed both their lips. Kendra pulled away and Madison pushed harder to stay on her heel. Kendra hurled her body over one last expanse of creek bed of broken rocks. The distance was simply too great for Madison to match. She was forced to bounce from one large rock to the next. It cost her twenty feet that she would never make up. Kendra bounded across the bridge. It rattled violently with her powerful steps. The beam below bounced twice and slid off the footing, shattering when the weight of the bridge above compressed the beam at an angle in the rocks below. Madison's first step onto the bridge coincided with the beams thunder-like clap. The bridge lurched to the side of the broken beam and dropping violently out from underneath Madison's feet. Her momentum carried her forward and down as she was sent sprawling forward. Her last awkward contact with the bridge threw her into a flying tumble which ended with a crash against the soft grassy ledge of the opposite bank. The impact was so great that she bounced off the wall of the ledge and was thrown back towards the edge of the embankment. Madison shrieked in pain as she rolled across the ledge and over the crest, reaching out to grasp a tree limb just before plummeting to the rocky creek bottom thirty feet below. She dangled over the ledge, clinging to the limb, too exhausted to pull herself back up.

Kendra heard the scream and returned to the bridge. Michael and Kevin had heard it as well. They were a hundred and fifty yards away and broke into a sprint when they realized there was trouble, Kevin leaving his faster partner behind when he realized Madison could be in trouble. Less than a minute later he had the fallen bridge in sight and could see Madison clinging to the side, and Kendra laying on the ground above her clasping her wrist, trying to pull her up, her hand slipping slightly as she struggled to maintain her hold. Kevin was within twenty feet and had already decided on the only possible action that could keep Madison from falling. He gathered himself for a running jump as he came to the edge, even though he realized he couldn't jump the full width of the creek's banks. He picked out the thickest looking vine among those that fell from the edge and dangled near Madison. At full speed he lifted himself up and out like a long-jumper, soaring across the crevice, and landing chest-first, vertically against the hillside, with a thud that pressed the wind from his lungs.

It would have been a wonderful opportunity to say something clever but he could hardly breathe. Madison's eyes were wide with surprise. The only word she could get out was his name, gasping it out and wondering if it would be the last thing she said to him.

His left hand found the vine and with the other he grabbed her at the inner thigh and with surprising force thrust her toward Kendra. Kendra jerked her forward at just the right moment, pulling her onto the bank, as she fell backward. The physics of Kevin's maneuver was costly. With one arm outstretched and holding his entire weight, he exerted three times the amount of weight the vine could hold. It held the stress just long enough for him to give Kendra the surge she needed to drag Madison to safety before snapping. With a 'pop' the vine broke and left him grasping for another as he fell backward, arms flapping as he struggled to keep his body upright. He bounced off the side of the rock wall and felt an icy pain shoot through his shoulder, just before he struck a large boulder that collapsed his legs and halted his fall. The impact with the rock sent his body sideways the few remaining feet to the river bed below. He groaned and went unconscious.

Michael reached the edge to see the last few seconds of the fall. He was already starting down the embankment by the time Keller's body came to rest at the bottom. Madison could see him lying motionless on the river bed. She cried out to him but got no answer, as tears streaked down a face unaccustomed to crying.

Michael slid to a stop next to Keller, putting a finger to his throat to find a pulse that was stronger than he expected. He tried to pry one of Keller's eyelids open, which caused Keller to shake his head and come to. It was a better sign than he could have hoped for.

"How bad is it?" he muttered, barely conscious.

"Just a scratch, hero. Lay back and let me look it over."

"Is Madison okay?"

"Yeah. Fine. You're not so good, though. Looks like a compound fracture of your leg and your shoulder is all messed up. Not in shock yet. How do you feel?"

"Like I ejected at twenty thousand feet," he groaned.

"You've seen worse. Just relax and we'll get you through it."

They were within a hundred yards of the Summit Center. Michael debated whether wrapping his sweaty T-shirt around the exposed fracture would risk infection, but was persuaded by the pooling blood that was pumping from the wound. He pulled it off, tore it into two pieces, and quickly tied a tourniquet above the exposed bone. He wound the second piece around the wound gently and moved close to Keller's face.

"Here," he said shoving a small tree branch into his mouth for Keller to bite down on.

"Trust me, this is going to hurt *you* more than *me*. Are you ready?" he asked, looking more deeply into his friend's eyes than ever before.

Keller nodded and bit down on the branch. The others had reached them and were peering down from the bank above. Kendra and Madison were leaning over the edge in a controlled panic.

Michael yelled up to them. "He's going to be okay, Maddy. Kendra, can you get back to the Summit and call an ambulance?" he said.

He turned back to Keller. "Here we go. You're going to have to help a little." He pushed Keller up against a near-by tree to get him upright. Keller cringed in pain. He slipped an arm under Keller's good leg and looped Kevin's arm over his shoulder. "One . . . two . . . threee-uh." He lifted Keller onto his shoulder. Keller groaned. Michael groaned.

"Hold on buddy. We're going to be okay," he said. Keller bit down on the branch.

Michael moved slowly along the river bed until he could climb up to the trail that ran along its full length. The blood from Keller's wound had soaked the wrap and was leaving splotches in the dirt behind them. Michael rocked back and forth as he walked, trying desperately to avoid the sudden jolts that would cause a muffled grunt of pain from Kevin. Kendra had followed the path back to the Summit while Madison wound her way back down to the path Michael was following. She met them fifty yards from the building, more composed now, and put her face to Keller's.

"Hi. How do you feel?" she said as calmly as she could.

He grunted and she noticed the branch in his mouth. She gasped lightly as she was suddenly aware of the pain he must be experiencing.

They came to the base of the wooden stairs that lead to the Summit above. The stairs were more like a ladder, climbing nearly vertical up the side of the hill.

"Madison. This is going to be the toughest part. Get in front of me," he said.

Michael put his left hand on her shoulder and gripped it firmly. It hurt but she didn't acknowledge it. He used her shoulder as a moving crutch. They climbed lock-step up the stairs slowly. Keller's eyes closed in pain as the climb jarred his leg.

Kyle and Ryan backed down the steep stairway and positioned themselves on either side of Michael, grabbing him by the elbow to help lift him through each step. At the top, they hurried him into the waiting ambulance, Michael and Madison hurrying in behind. Michael turned to Kendra, Ryan and Kyle who stood behind the ambulance.

"Ryan, I think everything will be fine, and the show must go on. It's almost nine now. Have everyone shower, eat a long breakfast and then get everyone into the room. If I'm not back by 10:30, I want you to calm them down, and introduce

Kendra. She's been through this before and can take it from there. Can you do that for me?" he asked. Ryan nodded.

"Kendra. Can you afford a delay?"

"Sure. Already got my workout for the day," she said with a reassuring smile.

"Thanks. We'll be back as soon as Kevin's stable."

The ambulance doors slammed shut as it pulled out of the lot and onto the highway. The paramedics were scrambling to relieve the pain and stop the bleeding, working around Madison as she held Kevin's hand. Michael kneeled next to Madison, both of them working up reassuring smiles for Kevin's benefit. Kevin was drifting in and out of consciousness, suffering from a serious head concussion.

"I would be laying there right now if it weren't for him," said Madison.

"Yeah . . . I know," said Michael."

"He doesn't do this sort of thing for people," she stammered.

"What gave you that idea?"

"He told me he wouldn't have sacrificed his life for mine on the mountain."

"He wasn't in love with you then."

Madison didn't answer. Instead she turned and stared at Michael for a long moment, and then back to Kevin. Her hand pressed harder against his, causing him to open his eyes long enough to see the tears in hers. He closed them again and smiled a brief, pained smile.

15

Scene of the Crime

Half the work that is done in this world is to
make things appear what they are not.

—*Elias Root Beadle*

Ryan was finishing his last sip of coffee as Shaw and Fischer strolled into the dining room and joined a small group at a nearby table. He and Kendra were rewriting the conference agenda to account for Michael's absence when he overheard Shaw's comment to the group.

"How was the run?" asked Shaw.

The words echoed in Ryan's ear, and played over in his head. *How was the run?* It was completely out of character for Shaw to show any interest. *How was the run?* Jock Shaw couldn't have cared less about the run.

Ryan turned to Kendra with a sudden jerk. "Come with me," he said.

"What? Where to?"

"Come *on!*" he said, already standing.

Kendra followed him from the dining room, down the stairs and out the door that lead to the path.

"What are we doing?" she demanded.

"Michael Cevanté *isn't* careless. How does a bridge collapse at *his* conference? I have a bad feeling about all of this. Come on."

They dropped down to the lower path that ran along the river. It still had the signs of Michael's awkward footsteps and drops of blood. They followed it back to the riverbed where Kevin had fallen. The bridge was partially collapsed, with one side remaining intact and anchored, the other dangling in the air. Ryan noticed two sets of tracks in the deep grass along the river's bank. One set was Michael's, the other lead to the concrete footing that had held the beam of the bridge. Ryan rushed along the second set of tracks. He could see the scrape in the concrete pad left by the beam when it slid from the foundation. The two-by-four lay to the side. There were tracks all around the concrete foundation. The beam had dropped off the pad and into the riverbed below. Ryan scurried down the bank to get a closer look. There he noticed a glint of something metal that was reflecting the sunshine. He reached down and pulled the bolt from a pool of water in the creek.

Kendra was standing on the bank. "What is it?" she said.

"The bolt that anchored the beam into the concrete pad," he said, stepping back up the bank beside her. "Look at the scar on the end."

"Yeah? What do you think that means?"

"It's fresh . . . you know. . . just made. The rest of the bolt is rusted, but this gash is very recent. Why?" he said, wondering aloud.

"Don't know. Maybe it banged against a rock or something," she said.

"No. This is steel on steel. But the only other steel is on the footing. There's nothing that could have marked the bolt in this way." He held the bolt near the concrete foundation and its steel brace, moving it back and forth to recreate the possible path of the bolt as the beam gave way.

Ryan paused for a moment, and then spoke slowly as though recreating the moments before the bridge's collapse. "*Someone* . . . removed . . . the bolt," he said. He and Kendra looked at each other in disbelief. "Son of a bitch. Someone did this on purpose."

"What do we do?" asked Kendra.

"I may know who did this," he said.

"What?"

"Yeah," said Ryan, his eyes burning with anger. "But how do we prove it? It's not much more than a hunch, but I'd bet my last . . . " Ryan's voice trailed off as he thought.

"Who, Ryan, damn it. Will you tell me what you're thinking about?"

"I'd rather not say right now if you don't mind. I'd hate to be wrong about something this serious. But I promise to tell you when I've caught him."

"Fair enough."

16

Reflections in the Mirror

When what I see in another,
is what I wish for in myself,
I have found my lasting friend.

—*Kevin Keller*

The ambulance squealed to a stop and Kevin was whisked away to the waiting operating room. Madison and Kevin followed the team of nurses and technicians through the maze of abrupt corners and swinging doors, finally arriving at the hospital's emergency room. A dozen people swarmed in and out of the room, and buzzed around Kevin. A nurse stopped Michael and Madison at the door. She pressed a white surgical gown into Madison's stomach, forcing her to grab it, turned, and did the same to Michael.

"Here. You'll have to wear these," she said in a slightly annoyed voice at the prospect of having non-essential personnel in the emergency room. A second nurse had slipped behind them and began fastening a surgical mask over Madison's nose and mouth. Once they were both outfitted they moved cautiously toward the operating table where Kevin was being prepared for surgery. He looked very alert, an effect of all of the activity, but in severe pain. An anesthesiologist stood over him asking questions about his weight and previous medical history. A nurse inserted an I-V into his arm and nodded to the doctor that all was ready to put Kevin under. The surgeon spotted them and with a sideways nod of his head and raised eyebrows signaled them to move away from the table. He held his glove-covered hands at eye level and followed Madison and Michael as they moved back toward a corner of the room.

"It's rather straight-forward," said the surgeon. "A compound fracture and head concussion. We're going to put him under and repair the leg. The concussion will be reviewed with scans. The whole thing should take no more than an hour." He nodded and returned to the table, hands still held high.

They edged closer to the table and the surgeon turned and motioned Madison to come to Kevin's side. "He's about to take a little nap. You can tell him you'll see him when he wakes up in a few hours," he said.

Madison drew close to Kevin's face. "Looks like it's not such a big deal after all," she said, smiling to acknowledge that her comment was a veil for her concern for him.

"Yeah . . hhh. . a . . hhh . .walk in the park," said Kevin, forcing his words through the pain.

"You saved my life," she said.

"No . . . I . . . just . . . hhh . . . saved you from . . . this," he breathed.

"You risked your life."

Kevin didn't answer. The anesthesiologist turned the plastic feed on the I-V.

"Why did you risk your life? You said you wouldn't do it," insisted Madison.

"I said I wouldn't trade . . . my life . . . for something I didn't . . . value," he puffed.

"Me?" she said as tears ran down her cheeks.

Kevin nodded and smiled. He was beginning to go under.

"I love you," said Madison, brushing the tears aside and smiling tensely through the extremes of her joy and fear for Kevin.

Kevin's eyes flattened as a serene smile came to his face. He was nearly unconscious and closed his eyes—the smile remained. Madison waited a moment longer. Kevin's eyes opened into a small slit just before he fell completely under. All he could do was mouth the words, "I-Love-You-Too-Madison."

She wiped the remaining tears from her cheeks and stepped back from the table. The surgeon offered a blank stare of wavering patience to signal that it was time for them to go. They turned slowly, looking back over their shoulder to capture one last look at the scene and walked through the doors. Hallie Cevanté had been notified by the emergency room check-in nurse and was waiting to take Michael and Madison back to the conference. She met them in the lobby.

"Hi, Dad. Is everything okay?" said Hallie.

"Hi, sweetheart. Broken leg and a head concussion. He'll be in a cast for a while, but he should be okay. It might give him a chance to make plans for his future," he said, looking over to Madison. She just smiled.

They made their way through the parking lot and got into Hallie's car. Once there, they began the ride back to the Summit. Hallie was driving and firing questions. "Dad, what happened?" she asked.

"I'm not sure, sweetheart. The bridge collapsed, but I don't know why," he said.

"Kevin stopped me from falling just before he fell," said Madison.

"Wow! You're kidding. What did he do?" asked Hallie.

"It was really great," said Madison, her voice starting to crack. "He jumped to the ledge and pushed me up before he fell himself."

"Kevin's really cool. That's really romantic," said Hallie.

Madison smiled her answer.

"Have you decided what to do with the lottery money, yet?" Michael asked.

"No! What did you think about my letter?" she asked nervously.

"I thought it was fine."

"You didn't like it, did you!" she pouted.

"Honey, it's not easy. You've considered two of the many different perspectives of the situation—Grandpa's perspective, and a subjective view of it. You're smart, you'll figure it out."

"Dad, sometimes I just wish you would tell me what to do," she said, knowing he wouldn't.

"No, Hallie, you know you don't want that," he said.

"Maybe I do. Then I could just be an ordinary kid, with a nerdy dad, who couldn't wait to leave home and get away to school," she teased.

"Why do you think I avoid being a nerd?" he said, mussing her hair and grinning to thank her.

Madison admired what a great father Michael was to Hallie. "Your dad's a pretty cool guy, you know?" she said.

"He's okay," said Hallie, looking sideways at her father, slightly embarrassed that she had started the exchange.

"Michael, I love the way you sculpt minds," said Madison.

"I'm not sure I would put it that way, but thank you," he said. "I don't try to mold minds into something that I believe they should be. I think it would be horrible to have clones of anyone. What I love are the things thinking people can achieve. I help to unlock the chains that keep them mired in uniform thought. I would hope you see me as a liberator of thought instead of a sculptor of a single type of thinking."

"How about a sculptor of terrific, independent people?" she said, tussling Hallie's hair.

"I like that. But it's still far too generous. I can't do much for those with closed minds. Sometimes nothing will unlock the chains, even the chance to be free."

"Michael," she said, changing tones. "I've never really had a passion for anything but my running. My job is like a shadowy connection to what I love about running."

"What do you love about it?"

"Disciplined freedom," she said.

"What does it mean?"

"Running represents all the things I love most about life, but mostly the unlimited opportunities of freedom. You know, what people can achieve when they're free to try."

Hallie had already taken a liking to Madison. It was difficult not to. She was listening intently to Madison's passionate description. "Where does the discipline part come in?" asked Hallie.

"The freedom I feel isn't cheap, in fact it's rather expensive. That's the discipline—paying for it," she answered.

"I don't understand."

"It doesn't just come to you. You can't wish for it, hope for it, or pray for it. You have to pay for it. For runners, it's weight training, intervals, the right diet, the right technique and mental preparation." She paused. "Michael, that's what you do here at the conference, isn't it?"

"Yes. And more. But that's a good summary."

"I'd be dedicated to those principles in working for you," Madison said.

"I don't hire workers. I take partners only," he said.

"No one would be more passionate in delivering the ideals of Sales Esteem."

"I have a feeling you would make enormous contributions."

Hallie grasped what was occurring. "This is the strangest job interview I've ever heard of," she said.

"What do you think, Hallie. Madison? A partner? I wonder if she could get along with Kevin?" said Michael. Hallie giggled.

Michael considered Madison to be the best student he'd ever had. If she were interested, he would happily add her to his team. Madison had been adrift seeking a career that focused on the things she held dear. She had never felt more at home.

"We can talk more about the specifics, but there's plenty for you to become involved in. The offer stands. Take some time to think about what it means and let me know when you're ready to go further," said Michael, wrapping up the interview and offer.

Madison looked over and nodded. "Won't take much more thought than I've already given it," she said, smiling.

A short silence followed before Michael spoke in an entirely different tone. "Hallie. Kendra McKinney is going to be speaking to our group today. I think you'd be fascinated by what she has to say."

Madison caught Hallie's eyes in the rear-view mirror. "He's sculpting, isn't he?" said Hallie. Madison nodded with encouragement.

"Sure Dad. Should be fun. I think."

17

Justice

We're not all created equal, but effort can make
up for the differences and then some.
—*Kendra McKinney*

The car pulled into the Summit parking lot and they hurried through a thundershower back to the conference center. It was the first rain to fall during the conference. The lightning danced from the black clouds to the surrounding hillside and long, rolling claps of thunder gave the moment a background setting like a theater with an orchestra. The class had finished breakfast and were gathered back in the conference room. Ryan had given them an hour's respite to confirm travel reservations home, and catch up on phone messages back in the world they would be returning to soon. Michael and Madison came in while part of the group was still returning, others were chatting in small groups.

Ryan rushed to meet them at the door. "How is he?" he demanded.

Michael nodded to Ryan. "Fine, he's going to be okay."

Ryan looked back over his shoulder at Fiscger, then pulled Michael back through the door. "Kendra and I found some rather interesting things at the base of the bridge." he said. "Would there be any reason for someone to have done maintenance work lately?"

"Everything is completed before I let people run on the path. Nothing was done recently." said Michael.

"At least nothing that you knew about, Michael." said Ryan.

They came back into the room where Michael turned to the group, knowing they would want to hear the news.

"Kevin suffered a compound fracture and a head concussion. He is in surgery right now and should be fine," he said.

"How did it happen?" came the same question from several in the room.

"The bridge collapsed as Madison crossed it. Kevin was helping her climb back up the bank when he fell." Michael looked over at Ryan. It had occurred to him immediately that the bridge's collapse was an unlikely event. He kept them well maintained and they had been inspected recently. The frown on Ryan's face validated his concern.

"I'm happy no one else was hurt. All in all, it's a difficult situation, but one we can get through. We've had an unusually active conference," said Michael, with enough emphasis to send some chills down Shaw's spine.

This was the moment that Fischer had waited for. He wanted to spread guilt across the entire incident—indict the run and its intended purpose—and hopefully the entire conference. He wanted a scandal, drummed-up and constructed, to blot out the vast amount of insight that had taken place at the conference. It was a terrorist's mentality seeking to tear down ideals.

"I'm surprised you can stay in business when this type of thing happens," said Fischer. "How much of our tuition goes to pay your liability insurance premiums?"

Michael hesitated momentarily. The statement was so callous and out of place given the circumstance that it shouted for attention. Michael's look was penetrating as he stared at Fischer. Fischer had made his mistake, gloating like a criminal at the scene of the crime and thoroughly underestimating Michael's ability to sort things out, down to their roots.

"Tug. I stay in business because I make certain this type of thing does *not* happen. The bridge should not have collapsed, but bridges don't just fall down on their own—do they?" His chilling stare did nothing to dissuade Fischer's arrogant gloat.

"What, exactly, do you mean?" Fischer said defiantly.

"Our ground crew inspects the bridges the day before the conference, and following the first run, to make certain they are safe. There are only a few possible explanations for it's failure—aren't there?" It was the way Michael ended each statement with a question that made began to make Fischer nervous.

"I still have no idea what you're talking about," he said less boldly.

"Oh, come on Tug. It's a rather stable scientific theory. Solid beams support the surface of the bridge and do so until something changes the structure. Some physical action would have to occur for the structure to become unsafe. It could fail because of a lack of maintenance, but we know it was recently inspected by competent people. The only other possible explanation is that something occurred to damage the beam. An earthquake perhaps? Maybe the concrete support shifted? Perhaps a landslide pushed the beam off its support." Michael paced. Fischer breathed easier as Michael maneuvered himself further from the truth.

"Who knows why it failed—at least right now. We'll know when we have a chance to inspect it," said Michael. Fischer tightened again.

Ryan looked at Kendra, who shot him a glance of encouragement to tell about their find, but he hesitated and held his forefinger to his lips to signal silence. He wanted Michael to decide how to use the information before he let anyone realize he had make the discovery.

"In any event," Michael continued, "the conference will continue. We will make certain that it won't occur again, and I will tell Kevin of your deep concern for his safety, Tug," he said without an indicting tone. He too knew that there was more evidence to be gathered before Fischer could be ascertained as a possible villain.

"For now, I would like to move on to our next speaker. And thank her sincerely for her patience. I promise each of you it will be well worth the wait. Ladies and gentlemen, please welcome Kendra McKinney," he said, stepping back from the front of the room.

Rousing applause greeted her. She would have been recognized by most of them without the prior introductions, but by now, the group had already been informally introduced at the trailhead and knew about the competition between Kendra and Madison.

Kendra came forward nodding appreciation for their welcome. "Thank you," she said to get started. "Michael invited me here to share a story that is similar to the kind of set-backs many people face, perhaps by many of you."

Kendra was a natural public speaker who used her intimate knowledge of the subject matter, and skills of timing and inflection from the evangelical speakers she had observed from the pews of her church. It gave her presentation a natural flow, with emphasis and drama blended in nicely.

"The story has been quite well publicized, but, because I myself struggled mightily with it, I am always fascinated to watch as others offer possible solutions. Many of you may have heard about the events as they unfolded just prior to the 1988 Summer Olympic Games. That's what I'm here for today—to retell the story and to solicit and then analyze your reactions." She paused, looking from face to face to build the drama.

"From mid-'87 through the first of '88, I was at the top of my sport—yet not at my *personal* peak. I had just established a new U.S. record and was ranked number one in the world and was the odds-on favorite for a gold medal at the '88 Olympics. There were two events that stood between me and the gold—the U.S. Trials and the Olympic event itself. I had worked for six years for the days that were just ahead, and I mean worked. Four hour workouts every day, resting one day a week. Distance, sprints, weight work, and cross-training. It was a regimen designed to accomplish the single goal of having a gold medal hung around my neck. I didn't drink a drop of alcohol, or eat fatty foods for eighteen months before the trials. I slept, ate and lived my Olympic dream. And . . . I was the very best when the trials came."

Tip Bailey remembered the '88 trials well. He had gone to the trials as the unpaid agent of an aspiring professional track star who would become a client soon after the games. He remembered Kendra and the pain he felt for her. He was captivated to hear her retell the story.

"I was a sports darling," she said with an amused smile. "And there were genuine fans who clung to everything I did or said. Reporters did the same." Kendra began to pace, injecting more drama.

"My qualifying heats went just fine. I was within two-tenths of my U.S. record and far ahead of everyone else. All except a newcomer from South Carolina named Cheryl Pandera, who was just trying desperately to qualify and running the best times of her life." She paused. "The trials boil down to one final race with the top two finishers receiving a spot on the U.S. team. I counted the days that I had been dreaming about that one race. I ate right, went to bed on time—didn't sleep very well, but finally got about six hours in." She paused again, gripping the table in front of her for the finale.

"As I settled into the blocks, I remember thinking that I needed to run hard enough to lock up a second-place finish. I knew that I shouldn't hold back too much, in spite of the feeling among other athletes that the trials were too close to the Olympic Games and we risked peaking too early. As the thoughts were going through my head, I lost track of the count, and ended up jumping early." Her eyes got wide to confirm a jumped start was a problem.

"Having a charged jump-start kept me in the blocks an instant longer than I would have liked, but I figured I could make it up with my finish. Then I thought about pacing myself again. Suddenly, my steps were off, and for a hurdler that's a disaster. The rhythm is where the microseconds are shaved off a champion's time. I had to take the third hurdle with the opposite leg forward—bad news. I hit the fifth hurdle, and then the sixth. I recovered over the seventh but had lost far too much ground. Cheryl Pandera, on the other hand, was concentrating perfectly and hit every one of her steps. I couldn't catch her and crossed the finish line third—almost a second off my qualifying times."

Now Kendra walked around to the front of the table and sat down on its top, slumping slightly and looking dejected. "I *didn't* make the *team*," she said slowly.

"I wanted to *scream!* I didn't *make* it? My mind replayed the two hundred meters that I had just run. No doubt about it. I was at fault. I looked around the stadium. There was a hush of surprise. My coach had literally collapsed to his knees in anguish. Someone put an arm around my shoulder and apologized. Cheryl was ecstatic. She had come out of nowhere to make the team. I sat down on the edge of the track, stunned. I wanted to cry." She stopped there.

Tip Bailey's memories shot back to that moment. It seemed as though the track world had wanted to cry as well. Cheryl Pandera, her family, friends and coach, were the only people on the planet who hadn't been pulling for Kendra. Tip was among her biggest fans. And it was painful for him to watch her fail. But for Tip it was more than just painful, it was unjust.

"And that's why I'm here. To pose the question of how you deal with perceived injustices—and just exactly what justice is? To tell you how I viewed it, how I dealt with it," said Kendra.

Tip blurted out, "Justice is not a word you should use in describing what happened to you, Kendra." His tone was as though he had lost something dear to him, that it had been taken from him.

"That was the general feeling. But tell me why *you* felt that way?"

"Everyone on the planet knew you were the best in the world. The *system* cheated you," he said.

There were nods throughout the room. Kendra didn't react one way or the other. She paced back and forth. "The *s-y-s-t-e-m* cheated me, hmm? Other comments?"

Sally Holiday had found a new heroine in Kendra. In a defensive tone she said, "I don't understand, Kendra. If you were the world's best, why didn't they take you anyway?"

"How many of you think an exception could have been made to add me to the team?" asked Kendra.

Two-thirds of the group raised their hands in agreement.

"Why?" asked Kendra, prompting looks of surprise among those who had raised their hands.

"Because you were the best," said Tip. "You had the best times in the world. You were clearly trying to avoid 'peaking'. The trials shouldn't be held that close to the games. All of the athletes complain about it. Even if you had a bad day during the trials, you would bounce back and win at the games. Didn't you win a major world track meet right after the Olympics—beating the Olympic champion?"

"Yes," said Kendra. "And boy did that *feeeel gooood*," she giggled. "But how can you suggest that I be selected to the Olympic team?"

"I don't understand," complained Tip . "Didn't you think you should have been selected anyway?"

"No. Absolutely not!" said Kendra.

The group was silent. Kendra was silent. Tip was as frustrated as he had ever been. He looked over at Michael, who had a very satisfied look on his face. "Why is Michael grinning, damn it," thought Tip. He looked back at Kendra, who still held an absolutely neutral look on her face. Many of the group members exchanged glances among themselves. They wanted to yell in chorus, *what? why not?*

Kendra waited a moment longer. Tip protested. "I can't believe you didn't *want* to be selected!"

"That's not what you asked. You asked whether I *'thought'* I should be selected. There is no line of *'reasoning'* or *'thinking'* that could justify being selected. Of *course* I *wanted* to make the team. It was all that I wanted, with one exception, above all else I wanted justice," said Kendra.

Puzzled faces filled the room. Even for those who thought they had figured it out, and were guessing that Kendra was willing to 'roll with the punches' of competition.

"Let me give you a little insight," she said, pausing and leaning back against the table. "I came from a world where justice was for other people. People confuse the meanness of the streets of the inner-city with the 'law of the jungle.' It's not the case. The streets are all about politics and nothing about justice. Politics are gangs and mobs. Politics are jobs for people less qualified but befriended to those who have the jobs to dole out. My world was the *opposite* of justice, except for one small piece—track," she said.

Here it was. The group knew this was the essence of it. The reason Kendra was there and the reason Michael was grinning.

"When I was growing up, I recognized something terribly important. Track was justice. Track was honest. Track was pure. No one decided anything for anyone else on the track, just you. If you're the fastest, no one can say differently. If you're the best, it can't be disputed. The politicians run and hide from that kind of justice. And track was the way that I unshackled myself from the politics—the meanness—of the streets. Track was justice for me. And it was my only chance to get to where I am today. My whole life, all that I have become, is tied up in the *justice* of those thirty seconds on the track.

"Freedom is opportunity to try without shackles, to move through life without the extra weight of someone else's hand guiding the outcome. Justice is to know— before you run—that if you are the best, no one can take it away from you. We often confuse justice with equality. They're not the same. I'm really not interested in a race where everyone is guaranteed—through someone's intervention—to finish equal. It's a fraud. I'm better than most because it's human nature to improve. A guy named Darwin spent a lot of time to show that we wiggled up out of the ocean, climbed out of the trees, and began thinking because of that human nature. Freedom is the opportunity to excel beyond the ordinary and the equal. Justice is the knowledge that no one will interfere with your effort. Only politicians want everyone to finish the race at the same time." She paused.

"With that as my philosophy, how could I ask for the intervention of politics to put me on the Olympic team. I would rather walk away. The foundation of everything I had was the *elimination* of politics. To rely on politics to 'grant' me a place on the team was as dishonest as the politics of the streets that I fled from. Yet, those who took up my 'cause' wanted to call it justice. No way. Justice didn't have anything to do with it."

The rationale struck them like a punch to stomach. She continued. "There would be another day. Heck, I beat the Olympic champion a month after the Olympics. I still had the world's best time. But none, and I . . . mean . . . none, of that could be true if politics determined who should run, and who should be selected to the team. If that were the case, I would never have gotten to the trials to begin with. If my life relied on politics, I would never have escaped the streets." She paused.

"But Kendra, we could have added a third spot on the team," said Tip .

"And bump who? A race-walker? An archer? A synchronized swimmer?" she replied. "And who decides, Tip? What politician—as noble and as well-intentioned as they try to be—decides, at that moment, that Kendra McKinney should go instead of 'Ruthy, the race walker from Maine'? No, the moment politics enter the decision-making process, it all comes apart."

The room seemed brighter and felt livelier. Heads were nodding and there were no more puzzled looks. Sally Holiday was certain she had found a heroine. Tip was still not satisfied.

"It cost us the gold medal!" he said in exasperation.

"Tip, how many gold medals were won because we *don't* play politics in U.S. Olympic athletics? You can't turn a blind eye to the success of justice and point a finger of blame when it doesn't suit you. For Cheryl Pandera, *justice* was served. She was better than I was on that day. She had been given a chance to succeed without regard of what anyone else 'wanted,' and she was successful. It may not seem that justice is served at each and every moment. But it works. It works so exceptionally well that any other approach is miserable in comparison."

There was no argument to be made. Even Tip, for all his good intentions, couldn't pull together an argument against Kendra's rock-solid logic. She waited but got no reply.

"Can someone explain to me why we equate justice with winning?" she asked. Again, there was a pause. She was razor sharp in her explanations about ideas that were generally vague and fuzzy. Few of them had considered the issues so closely. She waited patiently.

"Let me put it another way. From my point of view, we have substituted the notion of justice with equality. Does anyone in this room truly *believe* we are equal?" she asked.

"Yes!" said Kat Kelly. "I think we're all created equal."

"Thank you for speaking up—I'm sorry, what's your name?"

"Kat Kelly."

"Thanks Kat." she continued. "Have you ever considered the absurdity of that statement?"

"I *believe* it!" Kat said indignantly.

"What about it do you believe, Kat?"

"That we're all born equal."

"Do you believe in it explicitly . . . or in the political context?"

"Well, I suppose in the way that it applies to personal freedom."

"Good. Me too. But do you believe the statement is accurate outside of that context. In other words, do you believe we are all physically and mentally equal?" said Kendra.

"Well, I like to think all babies have the raw material to grow up to be whatever they want, regardless of the circumstances."

"Now really. Do you think you were born with the *physical* attributes to compete with me on a track? Or enter a boxing ring with a heavyweight boxer? Or sing in the opera, or fly the space shuttle?"

"No. I can't run very fast or box. And you never, ever, want to hear me sing," she said with a laugh. "I might be able to fly the space shuttle, though—even though I do get carsick." Kat went on as though she were giving serious thought to each endeavor.

Kendra laughed out loud. "Kat. Have you ever seen one of those things they strap astronauts into that go round and round and round? They're guaranteed to make people who get carsick beg to be put to death," she giggled.

Kat nodded. "Yeah. Maybe not an astronaut either."

"And *when* were you named a Nobel laureate? I guess I didn't realize."

"I'm not."

"But you were *created* equal. Guess the only epithet they can give you is that you were 'born with it all—but never figured out how to use it.'"

Kat's feelings were slightly hurt. "Maybe I never got the same opportunities."

"See what I mean? Justice and equality are believed to be interchangeable. Kat, I'm sorry to pick on you, but the fact of the matter is, few people were born with my physical attributes. A handful were, and now the difference between us is the amount of effort we exert to make ourselves the best. *That's* justice. And I was born with better than average intelligence, but nothing to compare with what Einstein must have had at birth. I'm sure there are many people born with the same mental makeup of an Einstein, but the difference is what he did to foster, develop and apply his intelligence. *That's* justice.

"We're not equal *at birth* or *in life*. The political ideal of 'equality' is that of rejecting man-made barriers that keep those who would try from realizing their full potential—regardless of who they are and where they came from. The barriers that would keep me from running or keep Einstein from thinking. It has *nothing* to do with pushing ordinary people up to heights of achievement. It has *everything* to do with *not holding* people back. Is that what you believe in?"

"Yes. Now that you put it in those terms."

"That's exactly what I believe in. I have no illusions about equality and justice. You and I weren't born equal in social terms. I was born a poor, black kid. Unless I am mistaken, *you've earned your way*, from wherever you started, as did I. *That's justice*. Getting what we deserve, without the intervention of others, at the cost of those we compete against—good or bad. Getting what is earned and deserved. *That's justice*."

Kat had an odd look on her face. Sort of a combination of dejection and discovery. Kendra noticed.

"I hope I haven't been too harsh," said Kendra.

"No. No, not at all," said Kat as she shook off her glossed-over look of deep concentration. "I'm amazed by how well you understand a principle the rest of us have come to take for granted."

"I think that's why Michael wanted me to come here today," she said with a smile to remind them all that it wasn't by chance. Michael came forward from his chair by the door. He stood by Kendra and reached down to grasp her hand as he spoke.

"There are few people who can speak as eloquently about the subject as Kendra. Please join me in thanking her for joining us," said Michael.

Kendra smiled and held her free hand up to the group to thank them for their applause. She hugged Michael, and as the group continued clapping, asked, "Can I stay awhile longer? I would like to hear the rest of the discussion."

"Yeah, I bet. You want to know how graceful I am in announcing the new record on the path." jabbed Michael.

"How did you guess?" she demurred.

"Justice as a principle? It certainly sounds like a principle. But how does it apply to selling?" he asked rhetorically. "And what could the possible action of *justice* be? And the emotional result? Let's take a look, shall we?" he said.

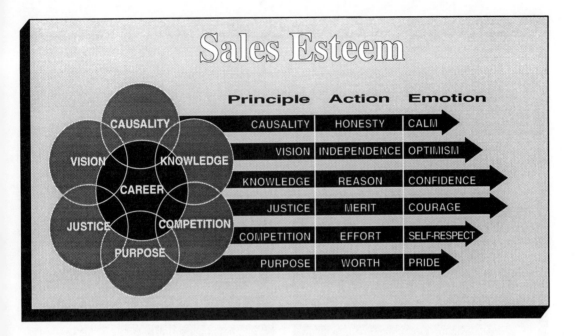

Principle	Action	Emotion
CAUSALITY	HONESTY	CALM
VISION	INDEPENDENCE	OPTIMISM
KNOWLEDGE	REASON	CONFIDENCE
JUSTICE	MERIT	COURAGE
COMPETITION	EFFORT	SELF-RESPECT
PURPOSE	WORTH	PRIDE

"Kendra has pointed out the opposing principles, *justice* and *politics*. The actions that follow are *merit* and *favors*. The resulting emotions are *courage* and *fear*. Justice defined is the realization of cause and effect without interference. Politics is the opposite, the fabricated result without regard to cause and effect. The action corresponding to the principle of justice is merit. Or, in other words, the expectation that knowledge and effort will be rewarded fairly. The emotional result is the courage to put forth the effort—and not just the minimal required effort—but everything you've got. The courage to be the best you can possibly be. The opposite principle of politics means choice—*someone else's choice*—based on their criteria. The actions are favors. The decision maker, after all, seeks something in exchange for delivering the rewards. And the end emotional result is fear. Fear that your knowledge, effort and hard work will never be rewarded, or worse yet, expropriated to be used by someone else. And fear that you will become enslaved to the favors and the politicians. Kendra is my favorite example of an individual who refuses to give up justice in exchange for politics, even in the instance when it would have benefited her most. It's max integrity," he said, turning to smile at Kendra. "The insistence of taking only what is justly earned and deserved, and refusing to be lured by favors. Favors make *slaves*. Merit garners rewards and the subsequent courage to continue to excel," he said and pressed the remote for the next slide.

"Fortunately, selling embraces the idea of justice primarily because we're paid only when the job is done. But it goes deeper than that. That's what I would like to examine. Let me ask, has anyone noticed what's occurring with our principles?"

"They're beginning to complement one another," said Ryan.

Michael smiled warmly at Ryan. "Yes, Ryan, that's right. And when you say complement each other, what do you mean?"

"Well, they're beginning to rely on one another . . . beginning to explain and support one another. If you choose the justice-to-merit-to-courage principle, you are likely to embrace the principles of causality, vision, and knowledge," said Ryan.

"Why?" demanded Michael.

"Courage comes from the expectation that things will turn out the way they should—that you'll get what you deserve. Getting what you deserve requires the effort of putting your knowledge to work to achieve something. More often than not, it takes time—or the principle of vision—to see it through, without taking any shortcuts. And at the base of it all is the principle of cause and effect. If justice is defined as the environment where the laws of cause and effect are not altered by someone else, then its justice *has to* assume cause and effect first. It's like a continuous circle—all of the principles relying on one-another." His voice was as rich as a child discovering the world's wonders.

"Mr. Matthews has made a terribly important breakthrough. If chance is your principle, you can't possibly hope for justice. If you ignore responsibility and abdicate it to someone else, you have to hope justice doesn't come looking for you when you stumble. And if you rely on emotions to guide your actions, their lack of substance will ultimately mean you don't achieve your goals and all that's left is the hope that someone will intervene and save you," Michael said, pausing as the class pushed through the mental work of making all the pieces fit.

"Justice wraps up the principles into a package. If you refuse to accept the shortcuts, like Kendra did, it reinforces your conviction of all of the principles. The inner voice that says, *'I seek only what I earn, and steer clear of the ransom of favors,'* asserts its corollary, *'I deserve all that I have, and owe no favors in return,'*" he said. "There are the occasional oddities of having a big ticket fall into our laps, or lose a sale we should have won. Lucky hits happen from time to time . . . as do small injustices. The world isn't always fair. But they tend to balance each other out. For those individuals who apply themselves and earn their way, through the principle of justice and the action of merit, as opposed to those who always seek to 'slide by,' the world offers rewards of immense proportions," he said, then paused.

"The more important question is what you, the individual, expects. Are you willing to rely on your effort—your merit—and nothing else. Or do you 'want' a free trip? The answer, the one that comes from deep down inside, will shape the way you see the rest of the world. It will shape the manner in which you apply your other principles. It's the backbone of 'integrity.' A contradiction exists if you hope for the luck of the draw—if that's your burning desire—but believe in cause and effect. How do you reconcile it?" he asked rhetorically. "There's just one way. Your principles have to agree to have integrity. If you're good at what you do, then justice is your only protection for receiving what you've earned. If you hope for a 'just world,' in which your merit is rewarded—as Kendra did—then you can't hope for its opposite when it will benefit you." He stopped and paced back in forth in front of them. This was abstract, but compelling, and he knew it was work to make it all fit.

"You're describing the subjectivity versus objectivity," said Kyle.

"Yes, Kyle. That's right."

"It's easier to think about than it is to live."

"I understand. But that doesn't change the fact that those who rely on luck will ultimately be done in by luck. There's a common saying that's invoked frequently these days, 'what goes around comes around.'" He paused, watching the nodding heads. "If it's so common, and so commonly believed, what is its cause?"

"People usually get what they deserve," said Shannon.

"How?" said Michael.

"I don't know," she shrugged.

"A lack of integrity doesn't always cause an immediate disaster. It often rewards the creeps, but not for very long. Given time, it catches up. If you've ever watched the full circle of 'what goes around comes around,' it usually occurs when the culprit does himself in. His own bad principles fail. It happens because at the core, his principles don't work. He may be able to fudge, and fake, and slip by for some time, but ultimately, they fall apart. Give it some thought. I would imagine everyone in this room knows of an example of this very thing. Think about what ultimately got 'em," he said, pausing as the group began to nod agreement in thinking out their own examples.

Michael continued. "The pay-off for good principles is the emotional rewards that come from justice and the energy they inject into our overall motivation. Courage is an interesting emotion. It's often misunderstood as blind guts, willing to try the impossible. But that's not courage—it's stupidity. Courage is the willingness to try the difficult, or the pioneering . . . and the willingness to risk failing. It's the contemplation of the likely outcome, and the guts to put your knowledge, skills, ideas and butt on the line to achieve something that's difficult. Don't confuse courage with gambling. Courage is calculating and strong. Gambling is risk taking without reasonable cause. They are not the same," he said.

"That sounds pretty lame to me. Winners are gamblers," said Fischer.

"Tug. Don't confuse the two. My wife loves to bungee-jump, but she's not a gambler. It would be gambling if the cord broke one-out-of-a-hundred times. She has courage to make the jump because she understands the physics involved. The cord, if fastened correctly, measured correctly, and manufactured correctly, will hold ten-times her weight even at the accelerated speed. Her intellect overcomes her fear and turns it into exhilaration." He paused. Fischer didn't answer, but others were shaking their heads in agreement.

"Courage can come from just one place—knowing that your brains and effort will win out in an environment that doesn't interfere. If you're beaten by politics and favors, courage flees, and your motivation goes with it.

"Most of today's sales motivators seek to replace real courage with false hope, or faith. It works just once. My favorites are the fire-walkers, who whip people into believing they can do the impossible, on faith, and then fabricate an event to demonstrate it. Sales Esteem is the opposite. Courage, and belief in yourself, comes from factual knowledge of your skills, of the legitimacy of the role you play as a salesperson, of the value you deliver, and of the integrity of your principles."

18

Of Eagles and Egalitarians

It's not the fierceness of the battle,
but of the adversary that counts.
—*Cherokee saying*

Michael got up from his seated position at the table, and walked back to the tote board. "Now that we've heard Kendra's story, I'd like to examine the event that unfolded right before our eyes this morning. Madison and Kendra were within a hundred feet of the finish when the bridge collapsed. We've estimated their times. I think this is close," he said, scribbling it on the board.

	Bobby	Sally	Madison	Kendra
Run 1:18:15:06	26: ?	18:10		
Run 2:18:09:11	22:33	16:55:12		
Run 3:19:31:03	19:35	16:00		
Run 4:18:10:00	18:30			
Record Held by Michael:		15:38	14:30	14:20

"Even if the estimate is off, the old record has been demolished. And the new record will probably stand for quite some time. Madison cut a minute and a half off her previous time. That's truly incredible. What in the world caused it?" he asked.

Madison eyes got wider as she shook her head in agreement. "I had the opportunity to compete against Kendra," she said.

"*Competition?*" asked Michael.

"I thought she would be the ultimate test—the best I would ever run against on the path."

"The standard of excellence?" Michael said. Madison agreed with a nod.

"Kendra? What was driving you on the path today?" he continued.

"Pride, I would say."

"I would be surprised by any other answer. Did the fact that you were running against each other have anything to do with your performance?"

They looked across the room at each other and giggled, shaking their heads as they turned back to Michael.

"You're all competitive people, in competitive careers. But how well do you understand competition?" he asked as he began to pace in front of them. "Is competition an instinct? Is it learned? Why does it bring out the best in people? Does it ever bring out the worst?"

The room erupted in discussion, some directed at Michael, the rest between them. Michael let it run its course. After a few minutes, he held up his hand to quiet them and returned to his questions.

"Tell me what you're thinking," he said.

Jock Shaw's lack of personal sales success had bred insecurity, which in turn had bred a peculiar mix of resentment and misfounded arrogance about competition. Michael frequently saw the inept portray themselves as topic experts in order to hide their insecurity. The fraud usually took the form of clichés and homilies, and a lack of fundamental understanding of the subject. Always opinionated without defense, it had the tone of arrogance without evidence. Shaw's comments about competition were about to betray him. He practically jumped out of his chair to say, "Competition is what life is all about. Competitors get life's rewards, weenies get churned up. It's the survivalist, animal instinct in us that comes to the surface," he said.

"Hmm," said Michael. "So it's instinctive. Uncontrolled. Unreasoning. Unruly. And primitive?"

Shaw hesitated, but didn't fully recognize the trap. "Uh . . . yeah," he stuttered.

Kat had found a new hobby: watching Shaw squirm under Michael's scrutiny. It was truly enjoyable for her. She wanted to play, too. "Jock. Did you hear what he said? Are you suggesting that competition is uncontrollable and primitive? Do you think your sales staff are lead around by the nose by their gut instincts to devour raw flesh?" she said, pleased with her precise mental dissection.

Shaw's arrogance sent him deeper into the crevice. "Honey, I wouldn't expect you to know anything related to devouring raw flesh. Real competitors understand what I mean. And if you don't, there's no way I can explain it to you," he spouted.

Michael burst out in laughter. "Jock? Perhaps you can enlighten us a little."

Shaw looked appropriately defensive, but dug deeper instead. "It's not that big of a deal. Everyone knows about evolution and survival of the fittest. We compete to survive."

"Yeah, as in Darwinian evolution," said Shannon. "Competition drove us from the trees to office towers."

Michael raised his hand. "Before we ascribe all of man's progress to competition, let's put it into proper perspective with some definition. Jock? You want to give it a try, or is it one of those things we can't possibly comprehend?"

"No! Competition is . . . the . . . uh . . . fight for . . . uh . . . between two people—uh . . . the race, by two people, to reach the same goal first," he said.

"Do you mind if I clean that up a little?" asked Michael. Shaw shrugged.

"How about this? Competition is the action taken by two living entities pursuing the same value." Michael glanced completely around the room. All were shaking their heads in agreement except Fischer, who gave a single nod when Michael caught his stare.

"I disagree," said Tip. "I can't tell you how often I've seen people who just love to compete, no matter what the incentive. They are driven to beat other people."

"Is it possible, Tip, that they are competing for a value that doesn't take the form of a tangible incentive?"

"I don't understand."

"Why do they want to beat other people?"

"Self-esteem I suppose."

"I would agree. It's possible that it may be misdirected competition. No one said we're always intelligent in the manner that we pursue values. But chances are, those people who seek to win for winning's sake, would feel differently if you were to dramatically change the value they were pursuing. For instance, let's see who can swim the furthest into the ocean without a life vest. Or, let's compete for the number of days we can run naked through the forest without food. Remember the primary value of happiness includes one of self-esteem, but it rests on value judgments of what is being achieved. Do you think your self-esteem competitors would change stripes in these instances?"

"I see your point. But I still know a few people who would take you up on such a ridiculous contest," said Tip.

"I understand, Tip. No one has claimed that everyone is rational," he smiled. "If you want, you can test it further by asking if they would compete again and again for an empty value. Ultimately they'll realize the foolishness of chasing a non-value, or end up as candidates for therapy," he said to grunted giggles from the group.

"The pursuit of values is the *nature* of *any* living thing. Competition is a concept, and as we will see shortly, a principle that describes the effort to gain something of value when it is finite . . . and when there are others after the same value. Competition isn't the starting point; *acquiring the primary values before they are all gone* is the starting point. Competition is simply the description of that process. It is a concept and a rather complex one, which means we can forge it into a . . . ," he waited for someone to fill in the blank.

"Principle," came a chorused reply.

"And what do we know about principles?"

Several in the room began nodding their heads, already aware of the answer. Kat was the first to announce it. "Some principles are right; some are wrong," she said.

"Good. The important point here is that there are different views of competition. And, it's rather easy to observe these different views. In fact, conceptually, there are a multitude of perspectives about competition. Since it is so central to life, everyone has an opinion of it—and many of them are negative. Let's sort through some of the various perspectives and see if we can forge a principle that we'll be comfortable with," he said.

Michael walked to the front and shifted the two easels side by side. "Let's do the positive-and-negative routine. Fire away. Positive views of competition first," he said as he faced the first easel, looking over his shoulder at them.

"Sets a standard of excellence," said Madison.

"Good." He scribbled it onto the pad.

"Sets a minimum level of performance," said Ryan.

"That's very perceptive." He scribbled furiously.

"Causes creativity."

"Why?" he turned and faced them.

"In order to get the value first, we create new ways to solve problems." It was Madison.

"Oh, that's *really* good. We need to dispel the myth that creativity is a special talent. We're all creative—we're all problem solvers—to a degree." He returned to the pad and added it to the list.

"More," he practically yelled.

"Ingenuity," said Ryan

"A measure of performance," said Tip.

"Separates performers and non-performers," said Kat.

"It's trailblazing," said Madison.

"What?" he said and turned around.

"It sets an example of prior achievement. We wanted to go to the moon. It couldn't be done at the time. The space race was born. Now, for the rest of history, we will know it's possible to get to the moon. It sets the parameters," she said.

"Oh, we're getting more and more clever all the time, aren't we?" he said and added to the list.

"It's fair and just," said Kendra.

"It brings out the best in people," said Sally.

"And the worst," said Kat.

"Positives first." scolded Michael.

"It elevates performance to its highest level?" said Kyle.

"It pushes us into new discoveries," said Kat.

"How about the things that we admire in athletes," said Tip.

"Like. . . ?"

"Power, determination, conviction, strength, agility," he said.

Michael added them to the list. "More," he said.

"It gives us a sense of accomplishment," said Kyle.

"Oh-oh. Now we're into the happiness values," said Michael as he scribbled.

"Pride," said Tip.

"Self-respect," said Ryan.

"Whew. Okay. I think we have a good start on the positives," Michael said as he moved over to the other easel. "Now, give me all the negatives you have heard about competition."

"Cut-throat."

"Killer instinct."

"Isn't a killer instinct a good thing?" asked Kyle.

Michael chuckled. "More."

"Law of the jungle—kill or be killed."

"Not civilized."

"Money motivated."

"Brings out the worst in people," said Kat.

"Not compassionate," said Sally.

"Winning is everything."

"There's always a 'loser.'"

"Puts the focus on the wrong thing," said Shannon.

"Explain that," said Michael.

"In business, for example, competition forces us to focus on profits instead of more important civic minded activities," said Shannon.

Michael circled it with a red pen. "We're going to come back to that idea," he said.

"Shortsighted."

"Hurts people who are too close to the action."

"Explain that," he insisted.

"If you're competing for the top sales award, for instance, and you sacrifice time with your family to make it, they get hurt," said Kat.

"Good. We'll come back to that one as well," he said circling it. "Okay. That should give us enough negatives. Let's talk about how we can have such diverse views of competition, shall we?"

Standard of Excellence Set's a minimum level of performance. Causes creativity Ingenuity Measure. Separates performers and non-performers. Trailblazing Fair and Just. Brings out the best in people. Elevates performance to it's highest level Pushes us into new discoveries. Power, Strength, Determination, Agility Sense of accomplishment. Pride. Self-respect.	Cut-throat. Killer instinct. Law of the jungle - kill or be killed. Not civilized. Money motivated. Brings out the worst in people. Not compassionate. Winning is everything. Always a 'winner' and a 'loser'. Puts the focus on the wrong thing. Shortsighted. Hurts innocent bystanders.

"Wow. Look at all those contradictions. How are we going to resolve these?" Michael asked as though it were far too difficult a task.

"There are times when they all apply, individually," said Kat.

"I disagree, Kat. Competition cannot be a standard of excellence and uncivilized at the same time. It's a consistent concept. If there's a contradiction, one of the two is not competition—even if someone claims that it is," said Michael.

"Remember, we said competition is a principle and we know how screwed up the wrong principles can be. Perhaps we can distinguish between conflicting descriptions of competition in order to identify the conflicting principles. What do you think?" He paused.

There were agreeing nods. He went on. "Okay. Integrity is . . . " he asked the leading question.

"When all your principles fit together without contradiction," answered Ryan.

Michael hopped to his feet and brushed his hand across the switch of the slide projector to bring it to life. He poked the control pad a few times to bring up the slide he wanted.

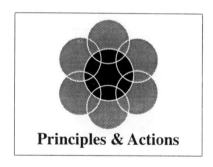

Principles & Actions

"You've seen this plenty of times. But let's talk about its usefulness as a decision making tool. Of course we know that this diagram symbolizes our approach, or master plan, to 'thinking.' It has two components, the first is the individual parts or the 'principles'. The second is the architecture that they fit into, which requires them to be capable of integration. This is the idea of 'integrity'." He pressed the control pad to bring the next slide to life.

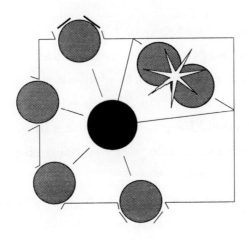

"The only other choice is to have principles that are distinct and not compatible." There was laughter from the group. "Here's a visualization of 'disintegrated' principles. As chaotic as the diagram appears, it probably doesn't do justice to what actually happens. It's probably a fairly accurate representation of the way most people think. This thought-process 'compartmentalizes' individual principles without ever realizing the conflict. The best example is the age-old 'double standard.' It's a pick and choose approach to applying principles. For the most part, it's simply ineffective—you can get away with picking your actions subjectively, you just aren't going to be all that successful. The problem occurs when you try to apply more than one principle—and they aren't compatible. Look around you, in business, in politics, in schools, in your personal relationships. If you find a failure, it's likely that you can trace it back to incompatible principles, or worse, colliding principles." He punched up another slide for drama.

"Disintegrated principles are bad enough, but real problems come up when you have a collision—a *contradiction*." Michael paused as the group absorbed the words.

"Aren't there some instances when you have a one-of-a-kind decision that doesn't relate to any other principles?" asked Michael.

"Well, I wouldn't step in front of a bus while it was moving," said Kyle.

"No, Kyle," said Madison. "That's a related principle. If you were trying to make it exclusive, it would have to be something like . . . 'crossing a street is an arbitrary decision completed unaffected by anything else," she said.

"I don't understand," said Kyle.

"To isolate that principle, you have to make it independent of any other, so crossing the street can't be dependent on the fact that you could die if the bus hit you," she said.

"That'd be stupid."

"It's your example," she said.

"No one would make a decision like that. Does that mean that it's impossible to have disintegrated principles?" asked Kyle.

"Not at all," said Michael. "You rarely see disintegrated principles when there is a physical risk involved. But when it comes to conceptual contradictions, you see it all the time."

"Let's try again," said Kyle. "How about the idea of Free Speech. It's a principle that stands on its own."

"That's an excellent try, but it's not a disintegrated principle. It relies on dozens of others," said Michael. "First, it requires principles of individual rights—specifically, that the individual has a right to independent thought. That may sound rudimentary to us, but you'd be hard pressed to find those two principles in most of the Middle East. It also requires many principles of law. For example, can you yell 'fire' in a crowded theater on the premise of free speech? Well, only if there is a fire. The principle of free speech does not integrate the principle of responsibility or consequence. There are many, many more, but I think you probably get the idea," he said.

"So you're saying that these types of conflicts can't happen," asserted Kyle.

"No. I'm saying they happen all the time. When they're identified or avoided, it's a sign of integrity. If they remain unnoticed, or worse, if the contradictions are ignored, then you have a 'lack of integrity.'"

"Give me an example," said Kyle.

"Isn't it true that you have a reputation for having been 'level-headed' during the junk bond frenzy?"

"Yeah."

"Was it arbitrary? Or did you have a reason?"

"It was crazy—all emotion. No one wanted to focus on the fundamentals. There was just so much money chasing the high rates," said Kyle.

"But you didn't let emotion persuade you?" said Michael.

"No," Kyle said, with a steely cold edge.

"Thousands of others did. Why were you different?" Michael pressed.

Kyle was shaking his head as he recalled his own circumstances. "I suppose I recognized conflicts that other people didn't see. They wanted to believe the outrageous corporate earnings forecasts that I knew would never occur," he said.

"How did you know?"

"They were ridiculous in some cases. Assumptions built upon assumptions built upon assumptions."

"Some people lost their life savings?"

"Yes."

"And there were honest salespeople who sold millions of dollars of junk bonds to unwitting investors, without recognizing the problems?" said Michael.

"Yes."

"Because they failed to integrate principles? Principles that you were aware of but refused to overlook. And what two principles were in conflict from your point of view?"

"They were truly quite simple. You must have the earnings to pay the interest payments. And the earnings appeared arbitrary given the history of the products being sold and the current state of the economy. The earnings were never going to happen and as a result, the companies weren't going to be able to make the interest payments."

"Is that integration?" asked Michael.

"Yeah, I get it," said Kyle, shaking his head.

"Equally interesting is that junk bonds are now considered to be taboo, simply because they pay high interest rates. But are *all* junk bonds bad?" asked Michael.

"No, it still depends on the fundamentals."

"Isolating the idea of *'junk bond'* into the category of *'lose-all-my-money'* is an example of a disintegrated principle," said Michael.

"I see," said Kyle. "But that brings up an even bigger problem. If there are so many principles floating around out there, how do you choose the principles you want to integrate?" said Kyle.

"Ahh, the best question of the day," said Michael. "There are fewer basic principles than you might think. There's a recent magazine article about selling that gives us an excellent example. We can diagram this if you like," he suggested.

"Please do."

Michael went to the white board and scribbled the word "deductive" across the top. "Here's the scenario. A salesperson is described as having made a gross error (something bordering on incompetence), and costing her client a considerable amount of money. The error, as it turns out, was actually committed by someone in the client's offices and not by the salesperson. Unfortunately, the mistake gained publicity and had the effect of embarrassing the client, and damaging the reputation of the salesperson who was blamed. She was probably losing business as a result. She approached the paper, making the editor aware of the error, and asked that they recheck their sources. The editor refused. The client, who was a big customer, did not come forward to clear the salesperson's name either. She decided to *weather* the storm and remain quiet." He paused. "Good decision or bad?"

The group jumped to life, asking questions, making comments, arguing.

Bobby Green answered first. "It was all she could do. A little embarrassment in exchange for keeping a good customer is no big deal." he said.

"That's what she reasoned," he said and then wrote "Keep big customer—suffer a little embarrassment" on the white board. Below it he drew an arrow facing upward. "What did she attempt to do?" he asked.

"Keep the relationship," said Kyle.

"And the motivation?" asked Michael.

"Commissions."

"And what is she putting at risk?"

"Her reputation," said Kat.

Michael put each answer on the board and drew arrows to connect them.

"Now let's see if all these are integrated. What has to come before the commission?"

"A decent product, and a good job selling it," said Kyle.

Michael scribbled some more. "Good. And what's required to have a good relationship?"

"Both parties must benefit," said Madison.

"Oh, very good." He scribbled some more.

"Now, take a look at the diagram. What principles are at the foundation of those ideas?"

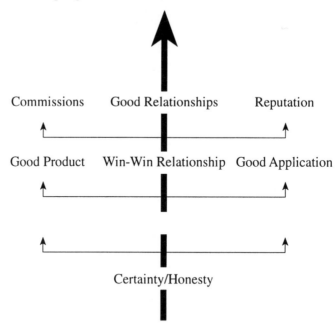

Keep big customer- suffer a little embarrassment.

Commissions   Good Relationships   Reputation

Good Product   Win-Win Relationship   Good Application

Certainty/Honesty

"I'm not sure about the left-hand side, but wouldn't it be 'legitimacy' in the middle . . . and maybe 'justice' on the right?" said Madison

"Very good! Especially justice. That's a difficult one to get in this circumstance and ultimately will be the crux of the decision. Anyone want to take a stab at what underlies 'good product'?"

"Purpose?" asked Kyle.

"Yes, that's right. We haven't spent much time on it yet, but you're absolutely right, Kyle."

Keep big customer- suffer a little embarrassment.

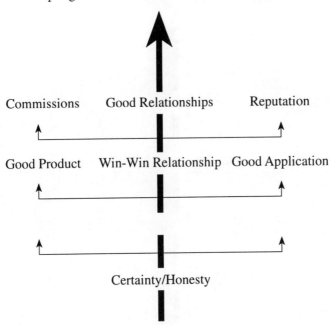

"Just in case anyone has missed it, this is classic deductive logic. It's an analysis on the basis of 'was it the right thing to do?' It's as simple as . . . do our more abstract ideas correspond with underlying concepts? If you run into a conflict as you move down the chain, the higher level abstraction is probably in trouble. Do you see the problem here?"

"Describe *embarrassment*," said Madison.

"You're going to fit in just fine here, Madison. In this instance, it means losing business because of a hit to your reputation," he said.

"There are plenty of contradictions," said Ryan. "Starting at the top you have a conflict if you believe reputation isn't a corollary of commissions. In other words, if your reputation goes, so will the commissions."

"How many of you agree?" asked Michael.

No one failed to raise a hand—not even Fischer. Michael scribbled an arrow from reputation to commissions.

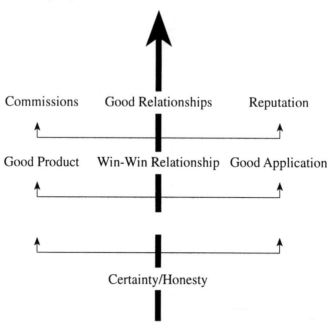

Keep big customer- suffer a little embarrassment.

Commissions Good Relationships Reputation

Good Product Win-Win Relationship Good Application

Certainty/Honesty

"Another contradiction," said Ryan. "Regarding the criteria for a good relationship; is it one-sided, and subservient? You know, 'am I willing to take any humiliation to make a buck'? It wouldn't be *my* definition."

Michael turned and waited for their reaction. When he got none he said, "Looks like we agree. Any more, Ryan?"

"Well, we've probably given enough reasons to change our decision already, but if you need more, the idea of *justice* has nothing to do with being blamed unfairly. And how can you feel as though you have purpose and legitimacy if you have sacrificed your self-respect for the commissions? Enough?" he asked.

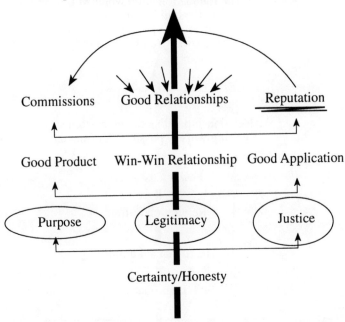

Keep big customer- suffer a little embarrassment.

Commissions   Good Relationships   Reputation

Good Product   Win-Win Relationship   Good Application

Purpose   Legitimacy   Justice

Certainty/Honesty

Michael drew arrows and circles and underlines on the graphic. He made a quick visual check of the group and said, "Yeah, I think you nailed that idea. You could have arrived at the same conclusion with inductive reasoning which is starting at the bottom and moving out. Inductive reasoning is a kind of 'looking forward' approach that would have been useful when making this decision initially If you start at the very bottom and work your way up the chain, what happens?" he asked.

The group worked through several possibilities on their own. Some muttered, some scribbled on paper. Michael crafted a new diagram.

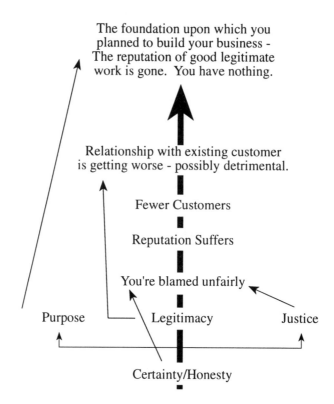

The foundation upon which you planned to build your business - The reputation of good legitimate work is gone. You have nothing.

Relationship with existing customer is getting worse - possibly detrimental.

Fewer Customers

Reputation Suffers

You're blamed unfairly

Purpose   Legitimacy   Justice

Certainty/Honesty

When he was done he pulled back from the white board. "What happens when we approach it this way?" he asked.

Ryan had a look of confidence. "It doesn't take long to discover where the conflicts will be. In fact, if you believe in the principles of certainty and honesty, you would do something to make sure it didn't go any further. If you weren't sure there'd be any damage, you might consider any of the other three principles and determine that you would never let such a mistake blossom to the point where it risked your reputation. You could avoid it all, or at least protect against, by starting at the principle level. It doesn't seem as though you need very many principles when you look at it this way," he said.

"Kyle? Do you agree?" asked Michael.

"Momma never told me there would be days like this!" said an exhausted Kyle to a round of laughter.

"I know this *seems* like an awful lot of *abstract* stuff, but actually it's the way your mind works naturally. You make this type of analysis, on a smaller scale, every moment of every day. The key, is whether your principles are correct and whether you make the effort to 'think' in a framework of integration. If your principles are wrong, integrating them is difficult or impossible. If you don't put in the effort to integrate your principles, for whatever reason—and trust me there are some less than honorable reasons—then you are condemned to poor-thinking."

"Now that we've had a glimpse of how you think, let's try some about our current topic—*competition*. Let's start with the negatives first," he said, turning to the two free-standing easels where the descriptions of competition stood.

Standard of Excellence Set's a minimum level of performance. Causes creativity Ingenuity Measure. Separates performers and non-performers. Trailblazing Fair and Just. Brings out the best in people. Elevates performance to it's highest level Pushes us into new discoveries. Power, Strength, Determination, Agility Sense of accomplishment. Pride. Self-respect.	Cut-throat. Killer instinct. Law of the jungle - kill or be killed. Not civilized. Money motivated. Brings out the worst in people. Not compassionate. Winning is everything. Always a 'winner' and a 'loser'. Puts the focus on the wrong thing. Shortsighted. Hurts innocent bystanders.

"Cut-throat," said Michael, circling it and turning to the class. "Does that mean that we would injure someone else to get whatever we're after?" he asked.

"Yeah," said Kyle.

"What principle does it collide with?"

"Everything," laughed Kat. "Justice, control, purpose."

"Throw it out?" asked Michael.

"Yes!" came a chorus.

"Killer instinct and 'law of the jungle' are pretty close. Are there conflicts? Tug, what do you think?"

It was a jolt to Fischer who had been drifting away from the class and was losing his edge. His nerves were getting frayed as he wondered about the futility of the bridge incident, and the risk of being found out. He was also showing signs of being careless. Among his character flaws was a propensity to talk too much when he was in trouble. It was exactly what Michael was hoping for.

"Competition means just one thing: beating the other guy," answered Fischer. "It's not a matter of falling across the finish line first, it's a matter of staying just ahead of your adversary. People find all kinds of ways to beat each other. Most people hope for the other guy to beat himself. The real winners help their competition to beat themselves."

"What do you mean?" said Michael softly.

"If I'm in a head-to-head duel, I'm not going to take my eye off the other guy. I'm going to throw obstacles in his path, try to surprise, bluff or deceive him into making mistakes," he said.

"Kind of like the bridge collapsing on Madison, *huh*?" said Michael without any hint of accusation. It had the tone of agreement so that it wouldn't be a warning. It was said as coolly as a trial attorney during prosecution.

Fischer hesitated for a second too long. His eyes darted to the side and returned. What was a momentary silence seemed to hang in the air like minutes. Then just as quickly, he gained his composure. "What do you mean?" he demanded.

"Just making a comparison to what you said about obstacles. If Kendra was employing your tactics, she would be hoping for the bridge to collapse, right?" Michael said, giving Fischer a way to extricate himself from the trap. There were grander traps to be sprung and he didn't want to alert Fischer to his suspicions just yet.

"Right. I mean. . . not really in that way," said Fischer. "I was speaking figuratively. I'd never want to hurt anyone." His tone carried the first hint of sincerity since he had been at the conference—a tone so uncharacteristic that it stood out like a flashing neon light. No one in the room believed him. Michael knew he had uncovered something. "Ryan and Kendra were probably right about their suspicions," he thought, but proving it would be a different matter altogether. Michael's thoughts were a moving stream of what ifs and probabilities. He needed a plan.

He continued. "Tug, do you see any conflicts with the rest of our principles and the idea of the 'law of the jungle'?"

"You're confusing your principles and mine," he sneered.

"*Right.* You're *exactly* right." He turned to the rest of the group. "Where are the conflicts with the 'law of the jungle' idea?" he asked.

"Michael, I'm not really sure. . . ," said Sally. ". . .would it conflict with our principle of vision?"

"That's right, Sally. How?"

"Euphemisms aside, we don't live in a 'jungle.' It's an excuse, a short-term excuse, to avoid the need for a conscience."

"How do you resolve the idea of 'kill or be killed' with 'power, strength and determination?" asked Michael.

"The first is a description of how animals survive—it's lame. The second is a human approach to survival," said Sally.

"You're not there yet, Sally. Power, strength and agility are physical attributes that would apply in the jungle," he said.

"Right, but none of us compete on that basis. We think in terms of 'mental strength,' 'mental agility' and 'powerful ideas.'"

"Now you have it. The phrase 'mind like a steel trap' is one that comes to mind. Power, strength, determination, agility, conviction. All of those are good descriptions of our cognitive processes as well. The environment, if it is a jungle, is one of thought, not brute force. So perhaps kill or be killed is an equally dramatic explanation, meant figuratively and not literally. But if killing is winning in the jungle, what is winning in the arena of the mind?" he asked.

Ryan smiled because the answer would sound more like an advertisement for Sales Esteem than discussion. "Integrated principles executed with strength, conviction and agility," he laughed at himself. The group laughed as well, recognizing the same tone.

"Okay. We've thrashed that one to death . . . so to speak. Next?" he said.

"Uncivilized is just a misinterpretation—kind of like killer instinct," said Kat.

"I'm satisfied with that."

"What about this?" he pointed at the word 'money-motivated' and underlined it.

Standard of Excellence	
Set's a minimum level of performance. Causes creativity Ingenuity Measure. Separates performers and non-performers. Trailblazing Fair and Just. Brings out the best in people. Elevates performance to it's highest level Pushes us into new discoveries. Power, Strength, Determination, Agility Sense of accomplishment. Pride. Self-respect.	√ Cut-throat. √ Killer instinct. √ Law of the jungle - kill or be killed. √ Not civilized. Money motivated. Brings out the worst in people. Not compassionate. Winning is everything. Always a 'winner' and a 'loser'. Puts the focus on the wrong thing. Shortsighted. Hurts innocent bystanders.

"Obviously they haven't heard your discussion on motivation or money," said Kyle.

"Then being motivated by money is okay, so long as it's in the context of value exchange?" he said.

"Yes!" came a chorus from the group.

"And how many people are motivated by more than money?"

Everyone lifted an arm into the air, except Fischer who had more on his mind than answering questions.

Michael went to the next white board topic "Brings out the worst in people. Hmmm . . . No argument if the definition of competition is disintegrated principles." He paused to determine their agreement, then continued, "How about 'not compassionate'. There's an interesting one."

Madison had been waiting for this one. "The question is . . . how do you define compassion?" she asked.

"You want to give it a try?"

"Can I answer with a question?" she said.

"Go ahead."

"Is compassion a physical action or a mental one?"

"Both," said Sally. "It's got to be mental first, though."

"Okay, how is the physical act carried out?"

"Charity," said Sally.

"Have you ever finished in second place, Sally?" asked Madison.

"Sure," said Sally.

"How would you have reacted if the winner offered you first place?"

"I would have turned her down."

"Why? Isn't that charity?" pressed Madison.

"It would be insulting. I didn't win. But compassion isn't meant for runners-up."

"Who then?"

"Those who aren't capable of competing."

"Then it isn't a question of competition, is it?"

"I guess not," said Sally. "What's your definition, Madison?"

"I think of compassion as admiration of effort and hard work. Admiration for the effort required to be second-place, or third-place. Admiration in ever decreasing degrees, depending on the amount of effort," said Madison.

"That's cold," said Sally.

"Really? Are you suggesting we admire second-place more than first, or third-place more than second?" asked Madison.

"No, I don't think we should admire them more than the winner. I just think we should be compassionate for anyone willing to give it a try," Sally said with conviction.

"What does that mean? Are you saying we should just *feel* it—or do you expect some *action* to follow?"

"I don't know, Madison, I haven't really thought about it."

"I'm sorry Sally, but that's true. You haven't *thought* about it."

Michael watched as they volleyed back and forth. There was something bubbling inside Madison and he was curious to see if it would come out into the open.

"What's the big deal, Madison? Why have you given it so much *thought*?" retaliated Sally.

Madison hesitated and looked at Michael. She was coming to work for Michael, but she didn't want it to appear as though she were trying to thrust herself in where she didn't yet belong. Her eyes asked whether she should proceed. Michael understood and gave a several quick nods of his head to hurry his approval. She went on.

"I *have* thought about it—but from a different angle. The idea that we should glorify anyone willing to try—regardless of how poorly they do—*feels* warm and fuzzy, but I wonder what impact it has," she said.

"Explain what you mean, Madison," said Michael.

"We know people are born with different skills, and that from that point forward, they have to put forth the effort to make the most of what they have." She paused. "It's a simple black and white fact that some people will finish last. It isn't fun to finish last. But suppose that you do, and the response you get—the feedback—is 'compassion.' At its center is the message that the *effort* is what counts—winning doesn't matter. Without arguing that point, let's just assume that you're the loser and you continually hear, 'winning isn't everything—it's the effort that counts.' What, and this is the critical question, what do you suppose goes on in the loser's mind?"

A smile had been building on Michael's face. The method in which Madison was attacking the subject was exquisite. No one answered Madison's question. Michael glanced around the room, and finally said, "Madison, build the scenario for us, maybe that will help."

"The reality is that winners get the rewards, losers don't. Winners get the admiration, losers don't. Winners get all that they deserve, losers get nothing . . . except mind games from the 'compassionate.' Mind games that send a message that they really won, because they tried, only that society—an 'unjust' society— doesn't recognize it. I admire the effort, but it's *just.* Some people win, others are runners-up. Some people lose. There's no hiding from that fact—unless 'feeling' takes on the illusion of being real. The implication is obvious, don't you think?" she asked.

There was still a lot of confusion. Ryan knew what Madison was getting at, but not certain how he could help her tie it together. "Madison, do you think the second and third place—or the losers for that matter—feel cheated?" he said.

"I think that's part of it. The winner is not always held in high esteem by the losers." She paused as it sunk in and everyone in the room made the connection of jealousy.

"Why do you suppose that is?" she asked. "Why do you suppose that frequent reaction toward the winner is one of *resentment.* How can second- and third-place strive for the same virtues that propelled the winner to victory and feel scorn when the winner has them. You can't value something and despise it at the same time—unless someone is leading you to believe that the value is not in winning, but in trying, and that you are a victim. A victim of the winner who has gotten all the rewards the loser deserves for trying."

"Come on, Madison. Don't you think that's a little too contrived?" said Kat.

Madison was calm and restrained in her answer. "Kat? I don't believe that jealousy is a *natural* human emotion. It's too destructive. I believe that people, left to think on their own, without this distorted idea of 'compassion,' would admire the attributes they seek, not hate those who have them. It's rare, but there are athletes I know who hold absolutely no resentment for their superior competitors. It's how *I feel*. I can't tell you how much I admire Kendra. She epitomizes the sport for me. She's an inspiration to me. But I am in a minority when it comes to that." She paused. "How do you feel about your competitors?"

"I admire their good work and am critical of the bad stuff they do," she said innocently.

"I'm sure you've been at the top from time to time, doing good work. Were you admired by all of your competitors?" said Madison.

"Well, no. Now that I think of it, we are maligned unfairly most of the time. It's a nasty business."

"So the effect is there. What's the cause, Kat? Is that just human nature? Is it competition? Or is it the result of a bad principle—a bad principle called compassion—turned and twisted—that engenders hatred because it tells the losers that the rewards for winning are unjust? Yes, I know it's a deeply woven theory, but I don't know of another explanation. If you're told long enough that losing is okay, trying is the key; and you never get the rewards, there is only one resolution—you either toss out the idea that trying is the main event, or you resent the winner. If you have another hypothesis, I'd love to hear it," she said.

Kat didn't. Neither did anyone else. They had never considered it. Most of them had been the victims of envy. Some had fallen into the trap of resenting others and couldn't disagree with the analysis. All of them, with the possible exception of Fischer and Shaw, wanted to believe that it was natural to admire skill and success.

"I think compassion has a place, though," said Madison to everyone's surprise. "I felt compassion for Kendra when she failed to make the Olympic Team in '88. Not because she was trying, but because she had all the skills I admire, and circumstances caught her off-guard. Would I argue that she was treated unfairly? No. Do I understand what it would be like to train, become the best, and then miss because of a fluke? You bet. The difference is I admire the person with the skills to stand at the top, and can understand the agony of failing to pull in the rewards. Would I intervene to change it? Never. Compassion is when stuff goes wrong for others who share your values but circumstances didn't allow them to triumph. It's not the way I wish it were, but it happens, and you move on. Compassion is the communication to those who share your values that you understand the effort, and you wish it had turned out differently," she said, falling silent. The group was stunned into deep thought. It was practically more than they could digest. They sat silently and contemplated her comments for a moment.

Michael cleared his throat and announced, "This looks like a great place to break. Let's take about fifteen minutes."

Kendra got up from her chair and walked over to Madison as the rest of the group emptied into the hall. She put her hand on Madison's shoulder and squeezed softly. "Thanks. I'm moved by what you said." Tears welled up in her eyes and they embraced. They stood for a moment and then pulled away from each other, slightly embarrassed by the public display of their feelings for one another.

The group wandered around the Summit's lobby, halls and outside deck with echoes of Madison's words ringing in their consciousness. Many felt anxious and uneasy. The kind of feeling one gets when some of life's philosophies are turned upside-down.

Shaw and Fischer huddled near a corner of the deck where they were certain they couldn't be overheard. Shaw spoke first. "Damn it! They don't seem to be disrupted at all by the bridge accident," he said.

"It's all we can do, Jock. I expected them to pack up and go home. I guess I underestimated them," said Fischer.

"Do you think they suspect anything?"

"Doesn't matter. They have absolutely no proof. No evidence. If they accuse us, we'll just deny it. They can't touch us," he said with defiance that Shaw wasn't sure he shared.

They saw the others returning to the conference room and followed them in. Michael was waiting patiently for the group to settle in. Once they were settled, he started.

"Okay. Let's pick up our conversation about competition at 'winning is everything.' Does anyone 'live' that idea?" he asked.

"I think I do—at least most of the time," said Bobby.

"You didn't win on the path," said Kat.

"What do you mean? Sally never matched my times," he protested.

"I wasn't talking about Sally. Madison's times were much better."

Bobby didn't answer and Michael interrupted to stop him from arguing a point he couldn't make. "Bobby, what exactly does 'winning is everything' mean?"

"Well, I suppose it means you don't give up on your goals. You persevere."

"Those are admirable attributes, but I don't think you really mean to combine the two. Will you give up your family? How about your freedom, or your conscience? Would you sacrifice those values to achieve your professional goals?"

"Of course not."

"So you don't 'live' the idea. Winning is a result of pursuing a goal with more expertise than others. It doesn't have anything to do with sacrifice. If it calls for a sacrifice of precedental values, then it's likely that the goal's not worth winning."

"I understand. And I'll save you the trouble of eliminating the idea that competition puts the focus on the wrong thing. It's essentially the same thing isn't it?" said Bobby.

"Yes, you do understand," said Michael. "What about the criticism that competition forces a distinction between winners and losers—and therefore always creates a 'loser.'"

"It's true though, isn't it, Michael?"

"Yes it is, by definition, and in reality. Competition means someone will be last. Is that bad?" he asked.

"It's unfortunate," said Leslie.

"From whose perspective?"

"The last place finisher."

"Then it isn't bad from the next-to-last place finisher."

"Come on, Michael, you know what I mean," she said.

"Sure I do, but I have to reject the idea without condition. Competition without interference must—it must—result in someone finishing last. You can't manage competition—because the moment you do, it's no longer competition. It's something else. You cannot pass judgment about a metaphysical certainty. It just is. And the moment you change it, you've obliterated the original circumstance," he said.

"I think I understand. But isn't it a noble cause to try to give everyone all they hope for?" she pleaded.

"I want you to consider the circular contradiction you get into. You can eliminate competition and have equality, but it takes intervention. To balance it, you must take away from the more competitive and give it to the less competitive. What happens when the more competitive realize effort is stripped away? When they realize that hard work is penalized. Do the more competitive try harder? If they do, more is taken. Once the more competitive are bloodied, and educated, they work less. Suddenly, the old losers are the hardest workers. But they see that they are penalized in order to bring them to the lower level of their once stronger competitors. They slow down, too. Now the goal is to find the lowest common denominator of motivation."

"Isn't that socialism," asked Leslie.

"Yes Leslie, it is. It's a terribly simplified version of why it doesn't work—and probably not all that well articulated—but it's not far from the reason it can't work. People are what they are. They need motivation. They need the freedom to reach their potential. Any attempt to reverse human nature is doomed to fail." He paused.

"I didn't intend to get that far off track, but I think you can see the connection. Kyle has taken care of the next on the list, which leaves us with 'shortsighted' and the idea that competition hurts innocent bystanders. Who would like to tackle those two?"

Ryan answered first. "The concept of shortsighted means you fail to view the full range of your actions. It's an impossibility to achieve the goal by falling short of the goal. But that doesn't mean there aren't shortsighted goals. Some are terribly shortsighted. But that's not an indictment on competition. It's an indictment on the principles pursuing the goal. Competition, in that sense, comes after the goals and the consequences of pursuing those goals are determined. It's a result—not a cause."

"Nicely put, Ryan," said Michael. "And what about innocent bystanders?"

"The same type of argument holds," said Kat. "There are injuries to innocent people caught in the crossfire of competition, but that's not the result of competition. It's the result of principles and actions which include the chance that someone innocent will be hurt."

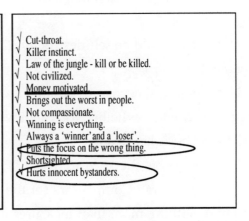

"Very good. One final idea about competition, what is the ultimate form of competition?" he asked.

Madison answered. "For me, competition is the challenge turned inward. Look at the negative comments again. Ask yourself if those views aren't all caused by action directed *at* someone else?" she said, as she walked to the board and scribbled some arrows.

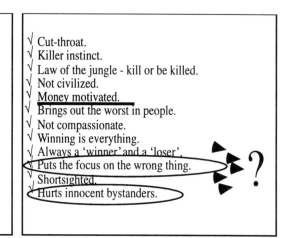

Standard of Excellence	√ Cut-throat.
Set's a minimum level of performance.	√ Killer instinct.
Causes creativity	√ Law of the jungle - kill or be killed.
Ingenuity	√ Not civilized.
Measure.	√ Money motivated.
Separates performers and non-performers.	√ Brings out the worst in people.
Trailblazing	√ Not compassionate.
Fair and Just.	√ Winning is everything.
Brings out the best in people.	√ Always a 'winner' and a 'loser'.
Elevates performance to it's highest level	Puts the focus on the wrong thing.
Pushes us into new discoveries.	√ Shortsighted.
Power, Strength, Determination, Agility	Hurts innocent bystanders.
Sense of accomplishment.	
Pride.	
Self-respect.	

"And if you are competing against yourself, would you ever think of it in those terms?" she asked.

"No! Most would be self-destructive," said Kat in a tone of discovery. "They're all directed outward."

"Now look at the positive comments. Can you apply this to everything you struggle to achieve—whether you call it winning or not?" said Madison.

Kat just shook her head.

"Competition is the *reference point*. Every great competitor competes against himself—not others. Competitors set the reference points, low, average and high, but they're nothing more than measures of whether you're realizing your goals. I ran faster than I thought possible because I could see it *was* possible. Kendra was ahead of me, running that fast. I didn't know whether I could beat her, but I knew that she represented a level that exceeded my goal. If reached, I would have exceeded my goal. My only interest is to what level I can push my performance." She paused.

"And look at it from Kendra's point of view. If she had been competing against me, she would have had to slow *down*." Madison finished the sentence with a laugh. "If she weren't competing against herself—she would be under-performing." With that Madison looked over to Kendra, who was nodding her head emphatically.

"Professional track is certainly head-to-head competition, but we all think—and compete—in terms of our *times*," said Kendra. "Did you know that most world records are set in the absence of a 'dead-heat' struggle?" In other words, it's not that extra effort that we associate with competition that pushes us beyond the old record. It's the individual performing against herself, against the clock, against the old record. It's the inward-focused goal fashioned by the knowledge of what it takes to be the best," she said.

The room was silent. The individuals in the room lived in an environment that was competitive on a daily basis. Every day they could tally up their activities and determine their performance. Each and every one of them thought they understood competition to the letter, yet their perspective was changing. They were applying their own experiences to determine if Madison and Kendra could offer them a new perspective. A new perspective that they could use in their competitive worlds.

Ryan spoke up. "Has anyone else in the room ever noticed that when you're competing with yourself you rarely ever do something damaging? And the times that you're competing solely with other people are the times when you mess up?"

"Oh bull, Ryan," said Jock Shaw. "Some of your best months came when we had you going head-to-head with Solly and Benjamin," he said.

"Jock, do you have any idea of the production I did before you showed up? That's when I set all the firm's sales records. Funny thing, I didn't think of it in those terms at that time. I wasn't competing with the others in the office. I was driven by my father's favorite ethic, 'always do your best.' Now I see that at that time, I was competing with myself." He paused as he was caught in the memory of his father's gentle, guiding words."

Ryan was discussing Jock's involvement as though he was solving a mystery, not fully aware that he was indicting Shaw in front of a room full of people. He was removed from the circumstances, searching for the truth. "After you showed up, everything changed. The focus was all wrong—beat the other guy into submission. Always an external conflict. Always a fight. You fostered that environment. You weren't bringing out our best, you were dredging up anger and emotion all focused on the wrong thing—other people. My production *never* got back to the old levels. And you're part of the reason." He finished, his eyes glossy and his stare vacant and removed.

Shaw sat stunned—disbelieving that Ryan was pouring it out for everyone to hear. The rest of the group was equally surprised. One by one they turned their gaze to Shaw.

"Ryan. I didn't know you felt that way," came Shaw's response with just a hint of understanding. "I thought everyone liked to compete in the firm. No one ever complained," he said. It sounded like an apology, but just as quickly, Shaw's attitude changed. "It's the way the business is. There's no room for wimps or second place. You fight, or you lose. That's all there is to it. And here we sit in this . . . this . . . sales conference, and listen to drivel about inward-focused competition. It's bullshit. It doesn't work. It's a fairy tale, Ryan, and I can't believe a star like you is getting suckered in by it."

Michael threw himself into the middle. "Jock, all the evidence seems to disagree with you. A world class athlete disagrees with you. I disagree with you. Your own salesman disagrees with you. Do you suppose that we're wrong and you're right, without evidence to support your position? Just how foolish do you want to appear? I strongly suggest you take control of your emotions and cut your losses now." Michael's voice finished with a tone so authoritative and powerful that everyone in the room turned their head to look at him. It was a command from the man they respected more than practically any other they had met. It was a refusal to tolerate the whining opinion of the pathetic loser. Shaw went silent. The room was quiet, but no one missed the moment of victory for Ryan. A cheer seemed to rise silently from each of them. They could see Ryan being unshackled from Shaw, and it was a beautiful sight.

Michael returned to the topic. "Competition is a principle, just like causality, vision, or justice. It's inaccurate to think of competion as a primitive human trait. It's a principle designed to achieve our values," he said. "Competition is setting your goals, knowing what standards there are for reaching those goals, and then measuring yourself along the way—against other people, benchmarks, or time. That's the *principle* of competition—a plan for realizing your values. It recognizes that there will be under-achievers, achievers and over-achievers—or if you prefer— winners and losers of various degrees. *Competition* is the principle—and its action is *effort*—effort in terms of striving, struggling, doing. The resulting emotion is self-respect. It's he knowledge that you *performed,* the knowledge that you reached for your dreams, struggled for your dreams, and realized them," said Michael, coaxing a slide into the projector.

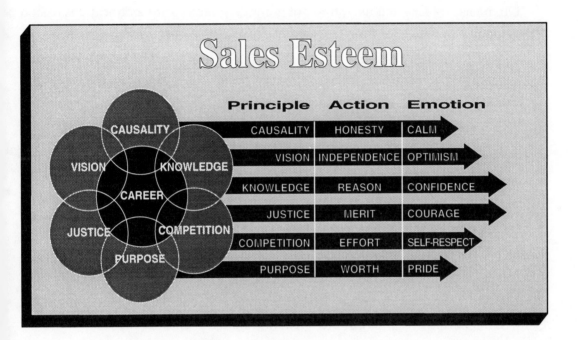

"And if *competition* is a Sales Esteem principle, it means there's a . . . ?"

". . . *a counter principle*." came a chorused answer.

"Yeah." Michael smiled. "This is a tough one, though."

Kendra waved a hand in Michael's direction. "A principle with the opposite intention of competition can only mean one thing," she said.

"That's right."

"Let me guess . . . *equality*. All winners, or more accurately, all losers to the same degree," she said.

"Does anyone know the correct term for that principle?"

There were no answers. Michael waited a moment longer before answering. "It shouldn't be surprising that it's a political term. An idea fabricated by society that can only exist with the support of intervention. The term is *egalitarianism*; and Kendra stated its goal perfectly. It's the notion that all can achieve the same goals, to the same degree, without regard to finite values, individual differences, or individual effort. If there is a more poorly constructed idea than that, I have yet to see it. It defies reality. To achieve it, requires force—either physical or mental. It takes pulling the weak up, and tearing the strong down. It is the act of taking from the best and giving to the weak," said Michael.

"Oh, please, please, tell us you're not going to go into some political discussion of the differences between competition and socialism," said Tug Fischer.

Michael looked over at Tug. "I hadn't planned to, Tug, but you're right, the two principles have been tried by millions of people, with a historically disastrous result. I'll leave it at that. Competition works because it is in step with reality, the differences in people, and the fact that there is not an infinite amount of values available for the asking. It works because gaining something requires effort, and competition brings out the best in us, pushing us along towards all of its positive results. The resulting emotion is self-respect, which should be obvious by now."

"Its opposite is *egalitarianism* and its action is *demand*. A claim that something is due to the individual and the action of *demanding* that it be delivered," he said. "The principle of competition, and its corresponding action of effort results in Self-Respect. Its opposite emotion is self-contempt." Michael paused for a moment. "Self-contempt, it drips and oozes disgust, doesn't it?"

"One last look at our positive reactions to competition. Keep in mind, the key distinction is the focus on the individual with competition as a principle method for measuring our progress, pushing us to excel, and encouraging effort. I like the list."

Standard of Excellence
Set's a minimum level of performance.
Causes creativity
Ingenuity
Measure.
Separates performers and non-performers.
Trailblazing
Fair and Just.
Brings out the best in people.
Elevates performance to it's highest level
Pushes us into new discoveries.
Power, Strength, Determination, Agility
Sense of accomplishment.
Pride.
Self-respect.

19

Purpose

A person is really alive only when he is moving
forward to something more.
—*Winfred Rhoades*

"And now we arrive at our final topic. It's been left 'till last because it asks broader, more encompassing questions of you and your sales career. Why did you choose your career? Why are you still here?" he said mischievously. "What's the meaning of your sales career? Why do you put in the effort? Why . . . why. . . why?" he asked, raising his hands.

"It's still a mystery why I started selling," said Shannon, laughing. "But I know why I stayed."

"Tell us."

"The money is good and the work is professionally fulfilling," she said.

"Both are important to you?" he asked.

"Yes. Money was more important when I started. But now it's a result of the things I find satisfying about the work. Enjoying the work is the reason to stay and the money follows," she said.

"Give me a broad name for it, if you can."

"I think I'd call it my professional purpose," said Shannon.

"Very good. We all pursue things we find to have *value*. Money is the medium of exchange to acquire the physical values. But it's not limited to the physical. There are emotional values to be had as well—as we have discussed all week long. As it pertains to the physical values, money is the result, but something must happen first. Who has the answer?"

Madison answered. "People come together to form social systems. There's just one reason to do so—to exchange their respective skills," she said.

"Right again," said Michael. "*Purpose* is a Sales Esteem principle. It leads to the action of being 'of value' to others as a method for pursuing our own values. It is the idea of exchange—one individual's skills in exchange for another's."

Michael flipped on the slide projector and punched the remote control a few times to locate the Sales Esteem paradigm.

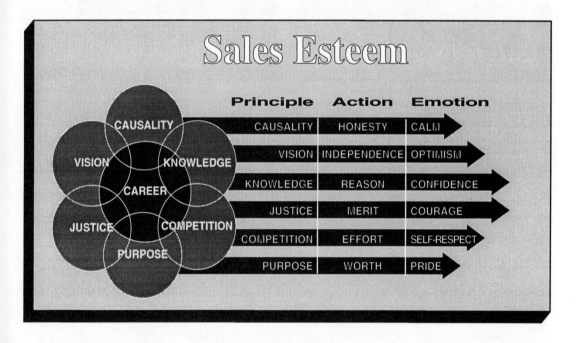

"*Purpose* leads to the action of 'providing identifiable *worth*' to the customer. The emotional result is *pride*. Purpose holds that there's a reason to acquire knowledge about your occupation. The reason is that you intend to provide something of value, for which you will be rewarded.

The opposite principle of purpose is *control*. Control is force—force used in opposition to the individual's own decision making. Control, whether consider necessary—or evil—occurs only when those who are controlled are considered to be incapable of their own guidance. Control can be physical or mental force. It can be threats or intimidation—or deception—all on the premise that those being controlled are incapable of self-sufficiency. The principle of control leads to actions of *manipulation*, either to hurry the ignorant customer toward a decision without their cooperation, or to deceive a competent customer about the subject matter. Either way, unless the customer is freely considering a value-selection, with accurate information, the only choice is manipulation," he said pausing for a moment.

Kyle Mitchell shifted in his chair. "Michael, I'm sorry, but most of us are taught that being in control is a good thing. I don't understand."

"It's an excellent point, Kyle. The question is, what can you control? Can you control other people, or is it possible that it's limited to 'controlling yourself'?" he asked.

"Both."

"Is controlling others effective?" he pressed a little further.

"Yes, Michael," Kyle said with some frustration.

"Okay," said Michael. "I challenge everyone in the room to take five minutes and come up with a circumstance where they have directly controlled—not influenced—but successfully controlled 'complex behavior.' The behavior of employees, customers, bosses, spouses, children, siblings . . . anyone. Complex behavior is defined as more than menial tasks like 'get-me-a-cup-of-coffee' or 'ditch digging.' Complex behavior is decision making. How does your child approach their education? How does your spouse approach his or her career? How do customers decide to spend their hard-earned money? Five minutes to see if we have any aspiring gods in the group," he said, thrusting himself up and into a sitting position on the table in front. He waited.

The group went to work. Some stared out the windows. Others doodled on the legal pad in front of them. Some clasped their hands, elbows on the table, and perched their chins on top in contemplation. A few minutes later Michael got up and walked around the room among them. He circulated through the room for a few minutes, looking over their shoulders at notes they had made, smiling at those whose eyes met his, clutching a few on the shoulders as he passed. When he got back to the front of the room he spun and asked, "Okay. Who is capable of controlling others? When has it worked?"

"I control my kids," said Kat. "They're not capable of making all their own decisions."

"How old are they Kat?"

"One is twelve. The other is eight."

"Do they ever rebel?"

Kat hesitated. Her twelve-year-old had become a handful, which was nothing new to most experienced parents, but was troubling to Kat. "My eight-year-old is perfect. My twelve-year-old is going through some difficult times," she said.

"Why?"

"She thinks I'm trying to run her life."

"Trying to control her?"

"Yes, I suppose," confessed Kat.

"Is there a chance that our children move from menial decisions to complex decisions?" asked Michael.

There were nods throughout the room. Michael continued. "I know that most of you have children . . . many in their teenage years. How many have watched in frustration as they insist on making their own decisions about complex issues?"

Hands went up all around the room. "Control?" asked Michael. "Consider how you felt at their age. Look at it from their perspective. Are children really different from adults when it comes to the three primary values? Do kids yearn for freedom values that come from independence? Perhaps the best method for examining control is to take a walk in the other's shoes. Kat? Think back to your time as a teen. Add the context of the world your daughter lives in and consider how you would operate. Does it change your perspective?"

Kat was nodding her head as she shuddered slightly at the thought of growing up again.

Michael continued, "Does anyone have a successful example of controlling others?"

Bobby raised his hand slightly. "Michael, I think it's a matter of degree. I mean managers control their workers all the time. They set tasks, and work schedules . . . and then discipline and promote their workers."

"Thank you, Bobby. And you're right. Supervision is thought of as control, but it relies on a loose definition, doesn't it? But take a moment to consider the word 'control.' If you have less than total control . . . do you have something different than control? I would argue that your manager has no control over you, Bobby, and here's why. The foundation of your relationship with your company is negotiated exchange—not bondage. Pay for work, or pay for ideas . . . there's nothing else. You could name a litany of actions that you would refuse to do for your employer, regardless of the pay. True?"

Bobby was shaking his head. "Sure. Do you want a list?"

"Why not. Go ahead."

"I wouldn't injure someone else for the company, or work longer hours without more pay, or move to the new plant in Guadalajara, or steal trade secrets, or lie to customers," he said.

"So who is in control?" asked Michael slowly.

"I am," said Bobby.

"That's only partly correct."

Bobby's smile faded. "What do you mean?" he asked.

"You have control of your actions. Your manager is in control of hers. Can she control you to the point that you willingly do any of the things you listed?"

"No. I'd walk."

"And can you control her?"

"No, she can fire me, but she certainly has the upper hand. She can choose to let me go at any time."

"Can you put yourself in her shoes for a moment, Bobby?"

"Yeah, sure."

"How does she view Bobby Green, as an employee?"

"I think she likes me a lot."

"No. I said put yourself in her shoes. No guessing. Real analysis. How does she view Bobby Green—objectively?"

"He's the top producer. His customers come back time and time again. He works hard and hardly ever misses work. He's independent and doesn't need much help," said Bobby, his face blushing from the complimentary self-examination.

"Are you going to get rid of Bobby?"

"Wouldn't I be a fool to do so?"

"Yes, you would. Where do you think her success comes from? Canning good workers and hiring their opposites, just in order to have control?"

"There are managers like that," said Kat.

"Yes there are. They believe in control as a principle. And what ultimately happens to those people?" asked Michael.

"They fail," said Kat.

"It's a generalization, I know. . . " said Michael. ". . . but consider the controllers you know. How many are very successful? How many end up with a staff of 'yes-men'? How many doers are there among the controllers you know? How many leaders?"

"And how does it apply to selling?" Michael asked.

Tug Fischer understood control very well. "You have to set up the circumstances so that there are few choices for the customer to make—if any," he said.

"What exactly does that mean, Tug?" said Michael, failing to hide his frustration.

"It means that if you wait for others to decide, nothing would ever get done. You have to press the customer into action—everyone knows that ninety percent of selling is *closing*."

Michael smiled broadly as though he predicted the outcome of the conversation precisely. "Tug? Do you believe that?" he asked.

"In case you've missed something here, Mr. Cevanté, I believe practically the opposite of what you are suggesting," he said, causing the others to turn and stare as his comments registered. Fischer was striking out, the only thing he had left. Michael didn't return the joust. Instead, he addressed the rest of the group.

"Selling in communication, the communication of concepts. The "close" tests how well you have communicated. There are just three things that can happen at the close: 'Misunderstanding,' which can be the result of poor listening skills as well as poor communication skills; 'Believing,' which implies faith or trust in some of the concepts being presented and relies less on evidence; or 'Comprehending,' which is necessary for successful communication. This is what I like to refer to as the 'purchase versus the sale'. In one instance—comprehending—the customer purchases. They initiate the action. In the other instance, the salesperson must 'sell,' asking the customer to substitute faith, trust, or some other 'feeling' for evidence." He paused and walked over to Fischer's desk, standing over him.

"In Tug's world . . . with Tug's principles . . . closing *is* ninety percent of selling," Michael said, looking down at Fischer, and then back to the rest of the group. "Tug's principles are chance, abdication and feelings. He's built a sales argument based on nothing more substantial than mist. There's nothing *left to do* but close by controlling the customer."

Michael's stare was as cold as steel when he looked back at Fischer. The look froze him into silence. Michael turned away and walked back to the front. He grabbed the slide projector's control-pad and poked it several times, searching for the slide he wanted. A dozen frames later he came to an architectural drawing of house plans for a large, modern home. The finished home was pictured above it. Its lines were precise and purposeful, leading the viewer to make the immediate connections between the design, its structure and the end result.

Next to that was a crude hand-drawn series of lines that formed vague boxes, jagged roof lines, and crude windows. Above this drawing was a crumbling, dilapidated home that looked as though it would collapse at any moment.

Michael chuckled. "This is intentionally dramatic, but I think you probably get the point. The beautiful home on the left was the result of an elegant, thoughtful, and precise design. Anyone, regardless of their knowledge of engineering, can follow an explanation of how the drafted plans will lead to the completed home. This is elegant communication—on the basis of substance—this is Sales Esteem communication. Foundations, solid structure, consistency and, finally, the integrated whole. As the salesperson builds their recommendations for the customer, it 'comes together' for the customer in just the same way that you would grasp the logical design and construction of the home. There is no need to control the customer's decision—he *sees* it for himself. It's obvious. The plans in this example are nothing more than a graphic communication of concepts. Words are the same thing. Symbols or sounds that convey concepts. Clear communication paints similar conceptual images for the customer. When they are based on substance, they are easy to communicate and, more importantly, easy to grasp by the customer. The customer is in a position to *buy* instead of *be sold*," he said.

Michael paused for their rebuttal, but none came. Fischer had begun to lose his will to fight. The potential of being implicated in the bridge accident was weighing on his mind. Its intended impact hadn't occurred. The ensuing confusion and disarray Fischer had hoped for never came.

Michael continued. "The opposite principle of control is *worth*. A word that is overused, superficially and frivolously, by far too many pretenders. In this context, it's the *value* you provide your customers. In Kendra's world, it's the value she has to offer to track fans, who seek entertainment. Her value is to deliver the visual impact of strength, skill, effort, and competition that thrills the audience at the track. In *my* world, value is the power of my ideas and the ability to increase *your* performance, the ability to communicate them clearly for you in a manner that you can grasp and retain. Whether we like it or not, we're all judged on the value— whatever its form—that we provide to others. It's the basis of all human interaction—even love and companionship. All healthy, human interaction requires an *exchange of value*."

Michael pushed himself up onto his sitting position on the table at the front, waiting for their reaction. Sally Holiday was fidgeting. "Michael?" she said, nervously. "Would anyone have tried to save my life if I had nothing to offer in exchange?"

Michael smiled warmly. "Frankly, we've never had cause for such a severe test of the principle of value. For the most part, the idea is quite easy to grasp, isn't it? Your company pays you for the value you provide. Your family appreciates you for the way you care for them. Your friends do things for you in exchange for the companionship you provide. The answer to your question is . . . probably not. The good news is that you were of *enough* value for Kevin, Madison and I to take the risks we did—which were considerable. But don't misunderstand the value we place on your life. It is not out of some altruistic sense of sacrificing our lives to save yours. Truthfully, I don't like the idea of people dying at my conference. It tends to make developing new business more difficult," he said to cautious laughter from the group. "Beyond that, the compassion we demonstrated for you could come from only one place; we seek in other people the values we hold ourselves. Your life is precious to the extent that your personal values are similar to mine. You are a reflection of the values I hold, and I have an interest, and a desire to protect those with similar values. It's the distinction we make when we point a gun at the enemy instead of our countrymen during war. And to draw the point more clearly, had you been a crazed murderer bent on killing me, with values of complete contradiction to mine, I would have pushed you off the edge instead," he said bluntly.

The group was completely silent. So was Sally.

"It isn't a pretty thought, is it? But it's honest." Michael paused.

"Business is an exchange of value. Selling is an exchange of value. The principle of worth holds that as the salesperson you deliver something that the customer seeks—something of value. Depending on the product and the customer's needs, the value may be transaction oriented or augmentation oriented. Bobby sells computer components to a price conscious market. The value he delivers is consistent, efficient delivery at a very competitive price. His value is transaction oriented. Ryan structures complex bond strategies for large pension plan managers, the value he delivers is the modeling he does regarding pricing and timing. His value is augmentation oriented. In all cases, the salesperson is paid for and commensurate with, the value he brings to each individual sale. Consider this diagram," he said, poking the projector controls to bring up the next slide.

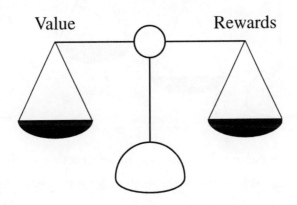

"Regardless of the actions you are rewarded for—work, friendship or ideas—you're rewarded in a manner that is relative to the value your action delivers to someone else. Value and rewards tend to be balanced. But what's wrong with the example on the screen?" he asked.

"It's not always in balance," said Ryan.

"Exactly. Value and rewards don't always have a perfect correlation in the short-run, but what happens over time?"

"They balance out?" Ryan asked.

"Right. Let's see how the diagram handles that." He punched up the next slide.

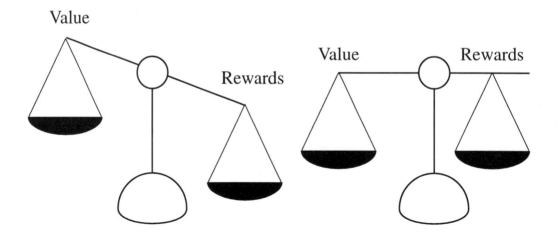

"The scales can be balanced by adding or subtracting to the quantity on each side, or by moving the placement of the scales along the arm. Some people prefer one visualization to the other, but for our purposes, the graphic on the right is more descriptive. If you have been overcompensated, no one will ask you to repay the company. If the value you provide is temporarily higher than the rewards, the rewards aren't returned. Instead of removing something from one of the trays, balance is achieved by moving the scales along the arm.

"The net effect is that Value and Rewards shift along the length of the arm until they reach equilibrium. For example, as you increase the Value side, the Reward side has to shift as well," he said, and brought up the next slide.

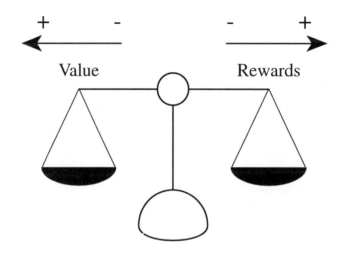

"I refer to this as Value/Reward Equilibrium because, over time, a balance will be reached. If your value is greater than the rewards, the rewards will shift and catch up. And the reverse is true. If you are over-rewarded relative to the value you provide, the rewards will shift.

"The department store chain Nordstrom is a great example of this. Their sales clerks increased their value by recommending clothes to match the customer's tastes, body type, personality, and so on. A segment of the populace was willing to pay for that extra value in the form of higher clothing prices, part of which was increased compensation to the clerks. A clerk who excelled at the service was not only more highly compensated on each sale, but increased the number of customers through referrals. It also enhanced the job satisfaction for the sales staff, not only from increased pay, but emotionally. Would anyone like to take a stab at the emotional result?"

Sally Holiday answered. "Pride."

"Absolutely. How?" asked Michael.

"The purpose of the job changed. Instead of chasing a customer around racks of clothes trying to locate the right size, the clerk 'designed' the look," she said.

"That's a nice way of putting it, Sally. Designing the look. *Purpose* is the principle here, *worth* is the action, and *pride* is the emotional result. Where's our paradigm?" he said, turning the carousel around to locate the right slide.

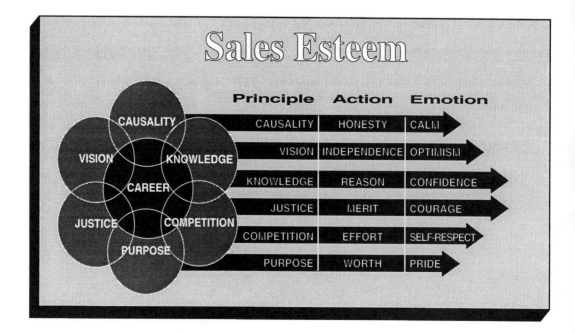

"There it is: *Purpose, worth, pride.*" Michael paused.

"By the way, we haven't had an opportunity yet to talk about today's run between Bobby and Sally. I think this is an appropriate time. Bobby, with all the confusion, were you able to check your time?"

"Yeah, eighteen, ten flat."

Michael went to the time-chart at the front of the room and scribbled it into place. "Sally?" he asked.

"Eighteen, thirty," she said proudly.

Michael jotted it down, and stood staring at it, rubbing his chin with the palm of one hand.

	Bobby	**Sally**	**Madison**	**Kendra**
Run 1:18:15:06	26: ?	18:10		
Run 2:18:09:11	22:33	16:55:12		
Run 3:19:31:03	19:35	16:00		
Run 4:18:10:00	18:30			
Record Held by Michael:		15:38		

"Hmm, Bobby what do you think?" asked Michael.

"I hate that run," he said in a monotone voice while he stared at the floor in front of his desk. It was said with such robotic disdain that it brought laughter from the others.

"But, Sally," said Michael. "You seem to like it. Your times dropped by one-fourth. You're within twenty seconds of that strong, young jock over there," he said pointing to Bobby.

"I know!" she giggled excitedly. "I can't believe it. I just love to go out there. I dream about it at night," she said.

The two personified opposites. Bobby fumed while Sally bubbled. Michael chuckled. Bobby? I think I sense a problem here. Give me your assessment of the path, physiologically."

"Are you asking if I am getting a good workout?" he grunted.

"Precisely."

"Yeah. It's too good. It's all tough running. I can feel my legs getting stronger, but my times just won't improve."

"You like to run on flat surfaces right?"

"You got it."

"Sally?" Michael said turning to her. "Before the path, where did you run?"

"The streets around my house."

"Did you like it?"

"Well, not really. It wasn't very enjoyable, but I had to do it to stay in shape." she said.

"Would you be willing to try a little experiment?"

"Sure, I guess."

"If we can persuade Bobby to join us, I think it would be fascinating to see what happens when we put you back on the street where you find running less enjoyable, and Bobby back on the street where he feels at home. It's up to you, I can speculate, but I would rather watch," he said.

Bobby sat up straight. "*Nowww* you're talking!"

"Sally? It's up to you. I think you've humiliated Bobby on your home turf. The street is his. What do you say?"

"I think I know what's going to happen," she said, hesitating. "But, what the heck. It should be fun to see."

"Okay. Let's break. Meet at the entrance to the hotel in ten minutes. The two of you can get changed and stretch. But first, Bobby, what's your fastest time over a mile of flat surfaces?"

"Five minutes, six-point-ten-seconds," he said.

"*Not* bad. Any bets on his time today?" asked Michael.

The room erupted in chatter. Michael smiled, waited for a moment and then said, "I guess so. Just for fun, Bobby, I'm anxious to see whether all the whining you've done all week is legit. Sally, you've improved dramatically. From your times on the path you should be able to keep up. Give it your best effort."

She nodded as the class was beginning to leave the room.

The road leading to the Summit formed a loop that climbed to the hotel's entrance and back down to complete the circle. The road ran along the ridge for about three-quarters of a mile until it started a descent back down out of the hills to the city below. The group was gathered on the lawn inside the semi-circle drive. Michael, Madison and Kendra were standing together surrounded by the others. Bobby looked happy for the first time in a week.

"Are we ready?" asked Michael.

"*We?*" asked Sally. "Why do you say we?"

Michael chuckled to let her know he had empathy for her stress. "Sorry, Sally. Are the *two* of you ready?"

"I suppose."

"Do you see the signpost on the right hand side about a half-mile down the road?" asked Michael. "That's the turn."

Both runners nodded.

"Before we start, I have just one thing to say. There's nothing like competing with one's self. Ready?" asked Michael.

Bobby and Sally glanced at each other with Michael's comment echoing in their ears. It was a refreshing distraction from the tense competition. They smiled. "Ready," said Sally.

"On your marks . . . get set . . . go!" he yelled.

The runners leapt forward. Bobby jumped to his running pace immediately, the one he could never find on the path. Sally was right on his heels, but clearly going faster than she should at the start. The runners stayed heel-to-toe for several hundred yards before Bobby began to pull away. Sally was surprised by her speed. She had never run quite this well before.

Because the group was at a higher elevation and had a view of the entire distance, they could gain a perspective of the overall momentum of the two runners. They watched the two separate after the start, then noticed a change of speed from each: Bobby getting faster, Sally slowing. They watched as Bobby rounded the signpost first and spun around it with one arm as though he were a school-kid at play.

The two passed each other as Bobby was making the return leg. As soon as Sally was within earshot he yelled to her. "How ya doin'?" he asked.

Sally smiled and nodded. "Fine . . . thanks." She wasn't breathing hard, but her gait seemed strained, and her body slumped slightly.

"See ya in a minute," said Bobby.

"Better make it two," she replied.

Bobby's mind was calculating his time. He had learned to do it with surprising accuracy, by counting steps subconsciously. He was running as fast as he had in some time. Sally would be a minute and a half behind him. He was sure.

From the hilltop the group could see Bobby's pace increase slightly as he began his kick. He crossed the finish in 5:01. He turned immediately to ask his time.

"Oh no! I just missed the fours."

The group's interest turned back to Sally who seemed to be struggling now. She noticed that their full attention was on her and she felt compelled to increase her speed. The group thought it was her kick, but in fact, it was embarrassment that made her sprint the last few hundred feet. She crossed the finish in 6:20, and to most everyone's surprise, didn't seem to be exhausted. She was breathing hard, but the group had hoped for something more dramatic, like a slow, rolling collapse to one knee, or at least a slumping torso, with a transition to a drop-seat plunk on the ground in exhaustion. Nothing. No bending over. No leaning on a bystander. Just hands-on-her-hips and heavy breathing. And a sort of pained look of having to put up with the experiment.

The group filed back into the conference room as Bobby and Sally headed for the showers. When they were gathered again Michael started the conversation.

"Well, that was interesting. Comments please," he said.

"I thought it was unfair to Sally," said Kat.

"Me, too," said Michael as he spun and wrote 'unfair to Sally' on the white board.

"I think Sally should have had a head start," said Tip.

"What? How chauvinistic," said Shannon. "Did you miss the whole conversation about justice? If we manipulated the finish so that they finished at the same time, wouldn't we be defeating the purpose?"

"You tell 'em girl," said Kendra.

"I think Bobby was holding back all week," said Kyle.

"Really? What possible reason could he have for holding back?" asked Michael.

"I don't know. Maybe he's allergic to the trees," said Kyle, getting some laughs from the group.

Michael smiled. "Maybe."

"I thought it was just what she deserved," said Fischer.

"Uh-huh," grunted Michael and pointed to Madison. "What do you think, Madison?"

Madison had the look of someone who knew precisely what had occurred but wanted to be certain she chose the right words.

"I saw *joy* . . . and . . . *pain*. It's exactly what they have shown all week. The difference was that today, the two were reversed," she said.

Michael smiled in appreciation of Madison's insight. "Why do you think it was painful for Sally?"

Madison pointed to the white board. "For the same reason you do," she said.

Michael smiled again. Madison was already at work at her new job. "Tell me what you mean," he said.

"You agreed with Kat that it was unfair, but not for the obvious reasons. It was unfair because you maneuvered Sally into doing something she otherwise would not have done on her own," she said.

"Excellent. And Bobby?"

"Bobby would have paid a second tuition to run today." she said laughing.

"So where do you think the joy and the pain come from?"

"Inside. Bobby wasn't seeking anyone's approval on the street. He loves to run fast—he does it for himself. That's joy. Sally's pain came from running for someone else and not herself."

Bobby came through the door smiling and with a slight bounce in his step. "Hi everyone," he said.

"*Hi, Bobby,*" the group said in unison.

He sat down triumphantly. "What did I miss?" he asked.

"We've just been dissecting your personality and rearranging your psyche. Nothing of too much importance," said Fischer.

"Very clever, Tug," said Michael. "Would you like to take a stab at explaining Bobby's passion for running on the road?"

"I'd guess . . . ," said Fischer, looking over at Bobby as though he were studying a car in a dealer showroom. "I'd guess that he's bored with the foolishness of running around in the trees and had an opportunity to demonstrate it to you."

"No," objected Bobby. "That didn't have anything to do with it. The path wasn't boring, it was tough. I'm not really into tough. I'm into constant speed. And as far as proving anything to Michael, that's bull. He's the one who got me juiced up at the start when he hinted about competing with myself. I've never run with such inward focus. It was great. Thanks, Michael," he said.

Sally walked in and sat down silently, but with a smile on her face. Michael ignored her on purpose to save her the discomfort of the spotlight.

"Bobby? Was that a personal best time?" he asked, knowing the answer but buying a respite for Sally.

"Yeah! By four seconds!"

"Sally?" he said. "I can't help but notice your smile."

"My Momma always said, 'when life gives you lemons, you make lemonade.'"

"It sounds like you've put things into perspective."

"I found something on the path that isn't possible for me when I run on the street. Your experiment made it that much more clear to me. I found a passion for running on the path that I don't have on the monotonous, flat, straight road."

"What do you suppose the difference is?" asked Michael.

"I don't know for sure, but I think I'm able to concentrate on the reason—you know, the purpose—for running when I'm on the path," she said.

"Hmm, the purpose, huh?" smiled Michael.

"So how does the competition between Bobby and Sally fit into all of this?" asked Michael as he stood in front of the tote board.

	Bobby	Sally	Madison	Kendra
Run 1:18:15:06	26: ?	18:10		
Run 2:18:09:11	22:33	16:55:12		
Run 3:19:31:03	19:35	16:00		
Run 4:18:10:00	18:30			
Record Held by Michael:		15:38	14:30	14:20

"We've got some interesting results here, don't you think?" he said as he studied the board.

"Bobby, you killed Sally on the mile run. But she's your equal on the path. How can that be?" he asked.

"I hate the path. She loves it. I'd rather run on the street."

"Sally?"

"He's right. It's as though we're complete opposites," she replied.

"And how do you explain the results?"

"You're better at what you love," said Sally.

"Not good enough."

"I don't understand," she said.

"Sally, why do you love the path?"

"It's the best way I've found to stay in shape."

"And that's your goal?"

"Well, sure. I like the scenery and everything, but I could get that by walking. No, the reason I love it is because it's the most enjoyable way for me to get my running in."

"But it's harder," protested Michael.

"That's exactly what I like about it. I get more of a workout in a shorter period of time. It just works better for me."

"Bobby, why do you run? To stay in shape?" asked Michael.

"Not really. At least it isn't at the top of my list. I run because I love the challenge of going faster every time."

"The path offers you the same challenge, yet your times remained practically the same?"

"It's not that simple. I like the steady, consistent pace I get into on the street. I like speed and refinement."

"So how do we explain this? Sally discovered energy she hadn't known before, but Bobby couldn't find another drop. Madison was once a world-class runner, no match for Kendra today, yet she stayed with Kendra step for step. Both Sally and Madison reached close to their physical limits. Bobby's passion—and his energy—was lost and his times reflect it. Does anyone see an important tie-in to selling?" he asked.

"You better believe it," said Kyle. "We've all experienced exhilarating highs from selling and we've all had days when we wish we delivered pizza for a living instead."

"So . . . what's the cause. How can there be such a difference in the outcome?"

"*Purpose*," said Madison. "It's purpose. Sally was seeking the very thing the path could give her. It shouldn't have been a surprise to anyone. In fact, that's why you picked her, isn't it?" she accused sincerely.

"Yes. It happens every time," Michael admitted.

"And what about me?" she asked.

"You too, Madison."

"You knew from the beginning?"

"For the most part. You've rediscovered your joy of running—that pleases me. But I'm even more pleased that you've found your life's ambition," he said.

Madison could only offer an embarrassed smile.

"Bobby, it's important to note that there's nothing superior about running on the path. Your purpose is no less noble—or no less difficult. Your purpose reflects your values. I find it fascinating that Bobby's position as a computer-component salesman calls for streamlined efficiency, and that Sally's job as a corporate recruiter demands more complex, less tangible actions. Bobby is transaction oriented. Speed and efficiency appeal to him personally and professionally. His job pays him on the number of transactions, and he's motivated to do them efficiently, quickly and in volume. Sally is an augmentor. She pours a lot into each sale, as it were. Greater investment, fewer transactions, bigger payoffs for each effort. Her personal purpose is similar. Neither one is 'better.' Recall the three primary human values. We each have a mix of all three. They're rarely the same from one person to the next. The best we can do is to work in a way that is matched to our individual purpose," said Michael.

"What if you ain't a natural born salesman, but you still have to put food on the table?" said Fischer.

"Should we argue whether salespeople are born or made first?" Michael asked.

"No. Point conceded," said Tug.

"There are plenty of easy answers. Answers you've all heard before," said Michael.

"Here's my favorite," said Ryan. "'We all sell something . . . and we're all salespeople.'"

"An oldie but goodie," chuckled Michael.

"'If it was easy, everyone would be doing it'," said Madison.

"Oh, there's one of my favorites. What's your reaction to those?"

"I suppose they're often true," said Madison. "But if someone believes they're mismatched to the job, they seem terribly hollow."

"Good. And so the tough answer is?"

"I guess . . . ," said Madison, ". . . if you can't stand the heat . . ."

"It's my fault. I shouldn't have gotten you started. A new rule for the rest of the day—no more clichés." Michael laughed. "But Madison is close. If you've objectively considered the function of selling . . . the legitimacy of selling . . . the value of selling, and the ethical technique of selling, and still have a difficult time matching your values with the *purpose* of selling, . . . it's simple—you should do something else. How do you know? Look to the primary values for a guide," he said, reaching for the projector's control in order to bring up a slide. He flipped through several slides before coming to the one he wanted.

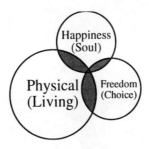

"The primary values are different for each of us. For many people, the physical values take precedence. This the 'American Dream' stuff. A nice home, travel, a boat, etc. If this is your value paradigm then selling may be among the best choices you can make. Skill, performance and hard work are rewarded directly." He brought up the next slide.

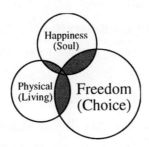

"Selling is also a good choice for those who seek freedom values. It's a wonderfully independent career. The relationship with the customer is generally a very personal one. If you choose to make your selling 'augmented,' then the relationship becomes the main event. Your style is up to you, and there are no limits to how hard you work. It also affords you the opportunity to act in the manner that you choose. No one can stop you from turning down a sale you believe is unwarranted. You have ultimate control over the company's interaction with the customer." He punched the remote control.

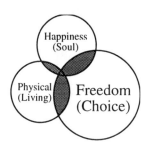

"And, finally, there are the happiness values. If traveling ruins the time you spend with your children, regardless of the amount of physical riches you can lavish on them, you may be hard pressed to find your purpose. On the other hand, selling might allow you to adjust your time so that you can spend more time with your family. And, don't forget the self-esteem issues of happiness. The point here is that Sales Esteem provides an honest look at how to realize each of the three primary human values without compromise. If your values are aligned with the needs and demands of the job, and you can execute the requirements of the job ethically, you've found purpose. If selling doesn't align with your values, for crying out loud, do something else. Life is too short."

Ryan leaned back in his chair. His thoughts turned to the early days of his career when he had made forthright decisions about why he 'wanted' to be a salesman. He hadn't thought about it for some time. Now, it all came flooding back to him. Michael had helped him discover his original intention and purpose for selling. He was relearning after all these years.

"We've saved a full discussion of the path until now for a reason," said Michael. "The path is, in many ways, the perfect metaphor for the Sales Esteem Philosophy. I want to begin to draw the analogies, and I'd like your help. To begin, I like the fact that the path is not flat; just like selling, it has ups and downs. A downhill propels you toward your next climb, just as a sale projects you to the next challenge in selling. There are changes to the terrain, some abrupt, some jolting, some that can be foreseen, others that spring out at you. Just as the endeavor of selling to a variety of people must take into consideration their different views, ideas, concerns and needs. There are obstacles on the path that will make you trip if you lose your concentration. It happens in selling as well. And the path is more difficult than running on the street. It forgives no shortcuts. It tolerates few mistakes. And it rewards you every step of the way with a reminder of why you're there in the first place. It cries out your purpose—to run. Just as Sales Esteem cries out its purpose to sell—for all the right reasons. Have you noticed? Can you give me more examples?" he asked.

The analogy wasn't difficult to grasp. The group had been noticing the comparisons all week. Most of them were integrating the principles from the classroom into the run.

"Well, just like out on the mountain, if you ignore causality and the physical world, you're probably gonna fall down," said Kat, laughing.

"It gets real tough to avoid responsibility for your own actions," said Kyle.

"Good, what else?"

"I don't understand how knowledge is better than emotions on the path," said Tip. "Getting psyched up has to make you perform better."

"Madison? What do you think?"

"All emotions rest on some cause. You can't get psyched up unless you have reason to believe you can perform. Think of it this way. Reason tells me that by eating well, and conditioning my body before I race, I'll run faster. Do you think it would be possible to ignore my diet, and my conditioning, and then rely on emotions as the source of my performance on the path?" she asked.

Tip looked confused. "No. But I watch athletes get themselves into a froth before every game. It's all emotion."

"Tip, don't confuse mental preparation and unfounded emotion," said Kendra. "I agree that they are emotional at that stage, but that emotion is a result. A result of the preparation they have gone through to get to that point. It's confidence and ambition. But those emotions have to be based on some knowledge of a possible outcome. Suppose you grabbed a construction worker off the street, put him in a football helmet, and landed him in the locker room before an NFL football game. What kind of emotions do you predict he would have?"

Tip laughed at the absurdity of the question. "Well, he'd probably be wondering where his mother was about that time." The group laughed.

Kendra smiled at the breakthrough. "Why?"

"He'd know he was about to have his head handed to him," said Tip .

"But suppose he's one of those *big* construction guys?" she asked.

"They may be dumb, but they're not stupid." More laughs.

"What if you gave him an incentive, like a month's pay, if he could play the entire game at nose guard? All he needs is a little courage, a little emotion."

"I see your point, Kendra. His emotion would also be a result. He'd be scared to death because of his *knowledge* that he would be carved up," said Tip .

Michael broke in. "Madison, I like your analogy of a good diet with knowledge. Good food equates to better performance on the path. Knowledge is like a good diet for the salesperson. You can have both good and bad knowledge, so you have to be selective, and your skills rely on the degree and quality of your knowledge. Remember. Emotion is an essential, but not as a preliminary to reason. It's the reward. And even an emotion like confidence begins with the knowledge that you have the skills, and the opportunity to succeed," said Michael. "Other metaphors about the path?"

"You can't control anyone but yourself on the path. The only way would be to knock 'em down, and who wants to win that way?" said Shannon.

"Michael, we've forgotten rational self-interest," said Ryan.

"Maybe we've just reserved it for you, Ryan."

"The tendency is going to be to take care of the path, our health, our diet . . . you name it, so that we preserve the value we find in the path. If we have the right purpose, the right rewards, the right principles, we won't intentionally damage ourselves through irrational actions. Cheating on the path—taking a short-cut for instance—would be self-defeating."

"Excellent, Ryan. More?"

"We know that the results from our efforts will be realized. In other words, if we work hard, the payoff will come. Just like justice. No one can take away the gains we make on the path," said Leslie.

"We've seen the power of purpose, but the real power comes from doing whatever we do for our own reasons, and not others. Sally was trying to run on the road for others. It didn't work for her here and it doesn't work anywhere else. I heard what you said to the two of them at the start—that bit about competing with ourselves. Regardless of what we do, it has to be our decision, our values, our drive and determination and our rewards," he said.

"Imagine the difficulty you would have running the path unless you exercised all of those principles to some degree," said Michael. "If you had none, you couldn't run at all. If you chose to use some of the right principles, but neglected others, you could still run, but with far less effectiveness. Bobby was a great example. He had all the physical attributes to run on the path—but lacked the purpose. His purpose lay in running with precision, and the right venue was the street. Without purpose, he lacked the full package. So it is in selling. It isn't an absolute requirement to use all of the principles of Sales Esteem—a minimum are needed just to survive—honesty, for instance. A handful of the principles will allow you to sell with moderate success, but the key is to grab as many as you can, integrate them, and let them all work for you. Madison rediscovered her love for running on the path and kept pace with one of the world's greatest athletes. We've seen Bobby's and Sally's relative performances. The sum of the Sales Esteem principles, their corresponding actions, and the resulting emotions is a 'greater-than-the-sum-of-the-parts' equation. No wasted actions, no wasted energy, no wasted emotion. At a mechanical level, there are reasons for an increase in sales since your efforts are effectively directed. At the psychological level—which is the energy source, there are even greater reasons for an increase in your sales. They are the resulting positive emotions, and often, the increase in energy that comes from eliminating the negative emotions. Better fundamentals and an increase in your mental energy—it's the essence of all that we've done this week combined into one integrated theory. At each turn, there are gains made, mechanically and emotionally, which feed the next element, which continues to grow. The end result is the most effective use of your skills, knowledge and emotional energy. It's Sales Esteem," he closed, pausing for a moment.

"We've had a memorable day." Michael said to a stir of laughter. "We have word that Kevin is doing well and will be released early next week." Michael looked at Madison when he made the announcement. She smiled in return. He intentionally avoided any eye contact with Fischer or Shaw to avoid tipping them off to his suspicions of their involvement. The trap was being prepared. Any unusual attention could upset his plans.

"We wrap up the conference at mid-day tomorrow. We've planned a fabulous meal, and some special entertainment for tonight. I'll be there to join you. It's a nice chance to unwind. Tomorrow is an important day—so don't unwind *all the way* tonight," he said with a smile. The group rose and emptied from the conference room. The nature of the conference fostered serious discussions after hours, and the resulting friendships that had been established were more substantial than most new relationships. Small groups formed in the lounges, or at poolside, or on the golf course during their free time, all with the common thread of enlightenment of their new philosophy. It was a brotherhood that would last some of them for the rest of their lives.

Hallie stayed in the conference room with Michael. She stood at the large windows that faced the lake below, staring out.

"Dad . . . do you think Kendra lost friends when she rejected their attempts to get her named to the Olympic Team in '88?" she asked.

"No. But my definition of a friend may be different, honey. My guess is that her friends thought more highly of her."

"Dad, no one is going to understand why I turned down the money."

He smiled. "Do you know, sweetheart?"

Hallie dropped her head and raised it again, pushing her long hair to the side and behind her ear. "It hasn't been easy. Kendra helped a lot. I mean, she loves justice more than she loves running. She knows she wouldn't have one without the other." Hallie paused. "Still, anyone who ever finds out will think I'm a fool."

"Not me. Not Kendra, or Madison or Ryan. And not Grandpa." He walked around her and squeezed her shoulders, massaging them in a reassuring way.

"Honey, we all need affirmation of our actions. The question is who do you look to for that affirmation. Friends? Family? Yourself? I'm not sure why I would include anyone else in that jury box."

She stared out at the boats on the lake. "Yeah, I know you're right. But it seems like it balances out the injustices of life, you know? Sometimes bad things happen and sometimes good things happen."

But I know that's only a rationalization. The world is full of little difficulties. And I get my share of little breaks, that's where the balance is. It could be the big breaks balance the risk of big disasters, but I know that there is no more satisfaction in being pushed further along in life by good luck, than there is in being held back by bad luck. They're not mirror images. It's all about what I do to push myself ahead. The rest is a shortcut."

Michael's pride for Hallie had never felt stronger. He looked through her light blue eyes and right into her soul. It was there to be admired—and it was his own flesh and blood displaying an understanding as rich as any he had known. Hallie sensed her father's emotions and moved to embrace him.

"I hope you understand," she said.

"Hallie, you've crossed over to a new level. I don't know how I could be any more proud of you. You're going to find life's celebration at every opportunity— and for that little miracle, a father's greatest gift is realized."

The group was gathering again as Michael brushed back Hallie's hair and kissed her on the forehead. "You done good, kid," he said.

Outside, on the Summit's outer deck, Ryan sat and watched as the fire of the sun's descent into the lake below lit up the horizon. The rest of the world seemed far removed. The Summit had become a mecca of knowledge, learning and energy for him. It would be hard to leave without some sadness. It seemed to be a feeling shared by most. The impact of the Sales Esteem principles were becoming clear— and he was feeling his spirits rise. He felt as though he were on a never-ending wake in the ocean looking out over the rest of the landscape from above and realize that he held knowledge that few possessed. Kat came out onto the deck with a look as though she had been searching for him. She leaned on the railing, staring out over the view, joining him.

"Hi," he said as though she were his kid sister.

"It's fascinating, isn't it?"

"What's that?"

"I've never really respected myself for what I do—you know—my career," her eyes still fixed on the departing sun.

"Yeah."

"Do you know what I'm feeling right now?"

"No, tell me."

"I'm proud of who I am and what I do . . . and I feel like I've cheated myself for never understanding that before." Her voice was crystal clear and without emotion. Ryan heard the strength in her voice and reached over to put his hand on her shoulder. He patted her gently.

"I think Michael manipulates time," she said thoughtfully.

"What do you mean?" Ryan asked with a slight laugh.

"This is how I expected to feel at the end of my career, not nearer to its beginning. It's as though I can look back on all the things I have done—right and wrong—and put them into perspective. I feel confident—like I have the answers to the questions I was unable to answer until now. I know I'll continue to make mistakes, but I don't know if I will ever make another fundamental error—you know—one of those where you're just completely wrong."

"I'm happy for you, Kat," he said sincerely, which jolted her into realizing she had ignored him.

"What about you, Ryan? I don't know if I will ever forget the image of you staring off into the horizon and agonizing about your son."

"I feel like I've gotten my son back. How does that song go . . . you know, 'The greatest love thing.' As simple as it might sound—it's true—you have to have self-esteem before you'll let others love you. It wasn't like that when I came here. I felt such self-disgust that I could hardly look at him any longer. It's as though I were blind before, not knowing how any one thing was connected to another. Even when I was doing the right things, I didn't understand. I can let Casey love me now. He can respect his dad, because I respect myself. I can't say there's ever been anything more important to me. I owe Michael a great deal."

"I know how you feel. But my guess is that he would insist it was you who made the breakthrough—that it was you who had to understand why you could respect yourself. I've never known anyone so committed to the idea that everything flows from the individual," she said.

"It's kind of frustrating, isn't it? I want to thank someone, but he won't have it."

"What do you think *he* gets from all this?"

"Besides earning a great living?"

"Yeah."

"My guess is that he's made the journey we have and thoroughly loves seeing others make the same breakthrough."

"It's a nice thought, isn't it?"

Ryan just nodded. The sun was halfway into the water now, and its fall seemed to speed up when it was this low. They watched it silently. Kat put her hand in Ryan's—both of them squeezing gently in a sign of friendship they would not forget. The air around the sun's corona boiled, a sign of the sun's final effort before dropping below the horizon.

20
The Sting

"There are no contradictions;
check your premises."

—Ayn Rand

The smell of coffee and bagels filled the Cevantés' suburban kitchen. Madison and Ryan had innocently invited themselves to breakfast the night before. They didn't give it a second thought, because they felt close to Michael and welcomed any opportunity to spend time with him. They were arguing when Hallie came in, still rubbing the sleep out of her eyes. She wedged her way in front of Michael as he stood staring into the refrigerator.

"What are looking for, Dad?"

"Cream cheese."

"I think Elizabeth had it last."

"Elizabeth doesn't like cream cheese."

"Of course. People's actions never betray their beliefs. Look behind the bean dip."

"What did you say?" He stared at her.

"Bean dip, Dad, bean dip."

"No, before that." He turned toward the table where Madison and Ryan sat.

"People's actions never betray their beliefs," she repeated.

"That's it!" his voice raised. Madison and Ryan turned at the commotion.

"Fischer will confess if we give him a chance. And people's actions never fully betray their beliefs. Just ask Hallie," he said with a smile.

"What do we know about Fischer?" He plopped down in a chair beside them.

"Besides the fact that he knows how to use a wrench?" Madison sneered.

"He's here at the insistence of the Securities and Exchange Commission for violation of fair practice laws," said Michael.

"Let see. He's a jerk," said Madison matter-of-factly. "He's arrogant."

"What else?" asked Michael.

"He thinks he's among meek people. He thinks he's a lion among lambs," said Ryan

"And how does that make him feel?" Michael said, knowing the answer.

"He thinks he's untouchable," said Madison.

"Exactly. And what do you think he'll do if he's threatened by the lambs?"

"Fight back. Lash out," said Ryan.

"Right. And how? He won't get physical cause we're both bigger than he is, but he will lash out," said Michael.

"He'll think he can use his wit," said Madison.

"Right. And what does he have to attack us with?" continued Michael.

"He hurt Kevin. And he knows we can't prove it," said Madison.

"His one weapon is the very thing we want . . . a partial confession, used to strike back at us. . . if. . . if we can corner him."

"That's the problem," said Ryan.

"What would cause him to feel threatened enough to attack?" asked Madison.

"His SEC-stipulated rehabilitation," said Ryan.

Michael nodded. "You got it. Suppose he didn't pass? Suppose the SEC thought he failed, and wanted to pull his license? A lifetime suspension from the securities industry would probably shake him up, don't you think?"

"How do we scare him into believing that?" asked Madison.

"What if we just called the SEC and explained the whole thing to them?" asked Ryan.

"Hmm, I don't know. What we need is drama—lots of impact in a short period of time so that he panics and strikes back without thinking. Fischer didn't pass and I'll let the SEC know. What they'll actually do with the information is up to them. I don't think we can rely on them to help us carry this off. And we won't stoop to trump up any charges," said Michael.

"I don't think we need to go that far. I bet he'll crack if we turn up the heat a little. We just have to lead him into believing he's being suspended," said Ryan.

"I think I have an idea," Michael said, leaning forward instinctively to speak in a quiet voice.

Hallie had heard the whole conversation and didn't want to miss anything now. She rushed over to listen intently as they crafted the plan.

A half hour later, Michael, Madison and Ryan joined the rest of the group as they were gathering in the conference room following breakfast. There was a serene calm that was lockstep with the still morning air and the mist that lay in the river valleys. Everyone was moving more slowly marking the symbolic end of the journey they had completed. The necessity of worrying about flight schedules and suitcases kept the conversation topical. Michael, Madison and Ryan came in together. The buzzing from the group continued as the three of them chatted about the upcoming session. After a few minutes, they separated, Ryan and Madison taking seats uncharacteristically away from the front and near the exit. Michael had to tap the glass of the overhead projector to get their attention.

"We're near our conclusion," he said. "All that remains is to draft our Sales 'Bill of Rights.' This is the objective of the conference—to explore the very fundamentals of your actions and then to forge them into your guiding principles. That act—putting them on paper—is the writing of a Sales 'Bill of Rights.' A good 'Bill of Rights' consists of principles that are so fundamental, they rarely need change. By contrast, a poor 'Bill of Rights' attempts to dictate all potential actions, which I hope you all agree, is absurd. A good 'Bill of Rights' does exactly what we have been discussing all week. It establishes principles which you apply to each individual action. Free speech, for example, as a principle of the U.S. 'Bill of Rights' can be applied to an uncountable number of individual circumstances— none of which need to be spelled out in the 'Bill of Rights' itself.

"The teaching method we use at the conference is abstract. We take real-world situations and draw analogies and generalizations about human knowledge in order to get down to our principles. The process is to take a concrete example, examine the conceptual issues, and then to forge something concrete again that you can apply to your view of selling. That final act is your 'Bill of Rights.'

"The 'Bill of Rights' you write today will be your own. It will consider the knowledge you've uncovered this week. As I said in my opening comments, the ability and effort required to make the journey would be yours. And some of you wouldn't pass. You may have noticed that Rick Kincaid is no longer with us. He left for this reason. His view of his career could not be reconciled with the Sales Esteem philosophy. I am troubled to say that there are others that have not passed," he said, pausing.

"In a moment we will take a break so that I may speak with those of you whom I believe have failed to grasp the essentials. We will refund your tuition and ask that you not rejoin us for the writing of the 'Bill of Rights.' I know the implication of announcing that some of you have failed and its potential harshness. However, I have an obligation to those of you who made it, and who rightfully deserve recognition for making the journey successfully."

As Michael spoke, each member of the group paused momentary to assess their participation and understanding of Sales Esteem. Most were certain they had passed—it was obvious from the individual responses that Michael had given them during the week. After some second-guessing, and tough self-evaluation, all were confident they had passed. *All but two.* Fischer and Shaw were suddenly gripped by panic. Fischer was at the conference in a fight to keep his securities license. He had made the mistake of believing that attendance was all that was required, and that any argument that needed to be made on his behalf, would still be an option. He knew now that the evaluation had begun from the beginning and he would get no other opportunities.

Jock Shaw knew he had been an antagonist for most of the five-day discussion. It had never occurred to him that the combative attitude he brought to the conference would result in a failing evaluation. His desire to prove he was a legitimate manager, to control Ryan, had consequences—consequences he was now just beginning to consider. A bead of sweat appeared on his temple and ran down the side of his cheek.

Fischer, in contrast, dealt quickly with his fear, and now pondered how he might extricate himself. His anger was beginning to grow.

Michael continued. "We're going to take a fifteen-minute break and then return to get started. Tug. Jock. Could I see you for just a few moments?"

With his last statement, the suspicions of everyone in the room were realized. Fischer's anger flared at the public disclosure. He would never know that Michael had never announced it in such a manner.

The rest of the group departed quickly in the wake of the obvious. Shaw, in a cowardly manner, put his hands to his head. Fischer crossed his arms—and began to fume.

"Jock. Stay here for just a moment. Tug, will you come with me?" said Michael, in the most serious tone he could deliver. Fischer glared at Michael, who returned the stare with steely resolve. In that moment of confrontation between the two men, Fischer's fate was undone. There would be no mental bluffing of Fischer's adversary. He could see it in Michael's eyes—and sense it in his intensity. The reality of it came rushing in as Fischer realized he was cornered. Michael noticed the look in Fischer's eyes turn from aggression to wild. Fischer got up and followed Michael into the hall and toward a small office.

As Michael held the door for Fischer to pass through, he motioned to a man sitting at a desk in the office. He was dressed in a suit and had an official look. On the desk in front of him were stacks of file folders, all arranged in such a way that they gave the impression of the formal findings of a judicial court.

"Tug, this is Ken Olley. Ken, you're familiar with Mr. Fischer's case." Olley didn't get up but simply nodded and reached into his jacket pocket to retrieve his glasses. Fischer surveyed the man as he put his glasses on. Olley's stare went immediately to the file folders in front of him as he picked one from the top of the pile and opened it. Olley was a large man, slightly overweight, but distinguished looking. His steel blue eyes drew attention away from his receding hairline. His features were all business. He looked like a judge. Fischer swallowed hard, his anger now mixing with a slight amount of fear. No handshake.

"Tug, you came here as a condition of a ruling of the Securities and Exchange Commission," Michael said as Fischer slunk into the chair across from Olley. Olley had yet to utter a word.

"That's right. Trumped-up charges."

"Uh-huh. Do you know that Kyle Mitchell participated in the Wholesome Foods merger that was the focus of the investigation?"

"What?" Fischer was incensed. "That little SOB was a plant?"

"Tug. The SEC sent you here hoping you would take advantage of the opportunity to return to the securities industry, with what might be termed, a new attitude. I agreed on the basis that I could fail you if you weren't learning the Sales

Esteem ethics. It's my observation that you have failed to grasp or embrace any of the principles the SEC believes to be the foundation for your rehabilitation. *However,* I wanted to give you an opportunity to respond before I made the final determination." Michael's voice was clear and without emotion.

The contrast between the composure of Olley and Michael, and the fear that was consuming Fischer was tangible. Olley had not spoken a word. Fischer assumed it to mean he was waiting for comments in his defense before making a judgment.

"I agreed to come to this ridiculous conference because I was forced at the threat of losing my license. No one—*NO ONE*—told me I would have to pander to the philosophy."

"Of course not, Tug. It would be rather foolish to tip you off so that you could fake it, don't you think?" said Michael.

"It was a trap," he said in desperation.

"No, Tug. It was a chance to observe your actions from the perspective of ethical selling. This is not a court of law, and there was no trap. It's only a matter of my interpretation as to whether you are likely to go forward with an honest sales perspective."

The trapdoor was opened. This was it. The confrontation had to be personified between Michael and Fischer. One man's view as compared to the other's. It was the only chance Fischer had to defend himself, which meant he would try. And, it was the only opportunity for Michael to beat him, intellectually, in such a way that Fischer would retaliate.

"What do you know about honesty," said Fischer acidly. "You live in an ivory tower where the real world never creeps in. I'll bet you were never successful selling on your own. I'll bet you had to run and hide here."

"No, Tug. Just the opposite is true. I witnessed early in my own career the laziness in which you rationalize your actions. I know *who* you are. I know *how* you think. I watched you reveal everything to me in class. Your soul opened up, Tug, and I peered right in."

"Oh, is that right? You really believe you know anything about me at all? What a joke. You're a simplistic idiot believing your idea of the world really fits other people."

"I see. Shall we discuss the Wholesome Foods acquisition? Shall we throw a spotlight on your peculiar mathematical shenanigans in valuing the pension? There's not a mathematician on the planet who would agree with your technique. Is that your perspective of the 'real world,' Tug?"

"Is that so? Well I say there's no way to value it, period."

"Tug, you're forgetting I have access to the records. The SEC was preparing a racketeering charge against you before your firm settled. Now, please tell me again why your view of *honesty* and the *real world* is more honest than mine?" Michael pressed harder for the man-to-man conflict. He didn't care about the SEC's accusations, he wanted the confession of the bridge incident. He needed Fischer's anger to send him into a vengeful attack.

"I'm sickened by what I see here. You finally get someone to argue against your pathetic idea of selling and all you can do is get the authorities to come to your rescue." Fischer looked at Olley, who sat rigidly, giving no response.

"Tug, I could have dismissed you on the first day. Or any *other* day along the way. I enjoyed thwarting your poorly conceived ideas in front of the group. You were the antithesis of all the things I wanted them to discover . . . only you weren't *much* of an adversary. Practically all of your arguments were weak, lazy constructs as transparent as you are. *You were fodder.* You argued against certainty because you didn't—and don't—*want* to be held accountable for your actions. You argued for emotions driving decisions because you *prey* upon the victims of greed and fear. You argued for cut-throat competition, only because you prefer the environment where *law is disdained*, where *force and coercion* are the law. You wished away justice because you have nightmares of justice in pursuit of you. You abhor the idea of your customers judging your value. You are the embodiment of all the immoral ideas *my profession* has been criticized for. You are the personification of the worst salesman there is. And like your weak, lazy, distorted ideas—you, too, are weak. You're an easy victory. *You're a toy.* And the only one who failed to notice it . . . was you."

Michael disliked the action needed to pry Fischer's hatred to the surface, but it was his only chance. He had to get him to break. "You're *disgusting,* Fischer, and deep down inside you know it. It won't be long before you collapse inward and wither away to nothing at all. You *failed*, Fischer. Not just here, but in life. You're *done*."

There it was. Michael's best effort to break him. He waited for the reaction. Somewhere—deep inside—Fischer knew the fight was over. He looked at Olley, who gave no reaction at all. Whatever the consequences, he couldn't reverse them. The hatred welled up in him. He was beaten and humiliated. At that moment he didn't care any longer. He wanted to strike out. He wanted to hurt someone as much as he had been hurt. "To hell with you and all you stand for. You assholes can take away my license, I'll be back. You think you've beaten me, but all you've done is hurt me for the moment. And there you sit, thinking that you've won every battle. Well, you're wrong. I won. *I got your buddy.* And I wish the rest of your lambs would have followed him into the ravine as well. Think of the pain he went through. I'll enjoy it when I think of it and know that I caused it, and I could tell you to your face, that it was me who arranged for the little accident. Only you'll never prove it and I'll think about it and gloat. To hell with you."

The words came out in a flurry. More of them than he had hoped for. Almost instantly Fischer realized he had said too much. He went silent as a smile crept over Michael's face.

Ken Olley rose from his chair. He was a large man with an imposing presence. He walked around the desk and reached behind him to pull a pair of shiny handcuffs from his belt.

"Mr. Fischer, I haven't had an opportunity to explain my involvement," said Olley. "I'm with the Travis County Sheriff's department. I'm here to investigate the accident on the bridge. I'm pleased you've offered to help in the investigation. In fact, I would say that was about as good a confession as I have had in quite some time. I'm placing you under arrest for willful endangerment of the life of Kevin Keller. You have the right to remain silent. Anything you say. . . "

Fischer went white, and started to shake and mumble. Olley lifted him to his feet, while he twisted one arm behind him and clicked a cuff around his wrist. The other arm followed. Michael nodded his head at Olley. "Thanks, Ken."

"Thank you, Michael. You made it real easy," said Olley, with a wink of admiration at the sting.

Fischer's head was down. He was beaten. He looked at Michael. Fischer's eyes were sunken, his chin rested on his chest, his back bent over like a cripple. There was nothing in his eyes but the remnants of hatred and defeat. Olley lead him away.

Michael walked to the chair and slumped into it as Madison and Ryan came running in. Madison gave him a bear-hug as Ryan watched.

"Justice?" asked Ryan.

Madison and Michael looked at him and repeated together, "*Justice.*"

"What about Shaw?" said Ryan.

Michael unfolded his hands and held them, palms open, at his side. "I think you're a better judge of that."

"The firm won't be happy with his failure, will they, Michael?" asked Ryan.

"No. And they're interested in the outcome because Shaw caused such a ruckus to come. I have a feeling he'll have a hard time explaining things."

"I believe you're right. I hope they ask for my opinion."

"Should we go see him now?" asked Michael.

Ryan just nodded. The three of them returned to the conference room where Shaw waited. He looked nervous and pale. Madison and Ryan waited at the door as Michael explained his decision. It was straightforward enough, although Jock appeared to be dazed. Michael knew Shaw's day of reckoning would have to wait. There was nothing to be gained by interfering. His part was played in handing Shaw a check for reimbursement of the tuition—designed to assure he would have to return it himself. Michael didn't spend much time explaining his reasons. Shaw would most likely betray his own shallow philosophy in an explanation to his managers, and Michael didn't want to help him to avoid it. Shaw didn't argue. He simply picked up his paperwork and left. On the way out, he had to pass by Ryan.

"What do you know about this?" he accused.

"You didn't *pass*, Jock. That's all I need to know." Ryan's voice was firm.

Shaw pushed by him without another word or even a second glance. They watched as he stood in front of the elevators, entered one when its doors opened, and stood forlorn while they closed.

Still staring at the closing doors, Ryan said, "Kind of poetic, isn't it?"

"I didn't know you liked poetry, Ryan," Michael smiled.

21

The Sales 'Bill of Rights'

What your company owes you.
What you owe yourself.

In a symbolic contrast, the doors on Shaw's elevator had closed just as the door on the elevator next to his had opened to reveal Kat, Tip, Shannon, Sally, Kyle, and Bobby. They were laughing in kindred spirit. They joined the rest of the group as they gathered for the last time. Michael stood before them. "A Sales 'Bill of Rights' is not an easy thing to arrive at. Had I put it on the board to begin the week, you probably would have walked out. After a week's worth of discovery, most of it on your own, without the insult of lecture, you have developed an understanding of Sales Esteem that should form the basis of your actions from here forward. We need to record it, write it in a way that will remind you of the principles you want to embrace, and keep it short so as to make it retrievable when the need arises, he said. "What is the centerpiece of your 'Bill of Rights'?"

"The primary values. And our right to pursue them," said Madison.

"State it in a way that it can be put into written form, will you?" Michael sat on the table with a computer keyboard in his lap. The computer's screen image was being projected on the large screen at the front of the room. When he typed, it was illuminated for them all to see. Madison spoke and he typed.

1.   *I have claim to my life, my happiness and the freedom to pursue my values. My career will help me to realize these values, and I will protect it fiercely from harm— from the outside, or from my own actions. I am independently responsible to*

pursue my values, and independently responsible to make judgments about the actions I take to do so.

"Very good. How about the principle of certainty?"
Ryan said it, Michael typed.

2.   *I see that the world works with a pattern. One thing leads to the next. Every action has a result and every result has a cause. My actions matter. Not only in how I affect the lives of others, but in how I affect the outcome of my career, and my own life. There are no shortcuts—no way to change the nature of cause and effect. I am guided by rational self-interest which embraces the idea that my actions impact others, and therefore ultimately impact me as well.*

"What about vision?"
Kyle began:

3.   *I have a unique ability to consider things long forgotten, and to project the result of my actions far into the future. I can consider the impact I have on events yet to happen. I can't predict what others will do, but I can make very accurate predictions about how my actions will affect me, my values, and the people with whom I interact.*

"Good. And how do we address being guided by knowledge?"
Madison answered.

4.   *All that we have achieved is the result of our conscious recognition of the world and how we mold it to reach our goals and aspirations. My intellect is the tool for realizing all that I want. First comes reason, then comes the emotional reward. Reason will rule my actions, and I will celebrate the realization of my values in the emotional rewards that follow.*

"That's excellent. Justice?"
Kat answered.

5. *My actions lead to an outcome that's either rewarding or harmful. Justice allows me to take all that I have earned, yet maintains a responsibility that I accept the consequences of my actions as well. They are two sides of the same coin, inseparable. From that knowledge comes the understanding that I will make mistakes, and the willingness to correct or accept responsibility for them. It also allows me to be proud of the accomplishments I have made.*

"Oh, you guys are good! Competition?"
Tip Bailey took his turn.

6. *Competition is the way in which I measure my progress toward goals. I compete with others so as to compete with myself. Competition cannot be self-damaging, otherwise it ceases to be competition. Competition marks the ever higher achievements I yearn for and announces the heights of skill, knowledge and effort to which I aspire. I will make mistakes, but they will not be fundamentally wrong. They will be the type of mistakes born of effort beyond the comfortable. Pushing the limits of what can be done.*

"And purpose?"
Sally knew this was her territory.

7. *I seek my own personal set of values. The pursuit of those values is my purpose. Regardless of what those values are, I reach them by providing value in some form to someone. It may be work or companionship or ideas, but my purpose is to deliver something of value in exchange for the things I hold dear. The more I deliver, the greater my rewards.*

"And what wraps it all together?" Michael asked.
Ryan answered:

8. *Integrity holds my principles together. Compromise regarding a principle allows them to fall apart. It's up to me to make certain I am never selective about the*

principles I use. They are there because they work. I vow to rely on my principles with the knowledge that they will ultimately make me as successful as I can be.

"There it is. Your personal 'Bill of Rights.' The words can be rearranged, but the essence is there for each principle. There are but eight. They correspond and rely on one another. They can be integrated. Practically any instance—any circumstance—any difficult decision can be tackled by going back to these principles. They are your guide.

"The distance you have traveled this week exceeds any measure in miles. You have the foundation for whatever degree of sales success you want to achieve. You are no longer bound to others' expectations, or their limits, or their mistakes. Life is about living it. Selling is about mirroring the way you live your life. You have no limits. And your horizon is built upon a foundation of substance—of principles—of knowledge—and of the emotional energy that will propel you as far as you wish to go. There are no longer any roadblocks. You will make mistakes. If not, you're not trying hard enough. But they needn't ever be unprincipled mistakes. You have principles. You have the framework for binding them together—which is integrity. You have more of both than most. With those tools, there is nothing you can honestly hope for that cannot be achieved. It is now, finally, up to you to determine. It's your life, your career and your world. It's at your command. I hope you make it exactly what you hope for. Thank you."

They rose without realizing why. There was a power and energy they knew would carry them forward for as long as they could recall the week at the Summit. Applause came without a second thought. It was an experience they couldn't forget, and a treasure they wouldn't let loose from their grasp. They didn't want it to end.

Michael smiled, raised his hand, mouthed the words 'thank you,' and left the room.

22
Coming Home

Michael pulled into the circular driveway of his home with more excitement than normal. The conference had been among the best ever, and he loved great endings. He had a week-long vacation planned with his family—far too little time, since Hallie would be leaving for school when it was over. But he'd deal with that when the time came. For now, he was ready to be immersed in the joy of leisure with the three of them. He came in through the door without announcing his arrival, looked around the kitchen, poked his head into his wife's office and headed upstairs to Hallie's room. She was sitting on the bed, studying. Books were scattered in front of her, and headphones were in place over her ears. She had the rhythmic bob most teenagers seemed forced to go through when the music was turned up. She looked up as he walked in and jumped up to greet him, sending books and the CD player flying. She threw her arms around his chest in a bear hug. She had always greeted him this way, even as she got older. It was one of his favorite things in life, and Hallie seemed to understand that.

"Hi, Daddy," she said.

"Hi, sweetheart. You look busy."

"No, just catching up a little. I've been waiting for you to get here."

"What do you say we grab Mom and Hannah and get an ice cream cone?"

"Sounds too good to pass up to me," she said. "I'll be down in a minute."

He spun to find the others as Hallie got up from the bed.

"Dad?" she said.

"Yes?" He turned around to see her.

"I love you."

"I love you too, Hallie."

Madison's long blonde hair blew in the gentle breeze. The buzz just inside the hospital foyer seemed unimportant and far away as the wheelchair attendant pushed Kevin through the automatic sliding doors. His leg was in a splint, and crutches lay across his body, extending up over one shoulder. He looked frustrated at the obligatory use of the wheelchair and rolled his eyes as he met Madison's stare. She walked with poise to meet him, struggling to hide her excitement. "Hi" was all she needed to say.

"Hi. Thanks for helping," was his clumsy reply.

The attendant helped load Kevin into the car, ignoring the indignant remarks that Kevin felt compelled to issue. Once in, he glanced up at the nurse and finally submitted. "Thanks, really," he said.

Madison spun around the car and got in. She was dressed in jeans and a man's work shirt and wore cowboy boots. It was out of character for her, but Kevin marveled at how terrific she could make work clothes look. She reached into her purse to retrieve two airline tickets, and handed them to Kevin. As he opened the cover, Madison reached into the back seat to add one final touch to her outfit—a floppy Australian hat with one side pinned up. It was chic. She flattened it onto her head and turned to get Kevin's reaction. He was shaking his head. "These tickets are for Phoenix," he said.

Madison looked eager. "Do you still want me to come?"

"Yeah. But I don't think they'll let you wear that hat there," he laughed.

"I like the hat."

"You'll come to Phoenix with me?"

"Are you asking me again, or do you want to reconsider?"

"What about the job here with Michael?"

"You make the trip for each conference, right. I guess I can too, I mean, if you want me to be in Phoenix with you."

It finally hit him. "Madison, I want to be wherever you are. I was trying to imagine what Portland would be like—whether I would ever get used to the rain."

"You'd go to Portland?"

He shook his head. "It's not where, it's who. I want to be with you."

She reached over to embrace him and banged her knee against his injured leg, sending him into a painful cringe.

"Oh! . . I'm sorry, I'm so sorry. Are you okay?"

"It's all right . . . really, it is," he said with a groan.

They both broke into laughter. Tears filled her eyes. "We can live anywhere you want. I'm not tied to Portland. You have a home in Phoenix. That's the sensible thing to do."

"No, you have to be here if you're really going to be part of Michael's group. I bet they have houses, grocery stores and theaters here, too. Will you move here with me?"

Madison's eyes softened. She reached out a hand and touched him gently on the cheek with her fingers. A kiss followed. Nothing else needed to be said. Madison put the car in gear and pulled out of the hospital parking lot. Kevin sat in the seat beside her and stared at her with a broad smile on his face. She noticed and brushed her hair behind her ear with her hand. She drove them to the airport. If they had spoken, they would have both expressed the same feelings, and they both knew that fact. It was far more poignant to ride in silence, acknowledging a connection that didn't need the help of words.

Finally, she said, "My dad will be very happy."

"You think he'll like me?"

"It will take years before he thinks you're deserving of his little girl" she laughed.

"Why will he be happy then?"

"'Cause he'll see how happy I am."

Kevin reached over to grasp her hand and then looked forward. Another moment of silence passed and he turned to her again. She returned his look.

"You're what I've always wanted," he said.

"Just wait. It's only the beginning," she said with a smile.

It was nearly midnight when Ryan pulled into the garage of his suburban ranch-style home. Amber and the kids had to stay with Grandma while Michael was away and wouldn't be back until the following afternoon. The waiting had become excruciating. He couldn't remember being so anxious to see them. From the moment he stepped off the airplane, his excitement had been nearly unbearable. His thoughts turned to the last six months, and he realized that period had been a living hell that had consumed him. It was an even greater contrast with his new state of mind. He couldn't believe how anxious he was to showcase his remarkable recovery with Amber and Casey. Not only in words, but in touches and hugs, and walks through the park, and laughter and smiles, and tender strokes of love at night before bed. He wandered through the house looking at every picture, picking up baseballs and toy trucks—holding each one for a moment longer than normal. He looked into Casey's room at the bed and longed for just one more day to pass so that he could see him lying there. He fell asleep with the television on.

The next morning was his first back at the office in more than a week. It hadn't occurred to him that Shaw's departure from the conference might have negative repercussions until he sat down for breakfast. It didn't really matter anymore. Both he and Shaw would always know what had happened. He took his time and got into the office at 9:00 AM—late by his ordinary standards.

As he walked down the aisles of cubicles, nodding at the other salesmen, patting a few on the back as he went by, he received a curious response—the kind of funny feeling he got when everyone else has news that he hadn't heard yet. He answered the same questions about his trip a half-dozen times before making it to the row of offices designated for vice presidents of the firm. His office was at the end of the hall, which announced his superior performance from an earlier time. It had become a symbol of his torment and declining sales before he left. Before, he knew he would be losing his office when the better producers tallied their numbers at the end of the year. But not now. He realized confidently that his newfound principles would put him right back into the top spot. He would have to play catch-up, but he would reclaim his status, and avoid the hassle of moving from his office, and rediscover his pride in being a leader among many talented people.

He turned the corner into his office and stopped short. It was completely empty. It had been cleaned out. None of his personal items remained. A bottle of window cleaner had been left on his emptied desk, adding insult to injury. He was caught completely off-guard. Certainly the firm was going to give him the opportunity to turn some good numbers again—after all they had just plunked down an enormous amount of money to send him to the conference. That couldn't be it. Wait a minute—SHAW! It had to be Shaw. The son of a bitch. Ryan spun around in a fury—ready to tear Shaw to pieces—and ran squarely into Bill Mallory—the firm's President. Ryan had to reach out and grab Mallory to keep the collision from knocking him over.

Mallory let out a groan as the collision caught him by surprise as well.

"Bill! I'm sorry. Are you okay?"

"I thought you were going to come back from that conference a little more relaxed, Ryan," he said.

Ryan thrust a finger toward his office and said, "Yeah, me too. Until I found my office cleaned out."

"That's why I'm here, Ryan," came the words Ryan didn't want to hear. "Come with me, will you?"

Mallory turned and headed down the hall briskly. Ryan was right behind and beginning to protest. "Listen, Bill . . ."

Mallory looked over his shoulder and had a peculiar smile on his face, which shut Ryan up immediately. It was out of place, the smile. It wasn't the look you would throw to someone if you were about to let them go.

They rounded a few corners before Ryan realized where they were headed— Shaw's office. The office adjacent to Mallory's corner suite. Fire raced through Ryan's head. Could it be that he would lose his job and have to face Shaw's scorn at the same time? If so, it might be time to . . .

Just as he was starting to voice his response, he caught a glimpse into Shaw's office and noticed the picture of Amber and Casey on the wall behind the desk. He entered and took a quick glance around the room. It was filled with his personal belongings—those removed from his old office the night before. He was stunned. He looked at Mallory and back to the desk and the view that it had over the city.

Mallory plopped into the chair in front of the desk and waved Ryan to the other side. Mallory's face was bright—almost glowing—from the effect his surprise had on Ryan.

"Welcome back. And thank you," said Mallory.

"Thank you? Why are you thanking me?" said Ryan in disbelief.

"If you were me, Ryan. And you learned what had taken place at the conference. Wouldn't you do the same?"

"Sure, but how did you know?"

"I know Michael Cevanté. I attended the Sales Esteem conference last month and what I learned made me re-evaluate , shall I say, Shaw's 'management' style. I only needed yours and Michael's confirmation to make my decision."

Ryan shook his head up and down in understanding.

"And then Shaw came in early this morning and confirmed it all. He blew. He went through the ceiling. Thank you for coming through at the conference. I thought you would. And I knew when you returned, it would be time to put your influence to work for the entire firm. You made us a lot of money as a salesperson—we'll miss that. But the impact will be much greater as the company's sales manager—if you'll take it."

"Uh . . . Yeah, yes. Of course. But, why do you think that I am . . . I mean . . . you don't know much about me . . . whether I can do the job or not," he stuttered.

"Michael Cevanté is sure. And so am I. Ryan, you've been with us for eight years. You think all I do is play golf? I spend an awful lot of time getting to know people, through actions, and reactions. You're the man I want. It was just a matter of getting you over the hurdle you faced. And building your sales philosophy at the conference," said Mallory.

Ryan's spirits were high. His mind raced with the opportunity in front of him. And he felt good about the justice delivered by Mallory. He smiled. "Yes. I'll do it," he said.

Mallory got up to leave and Ryan hopped to his feet to follow him to the door.

"Thanks, Bill," he said as Mallory left him in the office.

Ryan returned to the chair and spun around in it for a few minutes—like a kid—exploring every inch of his new surroundings.

A single, obnoxious knock on the door interrupted him. It was Shaw.

"Jock! What are you . . . "

"Moved in before the chair was even cold, huh?" asked Shaw.

"What do you want?" Ryan said without remorse.

"I left a box of my stuff in the corner. But it's also a treat to see the vulture dancing on the corpse."

"Jock, you blew it. And you almost ruined me as well. Don't play the part of the victim—it just won't fly with me." Ryan's voice was calm and controlled.

The strength of Ryan's voice was intimidating.

"I'm sure you're real proud of yourself, right now. But you'll get what you deserve. You'll see." Shaw was broken and pathetic.

"You haven't any idea of what is deserved and what is not. You have no concept of integrity or justice. Do you think this is an accident? The firm has been preparing to remove you from the moment you started screwing up. The conference was the capper. If you have any intelligence at all, you'll deal with it and change. But my guess is that you won't do that. I'm going to bet that you stay bitter—filled with hate. Frankly, I don't care enough to even recommend you try to avoid it. Remember causality, Jock? Remember justice? You're seeing the consequences of your actions now. Only you want to blame someone else. Just like your embarrassing confrontation about opinions at the conference. Your opinions, your ideas, your principles are lousy, Jock. And now you want to blame me for your failure? What a joke. Get out of my office." Ryan glared at him.

The years of incompetence, mind games, and politics had added up. Ryan didn't care about placing blame for his problems, they were behind him now, but he knew how much Shaw contributed to his misery. It was a fitting conclusion.

Somewhere deep inside, Shaw knew Ryan was right. He couldn't avoid it— and the thought of his own destruction was crippling. He couldn't speak. He just listened as though Ryan's words were the punishment for his actions. He stared blankly at Ryan for a moment, reached down and picked up the box he had come to gather. His eyes went dim. He didn't turn to leave. He backed out of the office slowly. There was no anger any longer. Remorse seemed to be slipping in. It was clear he wanted to fade away, and hope that something could be remade from the wreckage. At the door he mumbled his final words to Ryan.

"You're right. Good luck." Shaw turned and walked away. Ryan felt no satisfaction in watching the man crumble, but he felt a warm glow for the victory of his own decency. Justice dealt those feelings regularly, he guessed, and he knew it took courage to deal with both sides.

People began streaming into the office to congratulate Ryan. The most rewarding were the salesman who were once his peers and now under his stewardship. They seemed the most pleased. Ryan chatted with several of them for almost an hour, keeping his eye on his watch as he waited for the minutes to tick away. Amber and Casey would be arriving at the airport at 11:45 and the wait had become physically uncomfortable.

He left for the airport a half hour early, and paced like an expectant father in front of the gate. The plane was late. He could take no more. Finally, the door opened and a little boy pushed past the attendant. He had a teddy bear in pinstripes in his hands and stopped to look for his father. Their eyes met and Casey rushed into his arms. Ryan caught him, lifted him high into air and spun him around. They embraced tightly. Casey whispered into Ryan's ear. "I missed you, Dad. Don't go away anymore. Okay?"

"No, son. I won't. I'm back now," Ryan said, knowing it had more meaning than Casey could possibly grasp.

Amber reached them and the three of them stood holding each other for a very long moment. Amber looked up at Ryan anxiously.

"I have so much to tell you," he said.

"You look good, Ryan," she said, noticing the brightness in his eyes that was reminiscent of the man she had married but not of the man she had sent off a week before.

"I am, honey, I really am."

When they arrived home, Ryan unloaded the luggage and immediately pushed them back into the car. They drove to the family's favorite weekend retreat— Boardwalk Park, where Casey could play in the park, ride the train, let balloons loose into the sky, and eat lots of ice cream. All three were tired from their travels, but the fatigue seemed willing to wait for the reunion to be completed. By late afternoon, Casey was slowing down, which Amber welcomed, and soon they were back at home. Dinner from a carry-out Chinese restaurant made the task of unpacking a little easier, and they completed it just as the sky turned dark. Ryan had located Casey's favorite books and had them waiting for his most cherished time with Casey. Amber had noticed the differences in Ryan immediately. His happiness seemed anything but transient. The heaviness in her heart lifted as she realized Ryan's troubles were behind him.

Casey and Ryan settled onto his bed for a story as Amber crept out of the room. She stopped just outside the door so she could listen to the story and watch Ryan reclaim his role as proud father. Her thoughts returned to the memory of watching Ryan weep in sadness as he stood over his son, and her own tears which followed..

Ryan read through a book and a half until Casey could no longer hold open his drooping eyelids and gave in, letting them close for the final time that evening. Ryan covered Casey as he kneeled down beside him. His hand found its way to the familiar outlines of Casey's face. He pushed back the little boy's hair from his forehead and leaned down to kiss him gently.

Amber entered the doorway to watch. Tears came to her eyes when she saw the look on Ryan's face. There was more written there than she had even seen before. No fear, no guilt, no remorse—only happiness, and an overwhelming love for his life, for her and for the little boy who would never fully know the turmoil his father had been through. She saw more in Ryan Matthews in that evening than she had seen in their ten years together. Ryan looked up at her and knew what she was thinking. He looked back down at Casey, caressed his forehead, and paused for another moment.

"Son, I'm home."

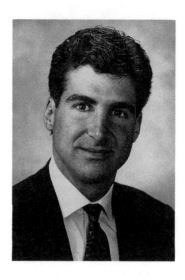

About the Author

For over a decade, Marc Ferguson has pushed the frontiers of selling, both in his personal selling and in training others. His first experience with corporate selling came from failing the well-known Merrill Lynch Sales Simulation during college recruiting. Undeterred, he established a rookie sales record for the John Hancock Denver agency that had not been achieved in its twenty year history. Looking back on the experience he would later recall; "Merrill wanted clever phone callers, Hancock wanted professional problem solvers." That distinction set the tone for a career dedicated to the customer.

In 1986 he was the leading New Business Development Officer for Capitol Federal of Denver while working from an undersized rural branch. Later that year, he developed the business plan to deliver comprehensive investment services in bank lobbies through commissioned salespeople - a rarity at that time.

Since 1987, he pioneered sales techniques that have produced substantially higher sales and greater customer satisfaction. He wrote the sales process for two bank marketing firms during the late 80's. The second firm, Essex Corporation, rose from relative mediocrity to the industry leader, partly due to the fundamental sales skills imparted through the author's work. In addition to authoring the corporate sales program, he worked the magic of Sales Esteem directly in the field - building the Southwest region into the company's most productive. It was during this time that the Sales Esteem Philosophy proved itself, yielding two and three times the sales productivity of both the East and West Coast regions. The region grew from $5 million in annual sales to $280 million in his first year in the field, and accounted for nearly one fourth of the company's total sales.

Marc has trained over a thousand salespeople on various aspects of Sales Esteem, and credits the philosophy for his industry leading success.